LONDON CORRESPONDENCE
JACK THE RIPPER AND THE IRISH PRESS

ALAN SHARP has enjoyed a varied career as a writer, theatre director and freelance IT expert. He writes for the two leading Jack the Ripper journals, *Ripperologist* and *Ripper Notes*, and is a contributor to the Casebook: Jack the Ripper website (www.casebook.org). When not writing about the Ripper he is an experienced mountaineer who hopes to one day tackle Everest. Of Scottish heritage he grew up in Gloucestershire and now has a home in Dublin. He is divorced with three teenage children who think their Dad is weird and like it that way.

LONDON CORRESPONDENCE

Jack the Ripper and the Irish Press

ALAN SHARP

with a Foreword by
ANDY ALIFFE

ashfield
PRESS

First published in 2005 by

ASHFIELD PRESS • DUBLIN • IRELAND

© Text Alan Sharp, 2005

ISBN: 1 901658 45 7

A catalogue record for this book is available from the British Library.

Typeset by Ashfield Press in 11 on 13 point Dante
Designed by
SUSAN WAINE

Printed in Ireland by
ẞETAPRINT LIMITED, DUBLIN

Contents

Foreword

By ANDY ALIFFE

Ripper researcher and commentator

I N 1997 I GAVE AN INTERVIEW to Stephen Ryder's well-respected web site – 'Casebook: Jack the Ripper'. In answer to the question: - *'What avenues of investigation were still open to researchers for the discovery of new information'* I outlined the following.

With the advent of technological advancement in telegraphic communication, the Whitechapel Murders became international news. Journalists around the world clambered to give accounts of the 'shocking' story. And so for a Ripper researcher it seemed worth checking the local library for newspapers, to see how the murders, committed between August and November 1888, were perceived on a 'global stage'.

The accessibility of historical archives has uncovered a wealth of contemporary press coverage. I predicted that new illustrations, witness reports and other fascinating information connected with the murders and ensuing investigations would be found, thus ensuring the subject matter of Jack the Ripper would remain ever popular.

So perhaps independently, or perhaps on my advice, some researchers and authors have followed my lead. Alan Sharp has done just that and used it to great effect.

In 1855, with the abolition of stamp tax duty, a dip into the 'daily rag' became more affordable. Coupled with the Education act of 1870, which meant that more of the working class could actually read, and with the mass production of newsprint in the 1880's, newspapers really became a readily available consumer product. A number of printed titles flourished, each one trying to outdo its competitor and win readership with ever more scandalous, exciting and tantalising reads. Jack the Ripper, in newspaper terms, was ammunition in a circulation war.

Over the past few years there have been several publications that address the 'press perspective' on the 'Autumn of Terror'. As a 'snapshot' they are all an excellent exercise on reported media whose attention was focused on a very localised series of crimes.

It is said that the newsworthy attention given to the Jack the Ripper murders invented the tabloid press or depending on how you look at it, that the tabloid press invented Jack the Ripper. Headline news creates headline news. The Whitechapel Murders gave rise to 'investigative journalism' on a monumental scale, and with this new found 'freedom of the press' everyone, from the richest man to the poorest widow could read about what was happening on their own doorstep, and hear it from a very different view point to that of the censored tones of the authorities.

We should realise that after the murder of Mary Ann Nichols, the Rippers first victim, the remaining four of the 'canonical five' were able to read, in all its lurid glory, vivid illustrated descriptions of their own fate, never knowing their tragedy would be known by the next.

They each had a moderate to good education, were from reasonably comfortable backgrounds and some like Annie Chapman were even well to do. So they would not have been alien to the horrific details of each and every murder, of what were quite possibly their friends; gruesome details of the inquests, which the press were allowed to print, and court hearing extracts, which they were able to publish. The vulnerable female class of the East End should have been alerted by the sensational headline cries of the 'street vendor' newsboys.

Mary Kelly was known to have specifically asked her boyfriend Joe Barnett to buy newspapers with reports of the murders. After reading details of the deaths of Nichols and Chapman in a newspaper in Kent, Catherine Eddowes returned from Hopping near Maidstone, believing she knew the identify of the killer, and the third victim, Elizabeth Stride, had purportedly spoken of what she had read of the murders to Dr. Barnardo, in the kitchen of her lodging house.

Provincial news-reporters were often outweighed by the 'nationals' and sought their own sources of information. They are known to have used a number of under-hand ploys and a variety of disguises to infiltrate the local residents for an 'exclusive'. Beware! In nearly all these cases of the hyped-up media attention, coverage was written often without regards for the truth, thus perpetuating many ongoing and incorrect facts, myths and legends.

For overseas consumption there were news agencies or the freelance London correspondents. This is the approach taken by Alan Sharp in 'London Correspondence – Jack the Ripper and the Irish Press'. On mainland Britain, the left wing 'rags' and the right wing 'broadsheets' were all quick to use the tragedy for a political stance. Some highlighted the poor social conditions, criticised the police and through the pages of their journals, publicly attacked figures of authority in a deliberate attempt to bring down the government.

Ripper aficionados will be aware of the mainstream 'enterprising journalists' who reported the Whitechapel Murders, and their names are to be found within these pages. New source material contained in this book comes predominantly from the words of anonymous London correspondents serving a number of Irish papers, and reported from an Irish viewpoint. Set against the background of Irish Home Rule, Alan Sharp follows the personalities and events leading up to the murders of 1888 and traces the evolution of these heinous crimes.

During the 1880's, the 'Phoenix Park Murders', the Parnell Commission and the mainland dynamite campaigns of the Fenian bombers dominated media attention, which continued to point an unruly finger at the rebellious nationalistic cause of Ireland and the Irish. The dastardly deeds of Jack the Ripper in London's East End quickly deflected the press coverage from the Irish situation, leaving the editorial agendas firmly in the hands of the Irish press who focused critical comment on the inabilities of England and the English. The tables had turned.

The Whitechapel outrages may have just been a continuance of enquiries for the British authorities involved up to that time with the Irish nationalists. All the main players on the field of Ripper lore, Abberline, Monro, Macnaghten, Warren, Anderson and Littlechild, had been connected in some way with the detection of the Fenian cause.

This may go some way in explaining uncorroborated reports and unsupported claims of a link between the plot to assassinate future British Prime Minister, Arthur Balfour of the Irish Office and the identity of Jack the Ripper.

In 'London Correspondence', Alan Sharp provides an entertaining and coherent narrative filled with informative, anecdotal reports. Ripperology, in the main, is time, location and event specific. 'London Correspondence' will broaden awareness for dedicated Ripper researchers; yet provide an informed insight for students of a wider interest in Victorian social history, gathered from a different and distanced perspective.

ANDY ALIFFE – DECEMBER 2004

CHAPTER ONE

The Beginning of the Terror

THE LATE VICTORIAN ERA was a period of change and turmoil. Scientific discoveries and inventions were changing the way of life for most of the population at an alarming rate. The British Empire was at the zenith of its power, and the industrial revolution had brought a new wealth and prosperity to the country. The old political systems were being crushed under the weight of the new independent middle-classes and the rise of Socialism. Yet behind the outward respectability and affluence of the era there lay another world, one of high unemployment and abject poverty, which found its home in the slum areas of the great cities of the Kingdom. In Whitechapel and Spitalfields were to be found some of the worst slums in the country, and the year of 1888 is destined to be remembered as the year that evil stalked the streets of those slums in the shape of a murderous fiend who would become known as Jack the Ripper.

Over the last hundred years a mountain of literature has been written on the subject of the Whitechapel murders; the story has been told time and again until it has grown to almost mythical proportions, and Jack has become a legendary monster on the same lines as Dracula or Frankenstein. Each writer has told the story his own way; some have told it well, others poorly. Rumours and inaccuracies have been added and demolished along the way. New evidence has been found, new suspects identified, and new theories formulated. Today the Ripper has become more than just an unsolved murder case; it has become its own industry.

The Ripper has been a flamboyant American quack doctor called Francis Tumblety, a mad Polish Jew called either Aaron Kosminski or David Cohen, an escaped lunatic called James Kelly. He has been a black magician, Roslyn D'Onston, drawing occult symbols across the map of London. Policemen involved in the case identified George Chapman, the wife poisoner, Montague John Druitt, a deranged barrister who committed suicide shortly after the killings ended, and Michael Ostrog, a lunatic Russian medical man. In the 1970s we had the Royal physician Sir William Withey Gull riding around Whitechapel in a carriage as part of a Masonic plot to cover up a clandestine marriage between the heir apparent to the throne and a Catholic shop girl, a wholly discredited theory which has nonetheless provided the plot for various movie versions of the story. A diary has been discovered implicating Liverpool cotton merchant James Maybrick, and, although roundly condemned as a hoax, science has so far failed to disprove its authenticity entirely. Most recently, and possibly most bizarrely, we have had crime novelist Patricia Cornwell insisting that the Ripper was the esteemed artist Walter Sickert whom she paints as some kind of villainous super-freak running around the country sending hundreds of letters in disguised handwriting to taunt the police with his evil cunning, leaving one wondering how he ever managed to find the time in between all this activity to actually paint!

Discovering the true details of the Ripper murders is a tricky business, particularly with such a mountain of books, many of which contradict each other and choose to ignore some items of evidence and overestimate the importance of others in order to emphasise whatever particular theory the writer is pushing. The best place to start is using one of the books that has no axe to grind and which simply tries to get to the root of the matter, such as Philip Sugden's *The Complete History of Jack the Ripper* or Paul Begg's *Jack the Ripper: The Facts.*

In this book, while I will endeavour to keep the reader as apprised of the actual facts as possible, a full presentation of those facts is not my aim. Rather the object here is to study the way in which the case was reported by the newspapers of Ireland, and the way in which those newspapers often used the crimes to further their own agendas in an era in which the Irish question dominated UK politics. The accounts of the crimes given, therefore, will naturally be based on the reporting of the time, which is a dangerous area to pursue where terms of accuracy are involved.

The newspapers are one of our major sources of information on the crimes today, but it must always be kept in mind that they were not always well informed. Sir Charles Warren, the Chief Commissioner of the Metropolitan Police during the major part of the Ripper scare, was a man deeply suspicious of newspapers, and he gave his force direct instructions not to co-operate with reporters. The result is that many of the early reports of each crime are garbled accounts patched together from the stories told by whatever rambling locals the journalists could lay their hands on. The radical London evening newspaper *The Star* commented on the phenomenon on November 10th after the last recognised murder of the series:

The desire to be interesting has had its effect on the people who live in the Dorset-street-court and lodging-houses, and for whoever cares to listen there are a hundred highly circumstantial stories, which, when carefully sifted, prove to be totally devoid of truth.

Many of these rumours and circumstantial stories have led to the inaccuracies which appear in countless of the newspaper reports and were repeated in books on the subject until quite recently, when access to the police files have proved them to be incorrect: the writing on the wall in Hanbury Street, the grapes found at the Berner Street site, polished shiny coins or wineglasses found at other murder sites; wrong names for victims, policemen and witnesses, the idea of the left-handed killer, the idea that the killer took the key with him from the Miller's Court murder. The newspapers even created an entirely fictional victim. The *Freeman's Journal* was among many newspapers to mention this victim in this report from October 1st, 1888:

> It will be remembered that the first of the series of murders was committed so far back as last Christmas, when a woman, whose identity was never discovered, was found murdered in or contiguous to the district known as Whitechapel. There were circumstances of peculiar barbarity about the mode in which the body was treated.

A search of police files and contemporary newspaper reports show that no such murder was ever reported. It appears to have been a mistake which first occurred in the *Daily Telegraph* on September 10th and soon became accepted by newspapers around the world as the truth. The date was given in that newspaper as December 26th and the location as the corner of Osborn and Wentworth Streets. From this information it seems likely that this was a garbled account of the murder of a woman named Emma Smith, and that the confusion arose from the fact that a witness named Margaret Hames[1] at her inquest stated that she had been attacked in a similar way the previous December.

Emma Smith was also frequently listed as the first of the Ripper murders. Her attack actually took place in the early hours of Tuesday, April 3rd, 1888, the day after Easter Monday. She was approached by three ruffians outside St Mary's Church in the Whitechapel Road and chased as far as the corner of Osborn and Wentworth streets, where she was brutalised outside a mustard factory. The three men assaulted and beat her badly, and stole her money. Then one of them concluded the attack by thrusting some hard blunt object, possibly a wooden stake or a metal railing post, deep into her vagina causing the internal injuries which would result in her death.

Smith managed to stagger back to her lodgings at 18 George Street, from where she was quickly conveyed by her fellow lodgers to the London Hospital.

She died from peritonitis the following morning, but not before she had managed to tell her story to the doctors. The attack was assumed to be the work of one of the various "high rip" gangs who operated in the area extorting money from the women of the night, and most likely this is the case. No arrests were ever made, and on the face of it no connection to the Ripper crimes exists, although some have theorised that Jack may have been one of her attackers and may have gained his taste for blood from the incident.

The next incident frequently connected to the Ripper crimes by the press, and one far more likely to have been Jack's work, was the murder of Martha Tabram on Tuesday, August 7th. Martha, whose surname is frequently given in the papers as Turner, the surname of a man she had lived with for a while, was a middle-aged prostitute who spent the evening of the 6th, again a bank holiday, in the company of fellow prostitute Mary Ann Connelly, known as Pearly Poll, and two soldiers. At around midnight the group had exited the White Hart public house at the entrance to an alley called George Yard. Martha then took one of the soldiers up George Yard while Poll went with the other to nearby Angel Alley for what were, she told the inquest jury "immoral purposes".

At two o'clock that morning Police Constable Thomas Barrett, on the beat in Wentworth Street which ran to the North of George Yard, found a young soldier loitering in the road, and, approaching him, was told that he was "waiting for a pal" who had gone off somewhere with a woman. Barrett and Pearly Poll would later be involved in numerous identity parades attempting to discover these soldiers.

At around the same time a young couple, George and Elizabeth Mahoney, returned home from celebrating the bank holiday and passed up the stairs of a block of dwelling houses, George Yard Buildings, to their flat. Elizabeth later went out to fetch some supper for the pair from a nearby chandler's shop. On no occasion did either of them see anything on the stairs. However, Alfred Crow, a cab driver, saw someone lying on the landing when he returned home from work at half past three, but in the darkness of the stairwell he assumed that it was a vagrant or a drunk sleeping there.

It was a quarter to five when the body was eventually discovered there by John Reeves, a young casual waterside labourer living in the building who was on his way out to the docks to look for work when he stumbled across her. He at once found Constable Barrett who sent him to fetch a Dr Killeen who lived nearby. The doctor examined the body and determined that Martha had been stabbed 39 times in a fury of violence, one of the stab wounds in the breast having apparently been caused by a heavy dagger or bayonet, the others by a smaller knife, possibly a pocket knife. The stab wounds extended from her neck down to her lower abdomen and genitals, although her throat was not cut as was erroneously reported later by some newspapers.

The murder was variously, but not extensively, reported by the Irish newspapers. This report from the *Cork Examiner* of August 8th is a typical example of the coverage it received:

> About ten minutes to five yesterday morning the body of a woman was found on the first floor landing at 37, George Yard Buildings, Whitechapel. Medical aid was summoned, and it was then found that a woman had been brutally murdered, there being knife wounds on the breast, stomach and abdomen. She was about thirty-five to forty years of age, and unknown to the locality. No disturbance was heard, and there is the utmost mystery surrounding the woman's death.

Although at the time this murder was not connected with that of Emma Smith, later newspaper reports would frequently report them as being committed by the same hand as the later murders. Indeed, Martha's killing would initially be associated with them by the police, although at some point this seems to have been discounted and the killing of Polly Nichols became the first "official" Ripper murder. In the years since, some theorists have included Martha in the canon of Jack's victims, some have not. My own personal feeling is that this was most likely to have been the work of the same murderer. Although there are differences from the later killings this is consistent with the development of the psyche of a serial murderer as he "learns his trade." The psychological make-up which allows for a person to be capable of brutality on this scale is not common, and it seems unlikely to me that there were two persons of this type operating in the area at the same moment in history.

It would be just over three weeks later that the Whitechapel murderer would first make his mark on the public consciousness. The first appearance in the Irish press would be in the *Dublin Evening Mail* on the evening of August 31st, the day that the murder took place:

> Another brutal murder was committed in Whitechapel, London, this morning. Constable John Neil found, at half-past four o'clock, a woman lying in Buck's-row, Thomas-street, with her throat cut across, and it was afterwards found that she had been stabbed in the abdomen, evidently with a large knife, leaving the intestines exposed. Her hands and face bore traces of a severe struggle, and her clothes were cut and torn. There is no trace at present of the murderer. The brutality of the crime leads the police to believe that the perpetrator of the crime must be a ferocious maniac. This is the third crime of the kind in the locality.

In fact it was Charles Cross, a carman on his way to work at Pickford's in Broad

Street at twenty to four that morning who first discovered the body. He passed along Buck's Row, a narrow darkened alley lit by a single lamp, when he noticed what he at first thought to be a discarded tarpaulin lying in a gateway to a stable yard. As he approached he realised that it was the form of a woman, and at that moment he heard footsteps behind him and turned to see another man approaching. His name was Robert Paul, and he was a fellow carman on his way to work, although the two men were unknown to each other.

Cross hailed the other man saying, "Come over here and look. There is a woman. I believe she is dead." The two men approached the body, but neither one having a light they failed to spot the injury to the throat. Cross felt her face and found it to be warm. Paul, in attempting to adjust her clothes to afford her more decency, felt a flutter in her breast and told his companion, "I think she is breathing, but it's a little if she is." The two men were both hurrying to their places of work, and resolved to continue on together and inform the first policeman they passed.

It was after they had left that Constable Neil made his own independent discovery of the body. He gave his account of the discovery to the inquest later that week, an account which was reported in the *Bray Herald* on September 8th.

> I was proceeding down Buck's row, Whitechapel, going towards Brady-street. There was not a soul about. I had been round there half-an-hour previously, and I saw no one then. I was on the right-hand side of the street, when I noticed a figure lying in the street. It was dark at the time, though there was a street lamp shining at the end of the row. I went across and found deceased lying outside a gateway, her head towards the east. The gateway was closed. It was about nine or ten feet high, and led to some stables. There were houses from the gateway eastward, and the School Board school occupies the westward. On the opposite side of the road is Essex Wharf. Deceased was lying lengthways along the street her left hand touching the gate. I examined the body by the aid of my lamp, and noticed blood oozing from a wound in the throat. She was lying on her back, with her clothes disarranged. I felt her arm, which was quite warm from the joints upwards. Her eyes were wide open. Her bonnet was off and lying by her side, close to the left hand. I heard a constable passing Brady-street so I called to him. I did not whistle. I said to him, "Run at once for Dr. Llewellyn," and seeing another constable in Baker's-row, I sent him for the ambulance. The doctor arrived in a very short time. I had, in the meantime, rung the bell at Essex Wharf, and asked if any disturbance had been heard. The reply was, "No." Sergeant Kirby came after, and he knocked. The doctor looked at the woman and then said, "Move her to the mortuary. She is dead, and I will make a further

examination of her." We placed her on the ambulance, and moved her there.

It was Inspector John Spratling of J Division, the Bethnal Green division of the Metropolitan Police in whose jurisdiction the murder had occurred, who discovered the mutilation of the body. He lifted the clothing while taking a full description of the victim at the mortuary and immediately sent for Dr Rees Ralph Llewellyn to return and examine what he had found. His report to the inquest is detailed in the same newspaper as the above:

> I went and saw that the abdomen was cut very extensively. I have this morning made a post-mortem examination of the body. I found it to be that of a female about 40 or 45 years. Five of the teeth are missing, and there is a slight laceration of the tongue. On the right side of the face there is a bruise running along the lower part of the jaw. It might have been caused by a blow with the fist or pressure by the thumb. On the left side of the face there was a circular bruise, which also might have been done by the pressure of the fingers. On the left side of the neck, about an inch below the jaw, there was an incision about four inches long and running from a point immediately below the ear. An inch below on the same side, and commencing about an inch in front of it, was a circular incision terminating at a point about three inches below the right jaw. This incision completely severs all the tissues down to the vertebrae. The large vessels of the neck on both sides were severed. The incision is about eight inches long. These cuts must have been caused with a long-bladed knife, moderately sharp, and used with great violence. No blood at all was found on the breast either of the body or clothes. There were no injuries about the body till just about the lower part of the abdomen. Two or three inches from the left side was a wound running in a jagged manner. It was a very deep wound, and the tissues were cut through. There were several incisions running across the abdomen. On the right side there were also three or four similar cuts running downwards. All these had been caused by a knife, which had been used violently and been used downwards. The wounds were from left to right, and might have been done by a left-handed person. All the injuries had been done by the same instrument.

This was the only time in the case that a left-handed killer was suggested, many of the doctors examining later victims contradicted the idea, and indeed Dr Llewellyn himself would later state his opinion that he was mistaken on this point. However, the idea of a left-handed killer took its hold on the public imagination and was frequently reported as fact.

The woman was identified from the mark of the Lambeth Workhouse on her petticoats. An inmate of that institution, one Mary Ann Monk, identified the body and records showed that she was Mary Ann "Polly" Nichols, a middle-aged prostitute who had passed her forty-third birthday in the previous week. A married woman with five children, she had split from her husband, a machinist named William Nichols, in 1879 or 1880. There is some argument regarding the cause for the split, her husband claiming it was due to her drinking, her father that William had had an affair with a midwife who had attended Polly during her last childbirth. Either way Polly was an inveterate drinker, and spent much of the remaining eight or nine years of her life in and out of workhouses and making a living on the streets.

For a while she had lived with her father, Edward Walker, but they had argued over her dissolute lifestyle and she left. They then appear to have lost touch with each other for some time, and at some point Polly began living with a blacksmith named Thomas Drew in Walworth. Walker next saw his daughter at the funeral of her brother who had died in an oil lamp explosion, something which appears to have been common and frequently commented on in the press at the time. At that time both he and Polly's eldest son stated that she was respectably dressed, although due to the family row they did not speak to her. Early in 1888 she had written a letter to him from Wandsworth, where she had found service with a respectable family named the Cowdry's. The style of the letter indicates that she was not an uneducated woman by the standards of the day.

> I just write to say you will be glad to know that I am settled in my new place, and going on all right up to now. My people went out yesterday, and have not returned, so I am left in charge. It is a grand place inside, with trees and gardens back and front. All this has been newly done up. They are teetotallers and religious, so I ought to get on. They are very nice people, and I have not too much to do. I hope you are all right and the boy has work. So good-bye for the present. From yours truly, Polly.
> Answer soon, please, and let me know how you are.

Walker wrote back but never heard from her again. On July 12th Polly absconded from the Cowdry's home taking with her clothing worth three pounds and ten shillings. From that time on she lived mostly at two common lodging houses in the Whitechapel district, mainly at 18 Thrawl Street, but for about a week before her death at 56 Flower and Dean Street in a place known locally as The White House.

On the night of her murder she had returned to 18 Thrawl Street and tried to obtain a bed, but was turned away for having no money to pay with. She had been drinking at The Frying Pan public house at the corner of that street until half past midnight. On leaving the lodging house she asked the deputy to keep a bed for her, telling him, "I'll soon get my doss money; see what a jolly bonnet I've got now." The bonnet she was wearing was not recognised by the other lodgers who knew her, but when and how she acquired it is not known. This is probably not important but some theorists since have suggested some significance in the fact.

She was next seen by Ellen Holland, a forty-five-year-old widow who had shared a bed with her at the lodging house for some time. She was on her way back from watching a major fire which had occurred in the docks, and ran into Polly at half past two on the corner of Osborn Street and Whitechapel Road. The timing of this meeting was confirmed by the clock of St Mary's Church chiming the half hour while they were talking. Polly told her she had had her doss money three times that day but had spent it on drink. Ellen tried to persuade her to return with her to the lodging house where she would persuade the deputy to allow her to stay on tick, but Polly stated that she would soon have her money and staggered away up Whitechapel Road heading East. It was the last time she was seen alive.

The dock fire which occurred that night is significant, as it would later provide part of the alibi of a major suspect. It was one of the largest fires in London for many years, and was said to have lit up the night sky with a red glow across much of the city. Many of the Irish newspapers reported the facts of the matter, and the London Correspondent of the *Dublin Evening Mail* provided a personal account:

> While the greater portion of the five millions of people [sic] who inhabit the great city were sleeping peacefully or otherwise in their beds, two of the greatest fires witnessed in the metropolis for some months past were raging with terrible fierceness in the heart of the London shipping. I had occasion to pass over London Bridge at half-past one this morning, and a more imposing spectacle than the fiery furnace seen from this structure I have not witnessed for a very long time. From out of the grim blackness of the well-known "pool" leapt lurid flames of gigantic volume, rising high against a canopy of fantastic clouds, and throwing the tapering masts into clear relief until they and their rigging looked like fairy cobwebs, illuminated by strange, unearthly light. The effect was grand, and, in the stillness of the early morning, distinctly weird. From afar came the rumbling whirr of the hurrying engines and the muffled shouts of the lusty firemen as they battled bravely with a sea of relentless flame. As one waited and watched and saw the fire fiend leaping, as it

were in triumph, until gradually it fell a victim to overpowering forces, it became evident that in a few short hours some hundreds of thousands of pounds worth of property had been sacrificed to the merciless enemy. The wonder is that the damage was not much greater. At one time it seemed as if nothing could prevent two or three miles of docks being hopelessly involved.

The murder of Polly Nichols was certainly more widely reported in Ireland than that of Emma Smith or Martha Tabram, but for that first week there was no indication of the media sensation that the story was soon to become. The *Irish Times* London Correspondent on the morning of Saturday, September 1st made a brief mention of the incident in his column:

> You will have from other sources an account of the horrible murder committed last night in Whitechapel, where a woman of 40 was found with her throat cut and the lower part of her body almost hacked to pieces. The aspect of this tragedy noted here is its suggestive resemblance to the atrocity reported about three weeks ago where a woman of like age was found in the open hall of a common lodging house, also with her throat cut and thirty-nine slashes and stabs in different parts of her person. The similarity in many points of these two crimes has stirred again suspicion that both poor women were victims of the same miscreant. We hark back to the time a century ago when "the monster"[2] prowled about London attacking women with a knife, and the theory is that some still more sanguinary scoundrel may now be gratifying a like mania. If so, it can only be hoped that he will speedily experience the punishment of his predecessor.

His contemporary at the *Dublin Evening Mail*, meanwhile, provided the readers of that newspaper with a far more detailed treatise, a pattern which would continue throughout the case. The gentleman in question appears to have developed a deep fascination with the murders, and provides the most thorough accounts of progress of any of the London journalists of the Irish papers. Referring initially to his account of the dock fires reproduced above he wrote:

> While this scene of hurry and toil and fear was exciting some thousands of people in different parts of London, a far more horrible drama was being enacted not very far distant from the same spot. I refer of course to the terrible murder committed in a squalid thoroughfare in the teeming district of Whitechapel. A more barbarous and sickening crime has not been perpetuated in the metropolis for a very long time, and the

mystery at present attaching to it has intensified the sensation produced ten-fold. A poor helpless woman, pounced upon, stabbed, and mutilated in a manner almost too horrible to describe, and then left dead or dying in the gutter. This is the story, in brief, so far as it can yet be told.

The removal of the clothes from the poor wretch's body revealed gaping wounds which had been inflicted in a perfectly fiendish manner, and apparently with a large knife, such as butchers use. Apparently, in the first instance, the knife had been thrust into the neck behind the left ear, and a horrible wound inflicted. Then the blade had been thrust in, in a similar position behind the right ear, and wrenched round with such force as to approach as nearly to decapitation as possible. In the lower part of the body the wounds were of a still more frightful character. The knife had been thrust into the lowest point of the body, and the woman deliberately ripped open to the breast, causing almost complete disembowelment. Again the knife had been thrust into the body under each breast and drawn down to the thighs in a zigzag fashion. A more terrible scene than that disclosed by the mutilated remains, as they lay upon the mortuary slab, I have never previously witnessed.

There are naturally many theories as to how the crime was perpetrated. By some people it is believed that the woman belonged to the "unfortunate" class,[3] and that she was attacked by one of the gangs who infest the neighbourhood after the public houses are closed, and levy black mail upon these miserable women. Others question the probability of this theory, holding that the woman's injuries could not have been inflicted while she was fully dressed and that the murder must therefore have been committed in some house and the body subsequently deposited in the street. Whatever the true explanation, such a crime can scarcely remain a mystery long. Something must have been heard or seen that will point more or less surely to the perpetrator of this diabolical outrage.

Other daily newspapers did not pick up on the sensation caused by the murder for a few days. The *Cork Examiner* reported first on the Monday morning, September 3rd. Their London Correspondent had this to say:

The ghastly murder of the woman who has been identified as one Nicholas [*sic*], a lodger in a common lodging-house in Spitalfields, has caused something more than a sensation in the East End. This atrocity strangely resembles two others that have preceded it. In all three cases we find the following points of resemblance. The victims are women of the town. They are not only murdered, but we might say savagely butchered in cold blood. The scene of each murder is within a circumscribed area within a radius of about half a mile. The crimes are committed in the early hours of the morning, when the police are naturally least vigilant, and they are done with so much precaution that the perpetrator leaves no trace of his existence behind. It is difficult to resist the conclusion that these murders must be traceable to a common source. They must be the work of one hand or of many. If of one, a fiend – a second Mr. Hyde[4] – must be abroad in the East End. There have certainly been no murders within living memory which bear so strong a resemblance to the terrible crimes which suggested De Quincey's essay on murder considered as one of the fine arts.[5] The chances are that the murderer must have confederates to guard him against surprise and secure retreat, which seems always to be affected with consummate foresight. In that case the theory that the murders must be the work of a gang who live by robbing and blackmailing "unfortunates" would be the most tenable.

This theory of a gang was common among reports of the murder. The *Waterford Citizen* of September 4th commented on this phenomenon:

> As the body was nearly drained of blood and there was little sign of stains on the footpath where it was found it is believed the crime was committed elsewhere. It appears a sort of "High Rip" gang exists in the neighbourhood which, "blackmailing" women who frequent the streets, takes vengeance on those who do not find money for them. Within twelve months two other women have been murdered in the district by almost similar means – one as recently as the 7th of August last – and left in the gutter of the street in the early hours of the morning.

The *Dublin Evening Mail* Correspondent also commented on this theory in his second lengthy essay on the subject of the murders printed on Monday, September 3rd. However, as usual, his was a more personal account and one which continued to set a precedent for the thoroughness of his reporting:

> All the talk in London is still of the horrible mystery of the East End. The evidence given at the opening of the inquest yesterday did little or nothing towards enlightening the public on those points which they are naturally most anxious to have cleared up. The woman's identification was made perfectly clear, and the medical testimony brought out with startling distinctness the details of the terrible mutilation to which the deceased had been subjected. But this was all. There was nothing whatever to throw the slightest ray of light on the manner in which the revolting crime had been committed.

The theories advanced are exceptionally numerous. They are one and all being discussed with an eagerness not often associated with the horrors of the worst of London crimes. The majority incline to the belief that the deceased was the victim of a "High Rip" gang who infest the neighbourhood after midnight and levy blackmail on abandoned women under threats of violence. The maniac theory is nothing like as popular as it was on the day after the murder, though it is still entertained by many people. The notion that the three somewhat similar tragedies of the past year have been the work of one individual or set of individuals is pretty generally accepted as probable.

The police for the time being seem nonplussed. They have, apparently, obtained no definite clue on which to work. The neighbourhood they have literally scoured. Scarcely a house remains that has not been visited. Offers of money have, it is understood, been largely made, with a view to obtain information that might supply a chain of the link [*sic*]. At present, however, all these exertions appear to have been in vain. It was thought yesterday morning that a coffee-stall keeper, who had seen a woman in the company of two men shortly before the discovery of the tragedy, might be able to furnish some useful information, but the man, on seeing the deceased at the mortuary, declared that she was nothing like the woman he had seen.

Both on the point of how and where the murder was committed, there is still great mystery. The fact that but little blood was found at the spot where the body was discovered at first convinced everyone that the crime must have been committed at some distance from the narrow street where the mutilated body lay. To-day, however, quite a new theory is started. It is held that the fact that there was but little blood upon the lower portions of the woman's clothing or upon the pavement, was due to the wounds in the abdomen, having bled inwardly. Although a small pool of blood was found near the head, the greater part from the throat had trickled down the neck and saturated the under garments. These surmises are held by some to be almost convincing proof of the fact that the terrible crime was committed in the secluded thoroughfare where the body was discovered.

I last night paid another visit to the locality, and was much impressed with the genuine panic which has seized upon all sections of the crowded Whitechapel community. I conversed with several men and women, and the purport of the remarks of the latter was something like the following:– "We are terrified to death. I do not mean to go out after dark any more. One may be murdered any night. I am really afraid of my husband stirring out at night. Surely it must be an escaped lunatic who is about. Nothing more horrible has ever been heard. Surely the police will find the murderer? If they do not they ought to be shot. Some one in the neighbourhood must know something about it. Why then don't they come forward? I believe we have murderers all round us. It is a horrible neighbourhood. I am persuading my husband to leave it. My daughters and all of us are frightened out of our lives." Such expressions as these are heard on every hand, and it is no exaggeration to state, as I remarked previously, that the neighbourhood is in a state of panic.

The East End waxwork showmen are already making a roaring business out of the Whitechapel tragedy. Several of them have produced an "exact imitation of the murdered woman as she appeared when found," and red-faced gentlemen with cheery but perspiring countenances proclaim the fact in blatant tones, and with a gesticulatory accompaniment perfectly bewildering. Crowds of curious open-mouthed, and in some instances awe-stricken individuals, willingly pay their pennies to witness the gruesome sight.

His next mention of the murders appeared that Friday, September 7th, and included mention of the man who over the course of the week had become the prime suspect in the case:

This afternoon I paid another visit to Whitechapel with a view, if possible, to glean something fresh concerning the recent murder. But there was little or no information to be obtained. A lot of talk was being indulged in concerning the horrible propensities of a man known as "Leather Apron," and not a few people expressed a firm conviction that this man was the murderer. So far as I could gather, however, the talk is all pure speculation. What is more certain is that the residents are daily waxing more indignant with the police for being unable to obtain some clue likely to solve the terrible mystery. Once more opinion has veered round to the idea that the murderer is a lunatic who takes delight in watching the death agonies of individuals under the most blood-curdling conditions, and it is now generally believed that all the terrible murders of the past eighteen months that have taken place in the district, but have never been traced, were perpetrated by the same sinister individual. The funeral of the woman Mary Ann Nicholls[6], which took place this afternoon, created intense excitement throughout the locality. The streets were lined with thousands of people.

A common feature of Irish press reporting, at least as far as the Nationalist press were concerned, would be criticism of the state of England. This would become more apparent after the second and subsequent murders, but it was noticeable even at this early stage, as this item from the London Correspondent of the *Cork Examiner* on Tuesday, September 4th shows:

> We are in the midst of a tornado of horrors. Murders, attempted murders, suicides, and all manner of ghastly crimes are being reported from all parts of the country. The exceptionally bad weather which we have experienced this year, no doubt, has had something to answer for in this connection. The spirits of the English are never very vivacious. A fall in the barometer has a noticeable effect upon people here. Lowness of spirits is followed by indulgence in stimulants, and that by crime.

It was not merely in England that such horrors were occurring, however. In Dublin that same week several major news stories were thrilling the public imagination, including an explosion in the Guinness Brewery in which several workmen had been killed. A more horrifying story, however, would disturb the public mind in the city for some time. The most complete report of the incident that I could find is this one from the *Dublin Evening Mail* of September 4th:

> One of the most revolting cases of self-mutilation that has ever taken place in Dublin, occurred yesterday afternoon in a field near the Royal Canal. The fact that the unfortunate individual, who is the victim, is a gentleman whose family occupy a good social position renders the occurrence all the more remarkable. The name of the gentleman is Mr. James E. Gannon. He is a medical student, aged thirty-six years, and resided at 20 Northumberland-avenue, Kingstown. For some time past he was the victim of many strange delusions, but yesterday morning at half-past nine o'clock he left his residence without his brother, Mr Edward Gannon, with whom he lodged, or anyone else, noticing anything very unusual in his demeanour. The unhappy gentleman seems to have made his way to Dublin, and at about one o'clock a girl named Bessie Carr, aged twelve years, saw him walking across a little pasture field which lies between the rear of the Cokeoven Cottages, Royal Canal, and the Liffey Junction Railway. He had a pocket handkerchief to his eyes, and he appeared to be bleeding very much. The girl ran and told her mother, who went out and found him lying in the field. Mrs. Carr assisted him to her house, where she bathed his face with cold water. He declined to give any particulars of the occurrence but said, "I am blind, let me rest for an hour." The husband of Mrs Carr, a signalman, in the employment of the Midland Great Western Railway Company, reported the occurrence to Police Constable 22D, who, in company with Constable 117D, at once

proceeded to Mrs Carr's house. The police found that the gentleman had both his eyes pulled out. His hands and the cuffs of his shirt were besmeared with blood. He said "My eyes are injured; take me to hospital," whereupon the constables procured a cab and conveyed him to the Mater Misericordiae Hospital. He was attended by the resident surgeon, Mr. Buggy, and resident pupil, Mr. Watt, and subsequently by Surgeon Hayes, who found that both the eyes had been torn out of their sockets, and expressed their opinion that the injuries had been self-inflicted. On being searched, a second class return ticket, 9s 11?d in cash, a watch and chain, a pocket book with some letters, and a bunch of keys were found in his possession. Police-constable 25D, with Constable Hall, examined the field where it is supposed the rash act was committed, and found in a dry dyke, about one hundred yards from where the gentleman was found lying, both the eyes, about two feet apart, amongst some nettles. The constables brought the eyes to Surgeon Buggy, who has them in his charge. A hazel walking stick and a piece of twisted wire, both of which were marked with blood stains, were also found in the field. The ground in one part of the field appeared beaten down and spotted with blood. Word having been sent to Kingstown, the injured gentleman's brother, Mr. Edwd. Gannon, and Dr. M'Dermott, of Kingstown, arrived at the hospital. The brother, who conversed with the patient in private, stated that he told him that he would tell him the whole facts later on, but at present could give no information. A telegram was also sent to Laragh, county Kildare, where another of the gentleman's brothers resides.

In London, however, it seemed that the horrors of the weekend were not enough for the enterprising journalists of the metropolis, and as the sensation surrounding the murder died down one enterprising reporter attempted to keep things going with a report of another attempted murder in the same district. The story was picked up and reported by newspapers around the world, including most of the Irish national dailies and many of the local periodicals. The account, taken directly from one of the wire services, generally appears in the same wording in all of these newspapers, and this is taken from the *Irish Times* of September 4th:

> Another desperate assault, which stopped only just short of murder, was committed upon a woman in Whitechapel on Saturday night. The victim was leaving the Foresters' Music Hall, Cambridge Heath road, where she had been spending the evening with a sea captain, when she was accosted by a well-dressed man, who asked her to accompany him. She invited him to her apartments, and he acquiesced, requesting her meantime to

walk a short distance with him as he wanted to meet a friend. They had reached a point near to the scene of the murder of the woman Nicholls, when the man violently seized his companion by the throat and dragged her down a court. He was immediately joined by a gang of women and bullies, who stripped the unfortunate woman of her necklace, earrings and broach. Her purse was also taken, and she was brutally assaulted. Upon attempting to shout for aid one of the gang laid a large knife across her throat, remarking "We will serve you as we did the others." She was eventually released. The police have been informed and are prosecuting inquiries into the matter, it being regarded as a probably clue to the previous tragedy.

The story was first published in an evening newspaper on September 3rd and appeared in several of the British daily newspapers on the next day, including the *Manchester Guardian* and the *Pall Mall Gazette*. The story appears to have caused some consternation among the police investigating the murders who were unaware of the incident and flew into action to discover the details only to learn that there weren't any. Although none of the Irish newspapers who carried it printed a retraction, several of their British counterparts did so, as, in the words of the *East London Observer* of September 8th, "inquiries made into the accuracy of the story have proved it to be absolutely false and groundless."

However, the major sensations of the week surrounded the mysterious "Leather Apron." This gentleman, who was stated to extort money with menaces from the women of the district, was identified to police and press alike by many of the "unfortunates" who inhabited the Whitechapel and Spitalfields districts, and quickly became the number one suspect in the eyes of the public. Initially just a name, reports of his appearance gradually turned him into a kind of monstrous freak, and it seemed no exaggeration was too great for his horrifying appearance. The *Star* newspaper fuelled the most grotesque of these accounts, and it was their version that quickly got picked up and reported elsewhere. It formed the basis for accounts of him in both the *Irish Times* of September 7th and the *Belfast Morning News* of September 8th.

The Irish Times account ran as follows:

The Whitechapel murder has taken a turn of most ghastly romance. Those whose sensations were not handicapped while they read it by a haunting idea that "the strange case of Dr. Jekyll and Mr. Hyde" was a performance at least as grotesque as it was grim will remember how the horrible Hyde in one of his transformations, butchered a woman just for the fun of the thing.[7] That is an effective passage in the book, and those whom it thrilled with a pleasing terror will snatch fearful joy from the story of "Leather Apron" as narrated in an evening sheet. "Leather Apron" whose soubriquet, derived from the constant wear of such a garment, has a ring of midnight deeds and darksome mystery about it, is a real entity, an actual man or monster, for according to the Star he is a mixture of both, who is very well known in East London where he has long been the terror and tyrant of females of the "unfortunate" class. He is described as a man of hideous aspect, with the strength of a bull and the spirit of a demon. His visage perpetually set in a malignant grin, and his sinister eye – a la Mr. Hyde as you perceive – are enough to give a nervous person fits. It seems, ever, that this Cockney Caliban has stabbed or otherwise maltreated scores of the wretched women on whose earnings he lived, for he never worked, but passed idle days on the blackmail extorted from his victims. He is suspected of worse crimes. It appears that his favourite threat to tardy or reluctant taxpayers, was that he meant to "rip them up" and as he always carries a sharpened shoemaker's knife it is certain that he has never been without the way to execute his will. All this is exciting enough, and quite a triumph for the sort which has thrilled the town with it. But there is a serious side to the business if it be true that a woman meeting "Leather Apron" in the streets a day or two ago called on a constable to arrest him for the murder, declaring that she had seen him a couple of hours before the mutilated body of Nicholls was found in company with the deceased. "Leather Apron," it seems, did not offer any denial at first to several repetitions of the charge of murder, but the policeman let him go, and we are now awaiting further developments of this very extraordinary proof that truth is stranger than fiction.

The *Belfast Morning News* version, appearing the following day, contains some of the same wording, demonstrating the way in which stories passed from newspaper to newspaper, sometimes picking up momentum and additional "facts" along the way. It is also highly critical of the police, another theme which would prove popular among the Irish newspapers of both political leanings:

SELDOM outside the pages of fiction has there been anything of a more revolting and mysteriously sensational character than what are popularly known as the Whitechapel murders. For a long time past that portion of London has been the scene of ruffianly outrages, committed by an individual who appears and disappears in the strangest manner. The chief objects of his fiendish attacks are the unfortunate women who haunt the Whitechapel district after nightfall. Many of them have been the victims of his brutality. His character, as far as can be ascertained, appears to be a mixture of the gross and unbridled ruffianism of Bill Sykes with the more cunning cruelty of Fagin the Jew. Indeed his appearance is said to be strikingly suggestive of the lowest Hebrew type, and his movements are silent, stealthy, and snake-like. On his feet he wears some kind of sandals by which he is enabled to move about noiselessly, and in front of him he wears a leather apron, from which his popular sobriquet of "Leather Apron" is derived. The recent horrible and mysterious murder of a woman at Whitechapel, forming as it does a fearful climax to the series of midnight attacks on women in the district, has aroused public feeling to a pitch of intense excitement. It is certainly a marvellous thing that in a populous portion of England's great metropolis outrage and murder can be perpetrated by a man who is known to hundreds, and yet defies detection or capture by the police. Is this but another example of the stale truism that truth is stranger than fiction. Did such a thing occur on the stage, or in the pages of a novel, critics would not be wanting to point out the absurdity of imagining that a man known to hundreds, perhaps thousands, by appearance, could range like a dangerous beast at large, and elude the vigilance of the authorities. Yet this is not the only case where the police have been at fault. Several murders have recently been committed, some in London, some in other parts of the country, and the murderer has walked away as free as air. Year by year swells the list of undiscovered crimes. Jackson, the convict who murdered the warder in Strangeways Prison, Manchester, was for weeks at liberty, and might never have been captured had not over-confidence betrayed him.[8] Even as it was, when he was retaken, his captors had not the slightest suspicion of his identity. There is, therefore, some reason for the prevailing feeling of dread that pervades the Whitechapel district. As soon as dusk descends houses are closed, windows barred, and women refuse to stir abroad. A veritable reign of terror has been instituted. The people fear to meet "Leather apron," whose ghoulish grin, silent movements, and dreaded knife have made him the terror of young and old. It is of course not known for certain whether this Cockney caliban, as he has been styled, is really the murderer of the woman whose hacked and mangled corpse was found upon the footpath at Whitechapel. But popular suspicion and the fact that no trace of him can now be found point strongly towards the conclusion that he is the guilty one. Certainly the fact of such a character eluding the police whilst they are seeking to arrest him on suspicion of being the murderer is not to the credit of the police force, and does not speak well for the protection which the innocent are expected to obtain from the law.

Such criticism of the police found its way into several of the columns of Irish newspapers commenting on the crimes, and this will be studied more closely in later chapters. The *Ballymena Observer* of September 7th was one such example, also moralising over the lifestyle of the victim:

> The crime is still involved in mystery, and as yet the efforts of the police have failed to throw much light on the act of unparalleled atrocity, and as far as we can see of motiveless ferocity. The theory which is gradually assuming shape adds still more to this sordid horror [in] which the whole affair is shrouded. The murder of the unfortunate creature who has been identified as Mary Ann Nichols, bears so strong a resemblance to two other foul assassinations which have occurred in the same neighbourhood that the police think it likely that they were all the work of one individual, or possibly of the same gang of degraded and savage miscreants who blackmail unfortunate women and murder them when their demands for money are denied. But without the strongest proof such a theory ought to be dismissed from our minds, for it is difficult to believe that fiends so inhuman can exist even amongst the debased section of wretches who fester and swarm at the lowest stratum of society. The history of the miserable creature whose life has terminated in a scene of brutal horror is as common as it is humiliating to our boasted civilization. One Mary Ann Nichols was the wife of a mechanic and was respectably connected. Some fourteen years of her life were spent apparently respectably enough with her husband, but whether from an inherited taint of vice, or from the terrible force of necessity that drives the poor and weak into headlong and reckless wickedness – that hunger which persuades to crime – spoken of by the Roman poet – she gradually sank into drunkenness, degradation and infamy. It is her death and not her life that has caused her to be singled out from the crowd of hopeless beings whose existence and evil influence are one of the worst evils of our over-crowded and struggling system. Drink seems to have been the first step in her downward career, as is usually the case; and it was this that compelled her husband to leave her, if we are to believe the evidence given before Mr. Wynne Baxter, the coroner, on Monday. The inquiry has been adjourned for a fortnight. Meanwhile it is to be hoped that the efforts of the police to trace the murderer may be more successful than in the other two cases. That such crimes should remain undiscovered is humiliating. It has been for some time suspected that the police force is inadequate for the manifold duties in London. It is impossible for 14,000 men to cope successfully over the wide area of the metropolis, with the army of criminals who war against law and order, and the percentage of

undiscovered murders is far greater than it ought to be in a well organ-
ized state. Certainly the intelligence shown by the officials of Scotland
Yard in following clues and tracing crime has in several cases failed to satisfy the public. That three secret murders should be committed in one
district in five months and the assassins still remain at large does not
reflect credit on their skill.

However, criticism of the police, at this early stage at least, is not wholly war-
ranted. It must be remembered that they were up against a motiveless murderer, a phenomenon almost unheard of in history up until this point. Jack was not
the world's first serial killer by any stretch of the imagination. But he was the
first whose crimes took advantage of the advances in communications technology to make the horrors a story of global significance. The first trans-Atlantic
telegram message had been sent thirty years earlier: a ninety-four-word message of congratulation from Queen Victoria to the new US President James
Buchanan, it had taken sixteen hours to transmit. In the intervening time, however, the technology had been advanced to such a point that by the time the
Ripper was terrorising East London, news of his crimes were appearing in the
pages of the world's newspapers within a few hours of their appearance in their
English counterparts.

Jack being the first serial murderer of the media age, then, the police force
of the metropolis had no terms of reference to which to refer in their efforts to
detect him. Today an expert criminal psychologist or profiler might be called on
to provide them with likely lines of inquiry. An incident room would be established, and a team of highly experienced detectives and forensic experts assembled. The Behavioral Science Unit of the FBI in America might be contacted for
aid and advice, and DNA and fingerprint analysis would be utilised to narrow
down the list of suspects. None of these investigative techniques were available
in the London of 1888, and the police had no better information to work on
than that which it could glean from a public who were inclined either to clam
up through distrust, or to exaggerate their own importance and level of knowledge. The following report from the *Belfast Morning News* provides an example
of the kind of misinformation they were forced to contend with:

Buck's row, where the body was found, is a narrow passage running out
of Thomas-street, and contains a dozen houses of a very low class. When
Police constable Neil discovered the body he roused the people living in
the house immediately opposite where the body was found, but none of
them had heard any sounds of a struggle. Several persons living in Brady-
street state that early in the morning they heard screams, but this is by no
means an uncommon incident in the neighbourhood, and with one

exception nobody seems to have paid any particular attention to what was probably the death struggle of an unfortunate woman. The exception was a Mrs Colville, who lives only a short distance from the foot of Buck's-row. She says she was awakened in the morning by a woman screaming "Murder! police!" five or six times. The voice faded away as though the woman was going in the direction of Buck's-row, and all was quiet. She only heard the steps of one person. Inspector Helstone [Helson] has, however, since stated that neither blood-stains nor wheel marks were found to indicate that the body had been deposited where found, and himself and Inspector Abberline had come to the conclusion that it was committed on the spot.

This not to say that Mrs Colville was a liar, but there is no evidence to suggest that her information had any bearing on the case. Certainly the police must have disbelieved her, for she was never called to testify at the inquest. Other reports continually state that cries of "Murder!" were common in the district, and so it is possible, even likely, that she was simply exaggerating an almost everyday occurrence in order to make herself seem more knowledgeable to reporters than she in fact was. Such stories became more and more common as the crimes continued, and they dog the final murder to such an extent that the true facts of the case have been argued almost constantly since.

CHAPTER ONE ENDNOTES

1   Reported as Margaret Hayes in some newspapers
2   Renwick Williams, see Appendix One for more information.
3   "Unfortunate" was a popular epithet for a prostitute in Victorian England.
4   R.L. Stevenson's *The Strange Case of Dr Jekyll and Mr Hyde* had been published only the previous year. In the week of the Martha Tabram murder a stage version of this story had opened at the Lyceum starring the renowned actor Richard Mansfield and had become the sensation of the West End. Throughout press reporting of the Ripper murders comparisons to Mr Hyde were common, and there were suggestions at the time that the murderer was inspired by having attended a performance of the play.
5   Thomas de Quincy published the essay "On Murder, Considered as One of the Fine Arts" in *Blackwood's Magazine* in 1827.
6   The correct spelling of Polly's surname is Nichols. However many newspapers gave different spellings. The spellings used throughout the text are those in the original newspaper articles.
7   In fact no such thing happens in *The Strange Case of Dr Jekyll and Mr Hyde* by R.L. Stevenson. Hyde murders only one person, a gentleman named Sir Danvers Carew, and at one point tramples a child in the streets.
8   John Jackson was convicted of the murder of a warder named Webb at Strangeways Prison, and was executed by hanging on August 6th, 1888.

CHAPTER TWO

Social Conditions
and Scotland Yard
Shenanigans

I N I R E L A N D , the Nationalist press were quick to jump on the Whitechapel murder case as an example of the hypocrisy of the English ruling classes towards their Irish brethren. The first of the hardline Republican newspapers to report in this way was *The Nation*, which included this item in its September 8th edition:

UNPUNISHED CRIME IN ENGLAND

Last week a horrible murder was perpetrated in London, the victim being a woman, whose corpse was found in the streets in Whitechapel on Friday morning. There is not, so far, a trace of the murderer to be had, and the police seem to have made no headway with the case. This is the third or fourth murder, in which the victim was a female, which has occurred in London recently, and for which no one has been amenable. Yet we do not hear the people of London denounced for their sympathy with crime. As the murder occurred in a densely populated district, it can scarcely have been perpetrated without someone knowing it. Had it been perpetrated on a lonely Irish roadside instead a whole nation would have been held responsible. But now even the Dublin Evening Mail, which surpasses the lowest Tory rag in Great Britain in this species of vilification, has not a word to say on the matter.

It was to become a common refrain, not only in the newspapers specific to the Nationalist movement such as *The Nation* and the *United Ireland,* but also in the Nationalist leaning mainstream press such as *Freeman's Journal,* the *Belfast Morning News* and the *Cork Examiner.* Even the more conservative, loyalist leaning *Irish Times* was not above taking the occasional swipe at the Dublin Castle administration, while the staunchly Unionist *Dublin Evening Mail* fought the opposite corner. A great deal of the local press also followed the Nationalist agenda and were quick to criticise the English authorities. Wicklow newspaper *The People* printed a short item under the headline "CIVILIZED ENGLAND!" on September 5th:

> The London evening papers of Monday are ghastly reading enough. We have in them such a feast of horrors as the inquest in the Whitechapel mystery, a child murder at Birmingham, a wife murder at Liverpool, the Poplar murder, the attempted murder and suicide by a Wrexham magistrate, the poisoning of a woman on Clapham Common, not to mind a score of less tragic and sensational atrocities.[1]

On August 31st, the day of the Polly Nichols' murder, the *Waterford Citizen* printed a commentary on an incident which had occurred in the previous week, again providing an Irish slant to the event. Under the headline "SCOTLAND YARD AND DUBLIN CASTLE" they printed:

> Mr. Munro,[2] Assistant Commissioner of Police of Scotland Yard, has retired, owing to differences with his Chief. Mr. Munro has endeavoured to build up sensations out of the supposed connection between some of the Irish Nationalists and the dynamiters, and it was believed that he sought to model the London police after the Dublin Castle model. It is hateful to the ordinary Englishman's mind to find a policeman who should be his servant converted into the tool of the Government of the day for political purposes. Sir Charles Warren, notwithstanding his many mistakes, sympathises with this feeling, and Mr. Munro's action did not, therefore, commend his approval. As London would not have these methods at any price, may we hope that Ireland will now be relieved of them?

The operation of the Metropolitan Police force during the late Victorian period was a complicated one, and the *Cork Examiner*, on September 12th, attempted to untangle it for their readers with a lengthy and highly critical explanation of the history and workings of that organisation:

> The appalling series of undetected crimes which have recently been committed in the East-end renders it necessary, in the public interest, to direct attention anew to two alternative plans for the protection of life and the detection of crime between which the authorities of the Home Office, who are responsible to the public, seem to be wavering at the present time.

A couple of months ago the organisation which was thought necessary for the purpose would have been briefly summed up as follows:– (1) An Assistant-Commissioner of Police, specially qualified by half a lifetime's experience in the directing of criminal investigations; (2) a superintendent who had served nearly 40 years in the detective department; and (3) under them inspectors and men in each Metropolitan district charged to report to headquarters every day and at all hours of the day or night on the occurrence of any serious crime, or with regard to any, even the faintest, clue that might appear to throw light upon any matter under investigation by the department. To-day what is thought necessary is to have a large body of detectives scouring the district in which a crime has been committed, to have no head or special organisation of the department, but to leave the charge of the inquiry in such cases as the latest East-end murder for example, to the inspectors on duty at Commercial-street Police-station, who are unfamiliar with detective work, and already sufficiently occupied with their ordinary routine duties. It seems hardly credible, and yet it is perfectly true, that when the first of the three recent diabolical murders in Whitechapel occurred about a month ago, Mr Superintendent Williamson, though attending daily at Scotland-yard, in charge of the Detective Department, received no notice whatever for a whole week that any such crime had been committed, and that this happened not accidentally or through carelessness, but in accordance with a deliberate plan on the part of the Commissioner of Police. We have not the slightest desire to exaggerate or misrepresent the present condition of things at Scotland-yard, but we think it but right that the public should understand that the changes which have taken place there are not merely personal ones, but that the whole system of the detective department is being changed, and changed, as we believe, for the worse, and that if Sir Charles Warren's plan is fully carried out it involves a return to the old system, which less than a dozen years ago gave rise to so much scandal, and was fully exposed and condemned in the course of the trial for fraud of Detective Inspectors Druskovitch and Meiklejohn in 1877. The history of the detective, or as it has lately been called, the Criminal Investigation Department at Scotland-yard, is curious. When Sir Robert Peel established in 1829 the Metropolitan Police, the principle he adopted was to create two chiefs, one a military man, accustomed to command large bodies of men, the other a civilian, to whom was entrusted the detective department. This system continued down to the year 1866, when Colonel Rowan died, and Sir B. Mayne shortly after became sole Commissioner, with two Assistant-Commissioners to assist him. On Sir B. Mayne's death Colonel Henderson was likewise appointed sole Commissioner with two Assistant-Commissioners, neither of whom, however, was specially responsible for the detective department, the heads of that department consisting down to the year 1877 of Inspectors who had risen from the ranks, two of whom, as has been already mentioned, were in that year tried for fraud and receiving bribes from the notorious convict Benson, and were convicted and sentenced to two years imprisonment with hard labour. In consequence of this trial a demand was made in the next session of Parliament that the department should be officered by men of higher status and greater intelligence, and as the result of a Commission which was appointed, Mr Howard Vincent, M.P., became the first Director of Criminal Investigations, but without any legal status as Assistant-Commissioner. When Mr Monro was appointed four years ago to succeed Mr Vincent, this anomaly was remedied, and Mr Monro, in order to give him the necessary power over his men, was made an Assistant-Commissioner, bringing the number of Assistant-Commissioners up to three. It is this fact that has indirectly led to the present disorganisation of the department. Sir Charles Warren having used his power as Commissioner to hamper the action of the Assistant-Commissioner, including the detective department, until the latter felt that he could no longer be responsible for its efficient working. Thus, for instance, however urgent might be the necessity for sending a detective to one of the seaport towns to track a criminal, or for any other purpose connected with his department, the late Director of the Criminal Investigation Department and Assistant-Commissioner found himself debarred from doing so by an order of Sir Charles Warren that no man was to be sent out of London without his permission. It is rumoured in the force that Superintendent Williamson, being also dissatisfied with the changes which have been made, and of which he is known to disapprove, talks of resigning, and should he do so, the condition of affairs will be almost precisely similar to what it was previous to 1877. There will be no one above the rank of an inspector in the department who has had any detective experience. It is needless to say that neither the present Chief Commissioner, nor any of his three Assistant-Commissioners has any practical experience of the working of this special department of police work, and a heavy responsibility will rest upon those in authority if they permit such a scandalous state of things to continue a day longer than necessary, while such murders are being committed in the East-end at the present time, and dynamite plots in the future are not wholly unexpected. The West-end may have to-morrow as much urgent cause as the East-end has to-day, for desiring that there should be a real direction of the work of the detective department, and that it should be placed in experienced hands.

Sir Charles Warren, forty-eight years old at the time of the murders, had been occupying the Chief Commissionership for two and a half years, having succeeded Sir Edmund Henderson in the role in early 1886. He was a popular appointment at the time, but he was the choice of Hugh Childers, the Home Secretary in Gladstone's moderate liberal Government, and when that Government fell a few months later, the new Tory premier Lord Salisbury appointed Henry Matthews as his Home Secretary. Henderson's downfall had come mainly as a result of a riot which he had failed to prevent, and when Warren seemed similarly unable to control the anarchist and Socialist protesters of the capital city his popularity likewise began to wane. Things came to a head on November 13th, 1887.

Early that week the Irish radical organisations of London had announced a major rally was to take place on that date in Trafalgar Square to protest the prison treatment of the Nationalist MP and editor of the *United Ireland,* William O'Brien, who had been imprisoned earlier that month and who was in dispute with the prison authorities over his refusal to wear prison clothes.[3] It was the latest in a series of protests over unemployment, Irish home rule and other radical issues to take place in the square, and which often ended in civil disobedience. Claiming that the square was the property of the Queen and not a public space, the authorities determined to act on the matter, as reported by *The Irish Times* on November 10th, 1887:

> The authorities have taken a decisive step with respect to the public demonstrations of the unemployed. The "centre of discontent" is declared a closed arena, and henceforth until further orders, Trafalgar square must be considered a proclaimed district. The notice issued by Sir Charles Warren is believed to be directed against the possibilities of other displays as well as against the actualities of the agitation which has its rallying point at the base of the Nelson monument. The Nationalist meeting which is in process of promotion was to have been held on the square, which, however, is now shut against that and all other forms of public manifestation.
>
> Apparently, however, the unemployed do not mean to accept the edict without an attempt at resistance. The evening journal which has constituted itself the champion of the people of the mob, comes out to-night with the defiant proclamation that in spite of the abuse of authority next Sunday will probably witness the largest meeting ever held in Trafalgar square. And Sir Charles Warren is further warned of the fate which befell Charles I when he tried to trample the people, or mob, who are suggestively reminded how the Hyde Park railings went down before the rush of the men who charged for liberty in 1866. Mr Stead[4] evidently

desires a conflict with the law, and it is believed that his desire will be gratified.

The organisers of the rally immediately issued a proclamation in defiance of the order, news of which was spread to almost every radical group in the entire metropolis. Sir Charles, meanwhile, was ordered by the Home Office to uphold the decision and ensure that the meeting did not take place. In fairness to Warren, the decision to prohibit meetings in the square was not his, but the responsibility for upholding that decision was nonetheless his responsibility, leaving him stuck between a rock and a hard place. Neither he nor the radicals were likely to back down and as the day of the meeting dawned, the whole of London held its breath in anticipation of the certain apocalypse that would follow. On November 14th *The Irish Times* described the scene in the square:

> Notwithstanding the police prohibition enormous crowds assembled around Trafalgar square yesterday afternoon, but were prevented entering the square by a triple cordon of police, mounted and on foot. Processions marched from the outlying districts with bands and banners, but were charged and broken up by the police after a series of fierce encounters, in the course of which many people were wounded by batons. About half-past four Sir Charles Warren, feeling himself powerless to control the enormous multitude around the square, summoned the military. The square was then patrolled by a detachment of Life Guards and several companies of Foot Guards, a magistrate riding with the guards ready to read the Riot Act. It appears that the sharpest scuffle took place at Westminster bridge, when two policemen were stabbed, one in the back, with an oyster knife, sharpened for the purpose, and the other on the chin. Processions from Bermondsey, Peckham, and Deptford met at Battersea section on the bridge, and by word of command formed one body. The police instantly attacked the centre of the procession, and wrested ten flags from the leaders. A hand-to-hand encounter took place, in which, as stated, two policemen were stabbed. Many were wounded by iron bars, pokers, stones, and sticks. Twenty-six processionists received head wounds from the batons which were freely used, while fifteen constables were injured. Shortly after four o'clock Mr Cunninghame Graham, M.P., and Mr John Burns, followed by about 400 persons made an attack upon the police forming a cordon round Trafalgar square. This manoeuvre was unsuccessful. Mr Cunninghame Graham was at once met on reaching the police by Inspector Hume and the police who drove him back. Mr Graham again pressed forward and according to the statements of the police used his fists freely on the con-

stables. Mr Graham was injured in the struggle, his forehead being cut open. He was immediately taken within the square, where his injuries were attended to by the police doctors. Later on he was brought up at Bow street, when, the charge having been taken, he was bailed out. Mr John Burns remained in custody. During the evening vast crowds still loitered in the neighbourhood of the square. There was no further disturbance, and order was soon restored.

The London Correspondent of that newspaper gave a personal account of his witness of the events of the day:

I have seen a good deal of rough work at public meetings during the last twenty-five years, but nothing to compare with the doings in Trafalgar square this afternoon. I was fortunate enough to obtain a place from which I could observe the proceedings in the lower end of the square where the conflict between the police and the people was the most prolonged; and a friend who witnessed what took place at the northern end tells me that there the police acted very much as their comrades did at the southern end, and that among the total of a hundred or more injured persons who were treated at the hospitals there is one with a bayonet wound in his back inflicted by a soldier of the Foot Guards. The mob consisted largely of idle people attracted to the spot by the expectations of a row between the police and the organisers of the meeting. There were the usual proportion of London roughs, loafers, and pickpockets. Up to nearly 3.30 everything went quietly. The mounted patrols advanced from the four-deep cordon of foot police, and after clearing the roadway returned to their posts. But at 3.25, when there must have been nearly 100,000 people massed at and near Charing Cross, a man on the pavement by the Grand Hotel began to address the crowd and to denounce Sir Charles Warren as the "bloody African butcher." Some of the people cheered and cried, "Down with the police." Immediately a body of foot police advanced on the crowd, followed by a dozen mounted men, and a scrimmage ensued, in which the police used their truncheons freely. The people retaliated, and one of the constables received an ugly blow on the head, I believe, with a stone. The bystanders hooted and groaned at the police and then the horsemen rode hard into the throng, scattering it in all directions.

Wheeling round by the top of Northumberland avenue, one of the horses slipped and rolled over on its rider, whose mishap was greeted with derisive cheers. Evidently exasperated, the comrades of the fallen constable went at the people standing on the "Refuge" in the middle of the roadway. Those who had sticks hit out at the police and the horses wherever they got a chance; others kicked at the horses' legs, and one fellow laid hold of a constable's cloak and tried to drag him from the saddle. At 4.15 the Lifeguards, with Mr Marsham, a police magistrate, rode slowly up Whitehall and were cheered, whilst the police were groaned at and hissed [sic]. The lifeguards rode at a walk round and round the square, the people cheering them as they passed. At the same time the mounted police, in detachments of from five to fifty, continued to rush their horses through the people, many of whom in escaping from one detachment were run down by another. After several charges had been made, the mounted police drew their truncheons. As darkness approached, the attack upon the crowd became more furious, and the horsemen not only cleared the roadways, but rode among the people on the pavements and drove them out of doorways. One body went helter skelter into a dense crowd on the pavement by the Old National Liberal Clubhouse, their horses rearing and plunging. Then the foot police rushed up and plied their batons freely. A quarter of an hour later the people had rushed back to this point to avoid a police charge lower down the avenue, and then they were again stampeded by about twenty police. The unarmed crowd, although vastly superior in point of numbers, was naturally unable to resist for any length of time such onslaughts, and by six o'clock most of the assemblage had dispersed, leaving behind upwards of a hundred in hospital, and about seventy in custody.

The victory belonged to the Government, the meeting was prevented, the agitation put down, but at the expense of the reputations of both Sir Charles Warren and Home Secretary Matthews. The public of Britain never forgave them for what happened on the day that became known as "Bloody Sunday", especially after one of the injured protesters later died in hospital. The Irish Nationalist press obviously vented their spleens upon the Government and their minion, Sir Charles. The *United Ireland* printed this in their edition of November 19th:

> To the present Government belongs the glory of having for the first time in history successfully invaded the right of free speech in the metropolis of the Empire. How far their popularity will be enhanced by the proceeding remains to be seen. The point at issue between the Government and the people was a narrow one. They wrong the Executive who introduce any question of expedience or convenience into the controversy. The people contended that free speech in the principal square in their own city was a national birthright; the Government argued that it was a

royal indulgence, revocable at will. The Government argued the question with the batons of the police and the sabres of the Life Guards, and carried their point – for the present. It was a strange sight, and scarcely a pleasing one to London eyes – the military and semi-military forces arrayed against their fellow citizens as for a pitched battle or a massacre, as chance might decide; a riot deliberately provoked, which might reach easily to the dimensions of a civil war.

Meanwhile even in their own country the action was seen as heavy handed and unnecessary, a staggering over-reaction on the behalf of the authorities, as expressed by the *Freeman's Journal* on November 15th:

> There was, of course, no talk of anything in London yesterday but Sunday's conflict in Trafalgar-square. It is not easy to find anyone who is particularly charmed with the results of the alleged attempt to vindicate law and order by the authorities. This is, perhaps, because no one can exactly understand how law and order were imperilled by the meeting which the police and military dispersed. There may be something to be said from the utilitarian point of view against holding meetings every week day in Trafalgar-square, but the considerations which could be urged against such a practice have no force when applied to Sunday's assemblage. This is an undeniable fact, and even those Tories who like to see law and order vindicated now and then, just to remind the people of the political force at the back of the authorities and of the readiness of said authorities to use it, think that the occasion selected was inopportune, and that the affair will not improve the position or reputation of the Government.

For Sir Charles Warren it was a turning point indeed, and his popularity as a man of the people vanished in an instant, to be replaced by a new reputation as a military martinet ruling the Metropolitan force with an iron fist.

What did not help the situation was that Warren began to be more and more in conflict with Mr Matthews over the running of the force. It was Warren's opinion that, as the man who bore all the responsibility for the force, he should thus have complete control over the decisions. One particular thorn in his side in this respect was the secret "Section D", frequently known as the Secret Irish Department, an elite anti-terrorist unit whose brief was to keep tabs on suspected Fenian agitators, which was under the direct control of James Monro. Although Monro reported to Warren as an Assistant Commissioner and Director of the Criminal Investigation Department, his activities as head of Section D were answerable directly to Matthews and by-passed Warren in the chain of command. It was a situation he found intolerable, and his relationships with both Monro and Matthews were showing cracks early into 1888. In the summer of that year things came to a head: Monro resigned his position in a letter to the Home Secretary on August 16th, stating that "Grave differences of opinion on questions of police administration have arisen between Sir Charles Warren and myself,"[5] and he officially left office on the day before the Polly Nichols murder, with his successor Dr Robert Anderson taking his place on the very day of that atrocity. On September 5th, *The Irish Times* printed an explanation of events that had led up to this situation:

> We are in a position to furnish the following additional particulars respecting the state of affairs at Scotland Yard. Friction between the Home Secretary and Sir Charles Warren commenced about the time of the Trafalgar Square disturbances, the immediate cause being that Mr. Matthews showed favour to the Commissioner of the Metropolitan District against whom the Chief Commissioner had brought charges of disregarding police regulations and giving orders to superintendents without consulting his official superiors. Sir Charles Warren protested against the course pursued by the Secretary of State, and finally threatened to resign, a threat which was repeated later on. It became necessary at length to bring the matter under the notice of the Cabinet, and Mr. W.H. Smith and Mr. Goschen were deputed by their colleagues to bring about a settlement of the points in dispute. Early in May Mr. Smith, Mr. Goschen, Mr. Matthews and Sir Charles Warren met in Downing street, and as a result of a conference which lasted nearly all afternoon the Chief Commissioner was adjudged to have made his case. The disputes between Sir Charles Warren and Mr. Monro arose out of representations made by the latter respecting the numerical weakness of the staff of the Criminal Investigation Department, coupled with a request for the appointment of an assistant chief constable and a few additional subordinate officers. Sir Charles Warren was not at first inclined to accede to Mr. Monro's request, but ultimately taking late account the fact that Chief Constable Williamson was at the moment absent through illness he agreed to the appointment of an assistant chief constable. A gentleman of large experience was recommended for the post with the acquiescence of the Chief Commissioner, and the recommendation was formally made to the Secretary of State; but before the appointment had been actually made Sir Charles Warren withdrew his recommendation on the ground that circumstances had come to his knowledge which made it undesirable that the gentleman in question should be appointed. The appointment was never made and the question of creating the new

post remains in abeyance. This did not improve the relations between Sir Charles Warren and Mr. Monro. Matters reached a crisis early in July when the Chief Commissioner and Mr. Monro went to the Home Office and had a lengthy interview with the Secretary of State, at which it was decided that Mr. Monro should immediately take a leave of absence with a view to his subsequent resignation.

The resignation was not an unpopular one among the Irish Nationalist press. Monro's Section D detectives, officially an anti-terrorist unit, had of late been most notable for highly public attempts to link Fenian terrorism to members of the Irish Parliamentary party. The *Freeman's Journal* had this to say on September 1st:

It is satisfactory to find that there is a pretty unanimous feeling among the London police that Sir Chas Warren's policy in Scotland Yard, which only last week brought about the resignation of Mr. Monro, the Assistant Commissioner, will have the effect of abolishing the Criminal Investigation Department or crippling its usefulness very materially. If any such result follows Sir Chas Warren's action all decent men will be ready to support the Chief Commissioner instead of holding aloof as they do now. The Criminal Investigation Department was up to some years ago a very useful institution in a big city like London, and it would continue always to be regarded as such if its functions were confined to the investigation of crime. But latterly it as been converted into a sort of political bureau. The hunt after the dynamiters completely demoralised it. Mr. Monro and his detectives, instead of confining their attentions to the men who come to London to blow up bridges, made a set upon all Irish Nationalists. They followed and dogged men who have as hearty abhorrence of crime as themselves. They swarmed about the House of Commons for the past two sessions, subjecting Irish members to the most offensive form of espionage, and creating such a scandal that English members like Mr. Bradlaugh and Sir Wilfrid Lawson avowed with shame from their places in the house that no such humiliating spectacle could be seen in any capital in Europe. This being the sort of work done by the Criminal Investigation Department, nobody will regret that Sir Charles Warren has given it a knock on the head. What would have pleased Mr. Monro was to be left a perfectly free hand at Whitehall-place, and to be allowed to do as he liked with his detectives and plain clothes policemen. Evidently Sir Charles Warren has very different notions. Sir Charles Warren is a very stern man, and his action in connection with Trafalgar-square shows that he cares very little for the rights of the public in the matter of open meetings, but still he has strong and not altogether objectionable views about the duty of every individual policeman under his charge.

If, however, it was Monro's actions against Irish Republicanism which made him an unpopular man in the eyes of that movement, had they but known it his successor was no improvement. An Irishman by birth, Dr Robert Anderson's antecedents were described in an article in the *Belfast Morning News* on September 3rd under the headline "FROM DUBLIN CASTLE TO SCOTLAND YARD":

> Mr. Robert Anderson, who succeeds Assistant-Commissioner J Munro at Scotland-yard, in the Criminal Investigation Department, is the third son of Matthew Anderson, of Dublin, formerly Crown Solicitor for the city and county of Dublin. He is forty seven years of age, and married in 1873 Agnes Alexandria, sister of Ponsenby W Moore, cousin and heir presumptive of the Marquis of Drogheda. Mr. Anderson was educated at Trinity College, Dublin, where he holds the honorary degree LLD, and entered a student of Middle Temple in 1860, and was called to the Bar 1870, having previously been called to the Dublin Bar in 1863.
>
> Mr. R Anderson served in the Irish Office in London 1867–8 and assisted in the Irish State trials of '67. Since '68 he has been attached to the Home Office, and has there held the appointment of Secretary to the Commissioners of English Prisoners since 1878 at a salary of £600 per annum. He will now receive some £1,300 per annum as Assistant-Commissioner of Police. He was secretary to the Royal Merchant Shipping Commission of 1864. He has contributed articles to the *Nineteenth Century*, is the author of "Prison Acts," and member of the National and Savile Clubs.

What this article did not say was that Anderson's tenure at Dublin Castle, arranged for him by his elder brother Samuel, the Solicitor General in the viceregal administration, had been one of monitoring the activities of Fenian groups, and his transfer to London had actually been to take up the role of deputy head of the anti-Fenian intelligence. In this role he became the personal controller of the notorious spy and double agent Thomas Billis Beach, who infiltrated the American Fenian movement under the false name of Major Henri Le Caron. He had been ousted from the intelligence service on May 9th, 1884 by the then head of the secret Irish department, Edward Jenkinson, but had unofficially returned to the work when Monro, who was a close friend, had taken over from Jenkinson. It was this close association with the work which had made him the obvious choice to succeed Monro as the CID chief.

Furthermore Anderson was, anonymously, one of the authors of *Parnellism and Crime*, a series of articles which ran in the *Times* newspaper beginning on March 7th, 1887, accusing Charles Stewart Parnell and the Irish party of involvement in agrarian crime in Ireland.[6] He was rumoured to have been among those involved in instigating the forging of letters implicating Parnell in supporting the assassination of Lord Frederick Cavendish and Thomas Burke, all of which will be discussed at greater length in a later chapter. On hearing of his appointment Edward Jenkinson, who probably knew more about the secret anti-Irish dealings of the Government than any other man alive, said, "What an infamously bad appointment it is! Anderson is not the 19th part of a man, and if it were known what kind of man he is, there would be a howl all over London."[7]

The job of the police was not made any easier by the arena in which these murders were taking place. The district, generally referred to as Whitechapel but in reality also including Spitalfields and the boundaries of Shoreditch, Bethnal Green and the City of London, was an area centred on the confluence of five main thoroughfares in the area to the east of Liverpool Street Station. If one takes the junction as the central point, then Aldgate ran westwards, Commercial Street to the north, Whitechapel Road and Commercial Road ran east, and Leman Street was to the south. Each of the murders occurred in close proximity to one or more of these main roads. Bucks Row was to be found in the east, just to the north of Whitechapel Road, and parallel to it, in the region of the London Hospital.

The horror stories which abound with regard to the desperate slum conditions in the region generally refer to the area between Commercial Street and Brick Lane, which ran northwards parallel to that road. In this area some of the worst streets in the city were to be found, including Thrawl Street and Flower and Dean Street, the two streets where Polly Nichols had lodged, together with Fashion Street and White's Row, and the notorious Dorset Street, known as the "Do As You Please," a street with such a bad reputation that it was said that uniformed policemen refused to enter it except in pairs. In these streets were clustered some two hundred and thirty-three common lodging houses which were home to something like eight and a half thousand abandoned wretches, of which the police estimated around one thousand two hundred resorted at least some of the time to prostitution to keep body and soul together.[8] The *Clare Journal* of September 17th tried to give its readers some idea of the conditions in this hellhole:

> It is difficult if not impossible to give readers who dwell in wholesome country towns or still more wholesome villages any idea of the conditions under which life goes on and still retains life, in the noisome dens of Whitechapel and the blind alleys by the docks. Were we to draw any-

thing like a true and faithful picture, in the first place it would not be believed, and in the second the details would be totally unfit for publication. Mr G R Sims[9] created a great stir in the columns of a London contemporary by his essays on "How the poor live;" but even he drew a discreet veil over the more ghastly portions of his canvas as that, shocking as his revelations were, they are not, as our American cousins would say, a circumstance to the real thing. The houses where the miserable wretches are huddled together are vile and obscene, the rooms they occupy in swarms are so many hotbeds of disease and vice; the food they eat is offal, their drink is but the scourings of the bar counter. They hide their nakedness with scraps of rags which no dog would look at. Much has been written by sentimentalists to prove that these people are superior to their surroundings and that they have only to be kindly treated to imbibe culture, and to become like their happier neighbours. This is a very pretty theory, but, alas! it is utterly worthless. The people of other quarters which are still called slums may be amenable to the unselfish efforts of philanthropists, but their slums, the slums of St Giles, of Westminster, or of Marylebone, are heavens of sweetness and light in comparison with those of Whitechapel. Here the nature of the inhabitants is subdued to that of the locality it works in, here, in brief, and to put it with brutal candour, the people are savages. Even this term is a compliment to them, for your natural savage has often lofty instincts and always some chivalry, and pride in his own person. None of these qualities exist in the London rough. He is a coward, a bully, he lusts after blood, he is a mean – unspeakably mean sneak. He subsists on the earnings of his wife, his mistress or his sister, and our readers need not ask how these earnings are obtained. He has no conscience, either public or private, and nothing, no not one rose from the dead, would impress him.

These were the streets where all of the victims of the Ripper lived. Life in the lodging houses was a constant grind, a struggle to make ends meet where every day, come rain or shine, the occupants would drag their weary bodies out onto the streets to scrape together a few meagre pennies to pay for food and drink and the next night's bed. These establishments did not keep permanent lodgers, the beds were rented by the night, fourpence for a single, eightpence for a double, and if you couldn't pay then you were left to walk the streets or to find shelter in a doorway or huddled under one of the bridges down on the Thames.

Even in the lodging houses themselves there was little by way of comfort or privacy. The London Correspondent of the *Dublin Evening Mail* would later describe one of the dormitory rooms in one such establishment as having "some thirty beds, let out to couples, who were only separated from each other by partitions that commenced a foot or more above the flooring and ended before reaching the ceiling." This only told half the story. On nights when the houses were busy mattresses would be thrown on the floor to squeeze in a few extra guests whose names would likely not appear on the official books, and for twopence one could spend the night slumped over a rope stretched across the centre of the room, about which the best that could be said was that it got the poor sod out of the rain and the cold.

E.T. Greaves, the London Correspondent of the *New York World*, gave his readers a description of the district which was reprinted in the *Belfast Morning News* on November 23rd and provides a good overall view of what life must have been like for the residents:

> Through this populous district the Whitechapel-road runs obliquely, much as Broadway runs through New York city. This thoroughfare is the Bowery of London, but twice as big, thrice as wicked and with four times the number of people pushing and crowding through it after nightfall. The dissolute and vicious of all climes congregate there – black "Lascar" sailors from India, crazed with rum; gay girls from Paris, who had to leave that city or go to prison for purification; men and women who have "done their time" in prisons; others who have escaped, and never stir out in the daylight; thieves and Thugs, housebreakers and harlots – they all are. The sky is aglow with the glare of splendid gin palaces, cheap theatres, and the smoking naphtha lamps of thousands of street vendors; you may see the reflection of it for miles. But they are not all wicked people that you see in Whitechapel at night. It is the shopping street of the respectable labourer and his wife. He may buy there at what we call in New York "Bowery prices." Not one in one hundred of the troops of Americans who come here every year goes to Whitechapel, or has even a remote idea where it is. Baedecker informs us in three lines that it is a district devoted to artisans and sugar refineries. That is very much like describing Brooklyn as a place devoted to preachers and elevated railways. So far as the condition of the streets is concerned, Whitechapel is cleaner than the territory I have referred to on the East side of New York. So far as the average appearance of the houses goes, it is not nearly as dilapidated as the Communists' quarter of Paris. But you will find more squalid, ragged children there, more half fed wretched-looking men and women, than you can scrape up in New York and Paris put together. It is the loose women of Whitechapel who make it one of the strangest and saddest spectacles in Christendom. Hundreds and hundreds of these forlorn creatures tramp the streets from dark till dawn. They have no home. It is seldom that they even sleep two nights under the one roof. These

unfortunates ply their vocation in the open streets, the hallway of lodg-ing-houses, and in the sheltered "squares" where they can gain privacy. In the bitterest weather they roam houseless, creeping into stairways to sleep, huddling in untenanted cellars, packed close together for warmth and heat. Until these murders began no policeman disturbed them. So long as they did not quarrel they were allowed to forget their misery in slumber. All that is changed now. The policemen are ordered to rout the unfortunate creatures out, and they tramp about all night and all next day till they can get fourpence to hire a bed.

The London Correspondent of that newspaper then carried on to provide her own opinion on the situation:

There are doubtless many people in these islands and in America who will perhaps think that this terrible picture is overdrawn, or painted in too lurid colours. Alas! it is but too true. It is drawn to life by a keen, obser-vant, and dispassionate observer. During my recent visits to the East End I have frequently been a witness of scenes of such absolute misery and degradation as no pen could adequately describe – which no painter could satisfactorily reproduce. The visitor is positively appalled by the widespread misery of the poor creatures, worn out with hunger, hard-ship, and fatigue, who listlessly trump in rags about the squalid streets or slumber on the doorsteps and in the dirty hallways. One has but to gaze upon their wan, pinched, and pallid features, thin, shuddering frames, and emaciated limbs, to read of a life of vice and misery, such as none of the writers of realism have yet given the least idea to the outside world. There was some years ago a picture in the Royal Academy in Dublin, entitled "The Castaways," which I recollect attracted much attention at the time. It represented shipwrecked persons on a raft at sea, in the last stages of starvation – gaunt spectres from whom all hope of relief seemed to have fled. An artist could get many models for such a picture over here in the slums, in the parks, on the iron seats beside the wealth of the palaces of Piccadilly, or in the embrasures of the Thames bridges. And yet, with such awful misery at our very doors, thousands of pounds are sent across the seas annually for the "conversion of the heathen," in flagrant opposition to the well-known proverb:– "Charity begins at home." It would be little wonder if the Buddhists, hearing from visitors away at the East End of the savagery, vice, and misery of this quarter of London, should entertain serious ideas of sending their missionaries here.

The overcrowded situation was exacerbated by the arrival in the years leading up to the murders of thousands upon thousands of continental Jews fleeing from persecution and pogroms in their homelands. They flooded into the East End as desperate refugees, and the captains of industry were quick to take advantage of this influx of potential workforce willing to survive on subsistence wages and undercut the traditional workforce. The results were the sweating shops which were described in a special report in the *Bray Herald* on April 21st, 1888:

A great deal of interest, and that of a painful kind, has been aroused in London by the revelations concerning what is known as "the sweating system" which prevails to such a lamentable extent in the East-end, and which are just now being made before a select committee of the House of Lords specially appointed to inquire into the subject. Of course, sweating is no new thing, as all readers of Charles Kingsley's "Alton Locke" published not far from forty years ago can testify. But its effects appear to have been intensified of late by the extensive immigration of Russian, Polish, and German Jews who, driven from their own land by persecution or poverty, are willing to accept starvation wages in order to keep body and soul together. A bootmaker from Austria has testified before the committee that he had to work from five in the morning until half-past twelve at night for about 15s. 8d. per week, out of which he had to live and pay rent; and a Russian Jew, turned out of his country simply because of his religion and race, deposed that, having arrived in this country three weeks before with only three shillings in his pocket, he had agreed to work for a month on trial for nothing but a cup of tea or coffee from his employer for a day's work. There can be no honest competition between British artisans and such wretched hand-to-mouth toilers as these, and the Select Committee has a very serious problem before it in endeavouring to suggest a remedy, for a state of things which, from every point of view, is altogether deplorable.

As bearing upon this grave question and as showing the growing proportion of foreigners who live in London it may be stated that no fewer than 662 Jewish in-patients were treated at the London Hospital, situated at Whitechapel, in the course of last year. Two Jewish wards, forming practically a distinct hospital for the Hebrew community, are now included in this establishment, a special Jewish kitchen, presided over by a Jewish cook, being part of the arrangement. This extensive provision for one alien race alone may appear astonishing to those who do not know how thoroughly some portions of the East-end are being Germanised and Hebraised. There are whole streets there in which one cannot see a single English name over a shop-door, and through which one may pass without hearing a word of our own language. The East-end is truly a home for all nations, but there is an uncomfortableness in the knowledge that an even larger foreign population is accumulating in our midst; for the greater it grows the less chance will there be of it being assimilated into English.

This was the world in which the Whitechapel murders were taking place, a dingy world of seedy back streets and alleys and blind courts, poorly lit and overpopulated with the dregs of humanity. Little wonder then that the killer could walk these streets with impunity, unmolested and undetected among the great unwashed whose appearance could be no less depraved than his own. If there could be said to have been one positive aspect to the murders it was the light that was thrown on the situation by the horrific butcheries taking place in its midst. The *Irish Times* of September 20th printed a lengthy leader column on the need for reform.

The marked attention of the entire English public has gravely been excited by the appearance of a letter in the *Times* over the well known signature S.G.O.,[10] dealing with the horrors that lately have been recounted from the infamous neighbourhood of Whitechapel. The writer uses strong language, and taking to task a class of social philanthropists whose energies might be directed into more beneficial channels than those they now occupy. The sentimentalism of philanthropy has been its bane, and indulgence in it has handicapped terribly many movements which more wisely directed, would have conferred a greater benefit upon humanity. The seed of evil, says S.G.O., has been sown, and we must expect to reap the harvest. "At last we are beginning to see what is the meaning and result of the existence in our midst of tens of thousands of our fellow-creatures, begotten and reared in an atmosphere of godless brutality, a species of human savage, the very drainage of the vilest productions of ordinary vice." Facts warrant the employment of such terms, for at this late hour in the modern day there are districts, not peculiar to London alone – though there the worst – in all great centres of population, where vice is born and reared, amidst a squalor and abandonment of which the citizen but a little removed knows nothing. These are the nests of social disease, from which proceed the monsters that vex society, and so frequently shock the moral sense of the community by appearing as the guiding spirits in an epidemic of crime. It is a commonplace reflection that criminals are educated with the utmost ingenuity of profligacy to take their part in the war upon society, and it is equally a known fact that the downward path in the majority of cases leads at last to that description of abandoned wickedness which of late in the case of the Whitechapel tragedies has so awfully been demonstrated. For this, who is responsible? The officers of the law may be blamed, and perhaps not altogether unjustly so, for a want of vigilance, but are they ultimately to be held accountable for the existence of the foul blot? The public must bear their part of the burden, for as the *Times* observes, "we seem to have listlessly acquiesced in the existence of these kitchen-middens of humanity; to have treated them as though society must keep a receptacle for the collection of its waste material. We have long ago learnt that neglected organic refuse breeds pestilence. Can we doubt that neglected human refuse as inevitably breeds crime, and that crime reproduces itself like germs in an infected atmosphere, and becomes at each successive cultivation more deadly, more bestial, and more absolutely unrestrained?" Mr BARNETT, Vicar of St. Jude's, Whitechapel, further writes to the journal quoted, with a special knowledge of the East End, and utters these startling words – "The murders were, it may almost be said, bound to come; generation could not follow generation in lawless intercourse; children could not be familiarised with scenes of degradation, community in society could not be the bond of society, and the end of all peace." And the writer, who has special means of knowledge, adds – "Some of us who during many years have known the life of our neighbours do not think these murders to be the worst facts in our experience, and published evidence now gives material for forming a picture of daily or nightly life such as no one has imagined." We thus were given to understand that worse remains behind, and the public can readily conceive how dread are the fatal influences of virulent social disease working at this moment in the slums of the densely populated cities. For the moment London has a bad pre-eminence, but can we honestly look around us as citizens of lesser towns and flatter ourselves that we are not as other men?

But how is this crying evil to be swept from among us? How is the light of purity to be let in upon these dens of iniquity? How are we at once to stamp out the grosser forms of crime and instil the sentiments of responsibility which so many hapless wretches are ignorant of? The problem is a vast one, but who will say that it is insoluble? To meet it is not the business of a department or a society of philanthropic visionaries. The duty is one that falls on all classes alike, and from their common stirring alone can good issue. The prominence given to the discussion has stimulated a multitudinous variety of suggestions. We do not propose to consider them at present in detail. But it may be noticed that the VICAR of ST. JUDE'S puts forward four primarily necessary directions which reform must take – efficient police supervision, adequate lighting and cleaning, the removal of slaughter-houses, and the control of tenement houses by responsible landlords. These would be radical changes, but they would represent nothing more than an initial step. Let the world ask itself, "Who is my neighbour?" and strive to supply the answer that humanity should dictate.

As far as the police were concerned, the first action taken by Dr Robert Anderson on taking up the role as head of the CID was to deal with this high profile crime by appointing one of his senior Scotland Yard detectives to the case. Inspector Frederick George Abberline, the officer whose name would become most associated with the case in the century to come, was sent to Whitechapel to co-ordinate the investigation on the ground, the last two murders having been committed in the different jurisdictions of H and J Divisions respectively. Anderson could not possibly have chosen a better man for this job. A softly spoken but highly intelligent detective hailing from Dorset, Abberline had spent most of his career in H Division where he had risen to take charge of the local CID, and there was probably no officer on the force who knew the streets and criminals of Whitechapel more intimately. On September 15th another senior Scotland Yard detective, Chief Inspector Donald Swanson, was appointed to take overall charge of the investigation.

In that first week of the investigation after the murder of Polly Nichols, everything pointed to the mysterious "Leather Apron" as the perpetrator of the crimes. On the evening of September 8th, the London Correspondent of the *Dublin Evening Mail* provided the readers with brief details of the progress of investigations so far:

> Still there seems to be no important clue in connection with the perpetrator of the Whitechapel murder. Even the man known as "Leather Apron," who is said to have been in the company of the murdered woman a few hours before the crime was discovered, cannot now be found by the much exasperated police. The individual referred to is said to be a terrible character for levying black mail upon unfortunate women, but even if this is true it does not, of course, prove that he had anything whatever to do with the murder. At the same time, it is felt that he ought, if possible, to be found. His evidence at the adjourned inquest might prove to be of considerable importance. As for the motive of the crime, some of the medical men in London believe that the assassin is a man who loves crime for crime's sake. They are of opinion that after killing the woman he horribly mutilated her remains out of pure devilment. Such cases are not uncommon in criminal history.

The report had been written and telegraphed on the previous

evening, at which time the journalist responsible had no way of knowing that by the time the printed version found its way into the paper, it would be surrounded by details of another horror which had taken place in the interval.

CHAPTER TWO ENDNOTES

1   See Appendix One for more details of some of these incidents.

2   The correct spelling is Monro. Various spellings appear in different newspaper reports.

3   William O'Brien's imprisonment is described in more detail in Chapter Five.

4   William Thomas Stead (1849–1912), editor of the radical London newspaper the *Pall Mall Gazette,* one of the few English newspapers to promote the Irish Home Rule agenda. Stead was a tireless campaigner for the causes in which he believed, and at one point even endured a prison sentence in order to expose the scandal of child prostitution. He died as a passenger on the Titanic.

5   Ref: HO 144/190/A464472C, National Archives. In a letter to his son Charles written from Darjeeling, India, in April 1904, Monro would state that he had resigned "not because of any quarrel with the Home Secretary, but because he had refused to do what he considered to be wrong." I will discuss what that might have been in Chapter Eleven.

6   Six articles in all appeared in the *Parnellism and Crime* series. The first three, dated 7th, 10th and 14th March 1887 were written anonymously and Anderson had no involvement in these articles. It was a subsequent series of three articles in May and June, subtitled *Behind the Scenes in America,* which were the work of Anderson.

7   Ref: KS 252, Althorpe Papers, letter from Jenkinson to Earl Spencer.

8   Ref: MEPO 3/141, ff 158–163, National Archives, report dated October 25th, 1888

9   George R. Sims (1847–1922), journalist, novelist, playwright and poet. Sims showed a fascination for the Ripper case and wrote about it often, under his own name and in a column he wrote for the Sunday Referee under the name of "Dagonet". Sims is best known today for his ballad "Twas Christmas Day in the Workhouse." His series of essays entitled "How the Poor Live" were published in 1883 in the *Pictorial World*.

10 Rev. Lord Sydney Godolphin Osborne, 1808-1889.

CHAPTER THREE

Dark Annie

ONCE AGAIN the *Dublin Evening Mail* was the first with the news, printing details of the latest atrocity on the evening of Saturday, September 8th, just twelve hours or so after the crime had been committed. Their correspondent sent in a special report which would be reprinted by several papers over the following week:

> The discovery this morning of another fiendish murder more diabolical and sickening in its details even than the Bucks-row tragedy of last week, has caused nothing less than a panic among the crowded residents of Whitechapel and Spitalfields. The woman whose mutilated body was found to-day can only have been the victim of a man who takes a malignant delight in the commission of the most ghastly form of crime. The scene of the tragedy is Hanbury-street, hardly a stone's throw from Osborn-street, and Bucks-row, where two other victims were butchered. Indeed through Hanbury-street on Thursday Mary Ann Nicholl's terribly mutilated body was carried on the way to its place of burial. The fourth victim to what must be a madman's insatiable thirst for blood, is like the other three, [sic] a poor defenceless walker of the streets. A companion identified her soon after she had been taken to the Mortuary as "Dark Annie," and as she came from the Mortuary bitterly crying she said between her tears, "I knowed her, I kissed her poor cold face."

Annie Chapman, or Annie Sivvey as she was sometimes known on account of having cohabited for some time with a sieve maker, was a forty-seven-year-old widow at the time of her death. She had been born Eliza Anne Smith, out of wedlock, in Paddington in 1841, and was married to John Chapman in 1869. From inquest testimony it appears that she told her fellow lodgers that her husband had been a veterinary surgeon in Windsor, but in truth he was a coachman, a very respectable position in those times. They had three children, the eldest of whom died of meningitis at the age of twelve, and another of whom was crippled. The marriage ended in 1884 as a result, as with Polly Nichols, of Annie's fondness for drink and promiscuity. Then she moved from Windsor to London, and lived in and around the district of Spitalfields for the remaining years of her life.

Initially her husband paid her an allowance of ten shillings per week to keep herself, and she shared a room at 30 Dorset Street with Jack Sivvey, but on December 26th, 1886, John Chapman succumbed to an illness which had kept him out of work for some time previously, and as the money disappeared, so did Jack. A report in the *Ballinrobe Chronicle* of September 15th takes up the story:

> During his sickness a wretched-looking woman, having the appearance of a tramp, called at the Merry Wives of Windsor, in the Spital-road, and inquired where he was living. She said that she was his wife, and that she had walked down from London, and had slept at a lodging house in Colnbrook. On her way she also stated that, having been told that her husband, who had discontinued sending her 10s. a week, was ill, she had come to Windsor to ascertain if the report was true, and not merely an excuse for failing to send her the money as usual. The woman quitted the house shortly afterwards, and the landlord did not see her again.

At the time of her murder Annie was living at 35 Dorset Street in a lodging house known as Crossingham's. Coincidentally in this same lodging house lived Pearly Poll, the woman who had been with Martha Tabram on the night of her murder. Although there is no evidence to suggest that any of the Ripper victims were acquainted with each other, there is a strong possibility that Poll was in some way acquainted with Eliza Cooper, a woman with whom Annie had a fight in the week before her death. The two were reported in some newspapers as having corroborated each other in a suggestion to the police.

Annie had a regular male friend named Ted Stanley, known in the area as "The Pensioner," who visited her at weekends and generally paid for her bed for a few extra days after he left. There was some disputed evidence about when the quarrel took place, Cooper stating that it had been on the Tuesday of the week of her death, but as others stated they had seen the bruising on Annie's face before this it was most likely a week earlier. On the Saturday morning Annie had asked Eliza if she could borrow some soap so that Ted Stanley could wash himself. According to Cooper she had not returned the soap, and when a few days later she asked for it, Annie had thrown a halfpence onto the table and told her to buy herself some soap, starting a quarrel which had got physical later that night in the Brittania Public House when Cooper had struck her in the face and chest.

The story told by Annie's friend Amelia Farmer[1] was somewhat different, and formed part of her testimony which provided details of Annie's movements in the week leading up to her death. Reported in *The Irish Times* on September 11th, she told the inquest:

> I saw the deceased two or three times during the last week. I saw her on Monday, September 3rd, standing in the road opposite a lodging house, 36 Dorset street. She had been staying there, and complained of feeling unwell. Deceased had a bruise on one of her temples – I think the right temple. I asked how she got it. Deceased asked me to look at her chest, which was also bruised, and said, "You know the woman," mentioning some name which I do not remember, but it was a woman who carried out books for sale. That woman and deceased were acquainted with a man called "Harry the Hawker." Deceased told me on Saturday, September 1st, she (deceased) was with a man called Ted Stanley – a very respectable man. She was at a beer shop with him – 87 Commercial street, which is at the corner of Dorset street. "Harry the Hawker" was also there, and was under the influence of drink. "Harry the Hawker" put down 2s for beer, the book selling woman picked it up and put down a penny. There was an ill-feeling in consequence, and the same evening the book-selling woman met the deceased and struck her in the face and chest. I saw the deceased again on Tuesday, September 4th. I met her as she was walking at the side of Spitalfields' Church. The deceased said she felt no better, and should go to the casual ward for a day or two. The deceased told me she had not had even a cup of tea that day. I said, "Here is twopence, get a cup of tea, but don't have any rum." The deceased was partial to rum, and I have seen her many times the worse for drink. She used to do crochet work, make anti-macassars, and sell flowers. I am afraid she was not particular how she earned her living, and I know that she was out late at times. She has told me so. On Fridays the deceased used to go to Stratford East to sell anything she had. I did not see her from Tuesday afternoon until Friday. On that day I met her in Dorset street about 5 o'clock. She then appeared perfectly sober. I said, "Aren't you going to Stratford to-day?" She said, "I feel too ill to do anything." I saw her again about ten minutes afterwards on the same spot. She said, "It's no use in my giving way. I must pull myself together and go and get some money or I shall have no lodgings." That is the last I saw of her.

In the same newspaper Timothy Donovan, the deputy of Crossingham's lodging house, takes up the story:

She has lived there for four months, but was not at No 35 last week until the Friday afternoon. At about 2 or 3 o'clock she asked me to allow her to go into the kitchen. I consented and did not see her until about 1.45 on Saturday morning. At that time I was sitting in the office, and I saw the deceased go into the kitchen. Deceased afterwards came upstairs, saying she had not sufficient money for a bed, and adding, "Don't let it; I shan't be long before I am in." The bed she spoke of was the one she usually occupied. The deceased left the house, and I did not see which way she turned, but I believe the watchman did. She had enough to drink when I last saw her, but she could walk straight. She was generally the worse for drink on Saturdays, but not on other days. When she left the lodging-house on Saturday morning I said to her, "You can find money for beer but not for your bed." She replied that she had only been to the top of the street to the Ringer's publichouse.

John Evans, the night watchman at Crossingham's, was the last person to speak to her before she left. "Brummy, I shan't be long," she said to him, "See that Tim keeps my bed for me." He then watched her pass along Paternoster Row, a narrow court which ran up to Brushfield Street and the Spitalfields Market.

Hanbury Street is a lengthy road which marks the northern extremity of Whitechapel. It was here that her body was discovered at five to six the following morning by John Davis, an ageing carman who lived with his wife and three grown-up sons in a cramped room on the top floor of a tenement house at No. 29. His story, as printed in the *Bray Herald* on September 15th, ran as follows:

Having had a cup of tea in the morning, about six o'clock, I went downstairs. When I got to the end of the passage I saw a female lying down, her clothing up to her knees, and her face covered with blood. What was lying beside her I cannot describe – it was part of her body. I had heard no noise, nor had my missus. I saw Mr. Bailey's men waiting at the back of the Black Swan ready to go in to their work – making packing-cases. I said to them, "Here's a sight; a woman must have been murdered." I then ran to the police-station in Commercial-road, and told them there what I had seen, and some constables came back with me. I did not examine the woman when I saw her – I was too frightened at the dreadful sight.

One of the men waiting at Bailey's Packing Case workshop was James Kent. His story appeared in *The Irish Times* on September 13th:

While waiting an elderly man called me. I believe his name is Davis. He

LONDON CORRESPONDENCE *Jack the Ripper and the Irish Press*

came out of his house and ran into the road. He said, "Men, come here.' I and James Green went to 29 Hanbury street. There were others standing about. I went to the passage and saw a woman lying in the yard between the back door steps and partition. Her head was against the house, and her body was flat on the ground. Her feet were towards our premises where I am employed. I did not examine her. I did not go down the steps into the yard. No one went in until Inspector Chandler arrived. She was dead. She had some kind of handkerchief round her throat, which seemed soaked in blood. I saw no blood running but she was smeared with blood – her face and hands – as if she had struggled. Her hands were in front of her, as if she had been struggling – as if she had fought for her throat. Her legs were wide apart, and on them were marks of blood. I did not notice whether there was blood on the clothes. I was too much frightened to notice very particularly. It seemed as if her inside had been torn out. I went then to look for a policeman, and I had some brandy. Next I went to the shop and got a piece of canvas to throw over the body. By that time a mob had assembled and the police inspector had arrived.

The first policeman on the scene was Inspector Joseph Chandler, who was the senior officer on duty at Commercial Street Police Station, at the end of Hanbury Street, that morning. In the September 14th *Irish Times* his story ran as follows:

On Saturday morning, about ten minutes past 6, I was on duty in Commercial street at the corner of Hanbury street. I saw several men running up that street, and I beckoned to them. One of them said, "Another woman has been murdered." I at once went with him to 29 Hanbury street. I went through the passage into the yard. There were several people in the passage, but not in the yard. I saw the body of the deceased lying on the ground on her back. Her head was towards the back wall of the house about two feet from the wall at the bottom of the steps. The face was turned on the right side, and the left hand was resting on the left breast. The breast was not exposed. The right hand was by her side. The legs were drawn up and the clothing was above the knees. Part of the intestines still connected with the body were lying above the right shoulder with some pieces of skin and flesh. There were also some pieces of skin over the left shoulder and a pool of blood. The body was lying parallel with the fencing. I remained there and sent for the divisional surgeon, Mr Phillips, and to the police station for the ambulance and other assistance. When the constables arrived I removed the people from the passage and saw that no one touched the body until the doctor arrived. I obtained some sacking to cover the body. The doctor arrived about half past 6, examined the body, and directed it to be removed to the mortuary.

Dr George Bagster Phillips was the divisional surgeon for the H Division of the Metropolitan Police. He was fifty-four years old at the time of the murders, and a highly knowledgeable police surgeon with over twenty years' experience of visiting crime scenes. Like Abberline, his name would be closely associated with the case in the century to come, and with good reason. Phillips would attend at least three, possibly four, of the Ripper crime scenes, conducted the post-mortem on Annie and one further victim and was present at two others, and was consulted on many other cases for his opinion on whether they were connected. In the same newspaper he described the scene as he found it:

> On Saturday morning I was sent for at 6.20 to go to 29 Hanbury street. I found the dead body of a female in the possession of the police lying in the back yard on the left hand of the steps leading into the yard. The legs were brought up, the feet resting on the ground, and the knees turned outwards. The face was swollen and turned on the right side. The tongue protruded between the front teeth, but not beyond the lips. The tongue was evidently much swollen. The small intestines and other portions of the stomach were lying on the right side on the ground above the right shoulder attached by a coil of intestine to the rest of the stomach. There was a large quantity of blood with a part of the stomach over the left shoulder. The body was cold except there was some remaining heat under the intestines left in the body. The stiffness of the body was not marked, but it had commenced. The throat was deeply cut. I noticed that the incision of the skin was ragged and reached right round the neck. There were about six patches of blood on the back wall of the house, and on the wooden paling there were smears of blood corresponding to where the head lay. These were about 14 inches from the ground. Clotted blood was near the severed throat of the deceased.

The body was loaded into the very same shell which had contained Polly Nichols just nine days earlier, and taken to the very same mortuary shed for examination. The shed was in the yard of the Whitechapel Workhouse in Old Montague Street, and was singularly ill-equipped for the purposes of acting as a mortuary, a fact about which both Dr Phillips and the coroner Mr Wynne Baxter complained bitterly, but there was no other facility in the district that could serve the purpose. Dr Phillips went on to describe the further condition of the body:

There was a bruise over the right temple and on the upper eyelid. There were other bruises on the chest. The stiffness of the limbs was now well marked. The finger nails were tinged. There were abrasions on the ring finger. On the head being opened the membranes of the brain were found to be opaque, and the veins loaded with blood of a dark character. There was a large quantity of fluid between the membranes and the substance of the brain. The throat had been cut from the left side. The cause of death arose from the throat being cut.

The dark blood was an important factor, as it suggests that asphyxiation had occurred prior to death, as does the protruding and swollen tongue. Asked to describe what sort of murder weapon had been used he replied:

I should say that the same instrument was used for cutting the throat as for mutilation. It must have been a very sharp knife with a thin blade about 6 to 8 inches in length – probably larger. It could not have been a bayonet or a sword-bayonet. The knife might have been one such as a slaughterer uses, well ground down. I think the knives used by cobblers would not have been long enough. There were indications of anatomical knowledge displayed by the person who mutilated the corpse.

The reactions in the newspapers, both Irish and English, were exactly as could be expected. The London Correspondent of the *Belfast Morning News* on September 10th had this to say:

A ghastly murder at the East End on Saturday has spread terror over London. People having business there on Saturday evening were afraid to go into the district of Whitechapel so great were the excitement and dread in the neighbourhood. The fact that five fiendish murders, all of women, have been committed in the same district during the past month, and that only a few days have separated the last two, shows that the murderer has carried out his work with devilish daring such as has scarcely ever been known even in London. The police are greatly blamed, and Scotland Yard has come in for fierce condemnation in connection with the crime. The generally accepted theory is that the murderer is a creature who takes a fiendish delight in shedding blood for the mere sake of seeing his victim writhe before him. All the victims up to this have been unfortunate women living in poverty.

Meanwhile in the leader column of that newspaper the emphasis on the leading suspect was strengthened:

For fiendish atrocity this hellish deed is without parallel. Everything tends to lend additional horror to this inhuman outrage. It is the fourth murder that has been committed in the same district within a very brief period, three of them having been committed within the past three weeks; it has taken place at a time when a widespread horror has seized the people in the locality, and when the name of the mysterious "Leather Apron" was on every tongue; it has been characterised by all the deliberate and diabolical fiendishness of the previous crimes, and the police have no clue to the murderer. It may easily be imagined that the terror in Whitechapel has been intensified to an extraordinary pitch. The wildest rumours have been in circulation, affirmed one moment only to be contradicted the next. Who has committed this latest murder? Popular opinion now points with renewed force to the terrible monster "being" identical with "Leather Apron." Widespread discontent prevails with regard to the inability of the police to solve the dreadful mystery, and suggestions have been made for the establishment of vigilance committees. A London contemporary comments with much point on the unwonted activity of the detective force in spying upon Irish members, whilst murderers walk about and perpetrate their crimes with impunity. Certainly there must be something radically wrong when a populous district of London can be made the scene of murder after murder whilst those who are responsible for the peace are powerless to prevent the crime or punish the criminals. Of course, for the present, the panic is principally confined to the East End, but it is quite possible that the author of these murders may find it convenient to betake themselves elsewhere. If this inhuman monster should commence his attacks on the wealthy denizens of the West End perhaps those in authority might waken up to the necessities of the case. The public not merely of London, but of the Three Kingdoms, will look forward with the deepest interest to the further developments in connection with this terrible chapter of crime.

In the *Dublin Evening Mail* the London Correspondent provided another of what were becoming his familiar in-depth reports on the case. It began as follows:

The murder of yesterday has positively thrilled London. Not only in the East End are the diabolical details discussed by one and all, in the West, in the mansions of the wealthy and the great, the atrocious nature of the latest crime, and the mystery which surrounds it, form the staple of conversation. Few people can recall anything as truly fiendish. There is a sickening fascination about the terrible discovery, and the probable motive which prompted the ghastly mutilation of the wretched woman's body that has seized upon the imagination of every section of the community, and filled one and all with astonishment and indignation.

No one now believes otherwise than that the three murders of the past month, committed in the same locality, were the work of the same assassin or band of assassins. The most popular theory is that a crafty maniac, with a thirst for gore, is abroad in the neighbourhood. By many, however, it is believed that the murderer is a foreigner – probably a Malay – who has some grudge against the class of women to which the deceased belonged, and is actuated by a ferocious spirit of revenge, which has its outcome in the most revolting and morbid form of crime.

The *Freeman's Journal,* predictably, managed to squeeze a comment on the Irish situation into their commentary on the crime:

The terrible murder at the East End on Saturday morning has thrown the whole of London into a state of intense excitement. The fiendish crime, occurring immediately after four others of equal atrocity in the same neighbourhood within a short space of time, has generated in the eastern portion of the metropolis a feeling of positive fear of their lives among the majority of the inhabitants. The fact that a woman was the victim in each case, and that she was poor, takes away the suspicion of robbery and suggests some unutterably fiendish motive such as that which is supposed to animate the mystical character of Hyde in Mr. Stevenson's book. When the devilish nature of Hyde was pictured in the novel nobody could believe that his prototype could be found in real life. These atrocities and apparently causeless murders show that there is abroad at the present time in the East End a human monster even more terrible than Hyde. The murders were committed apparently for no other reason than the satanic delight of spilling the blood of defenceless women and hacking up their writhing carcasses. The simple act of taking the life did not satisfy the murderer. He cut and mangled the bodies in each case in a perfectly horrible manner. That all the murders are the work of one person seems conclusive from the similarity of the circumstances in each case. The theory of the police is that it is a man, but there are some who think it is a woman. The latter suggestion has not been made in the papers, but some of those who have visited the East End and inquired into the circumstances believe there is ground for supposing that a woman is the murderer. In support of this idea it is urged that a woman would at least have the motive of jealousy, whereas the wretched and unfortunate condition of life of the victims could furnish no motive to a man. The woman theory is, however, I think, the least probable of the two.

The question which every Londoner, east and west, is now asking is, what are the police doing. Here are five revolting murders committed within a week of each other in the same locality, in one of the most populous parts of London, and yet the police have not the faintest clue to the murderer in either case. This is an alarming state of things. There are nearly fourteen thousand police in London, and competent authorities say that with this number the metropolis can be most effectively patrolled. It is quite clear that the scene of Saturday's murder was not properly patrolled. A man whose movements attracted suspicion was followed through several streets by a civilian even before the murder was heard of at all, and not a policeman was to be seen along the route to take the man into custody. I am glad to see that in this connection the *Pall Mall Gazette* supports the complaint which I have frequently made as to the withdrawal of large numbers of London police from their proper duties for the purpose of keeping irritating and needless watch upon politicians and men who have about as much connection with crime as the Archbishop of Canturbury. If Mr. Munro would turn his attention to the discovery of the Whitechapel monster he would do a much more substantial service to his country than he did when he tried to connect an Irish member with a conspiracy to blow his colleagues in the House of Commons into small bits with dynamite.[2] It is ridiculous speculations of this kind that occupy the wits of the London detectives, not the discovery of monsters in human form who go about hacking their fellow creatures with knives in the broad daylight.

The *Belfast News-Letter* discussed the opinion current in London at the time that the crimes were of an "un-English" nature, and must thus have been committed by some foreigner:

The ignorant denizens of Whitechapel have become possessed of the idea that some dissolute Jew has committed the horrible crimes upon two outcast women. They argue in their own rude way that a person born within the pale of Christian society could never have committed crimes so appallingly savage. Therefore, they jump to the conclusion that only a monster among the Hebrew community committed the atrocities. At present there is a fear that an anti-Jewish agitation may spring out of the present unreasoning prejudice. The police are said to have a clue of some sort, but there is reason to doubt the statement. Suspicion in some quarters points to a mysterious "character," who is locally known by the soubriquet of "Leather Apron," – a short, dark man who wanders forth nightly amid the purlieus of the East End in his slippers, with most of his squat figure enveloped in the aforesaid apron. His habit is to glide into the gin palaces, paying each a short visit on his rounds. This is doubtless one of the countless stories that the recent crimes have given rise to, and which may be as destitute of foundation as the statement that there was chalked over the wall where the unfortunate woman was found yesterday, "Five. Fifteen more, and I give myself up."

On this last point Dublin's *Evening Telegraph* would comment a few days later on September 12th:

An amusing incident is related with regard to the terrible tragedy at Whitechapel. The story of the "Five and Fifteen More" being written on the wall, close to the scene of the latest of the awful murders at the East End is now regarded here with a good deal of scepticism. It is hinted that the inscription was the conception of one of the smart individuals who belong to the fraternity of London "penny-a-liners," and who bear about the same relation to the Press as jackals do to the lion. Such at least is the opinion of some of the shrewdest authorities at Scotland Yard. Inspector Shore was interviewed by one of the "lining" tribe on the subject recently, and observed reflectively and with a meaning smile – "I should like to see that writing. I fancy that I would be able to recognise the handwriting of most of you gentlemen." The interview closed abruptly, and nothing has since been heard of the sensational "writing on the wall."

With regard to collecting the "scoop" however, the day belonged to *The Irish Times*. Their London Correspondent had taken himself down to Hanbury Street to join the crowds of sensation-seekers who had gathered around the house as the day wore on. His report is one of my personal favourites from any newspaper over the whole period of the Ripper murders. It gives one an idea of what it must have been like to be part of the crowd that day, pushed and jostled in all directions, and finally to gain what must have been the ultimate thrill for those present:

The scene yesterday afternoon at the East End gave an instructive insight into what we might expect in periods of public panic when the crowd loses its head under the pressure of mixed anger and fear, and the popular temper heats to the danger point. The locality in which the butchery of Friday night was committed is also the theatre of the previous three murders charged with good reason to the same hand. It lies off the Whitechapel road, part of the main artery through the vast region lying east of Aldgate pump. There are many dangerous slums in this poorer

London, with its million and a half of a population – it does not include the entire east – and the district which has been the theatre of such horrible tragedies has always borne a bad name. Anybody who walked in the Whitechapel and its continuation, the Mile End road on a Saturday afternoon when the cosmopolitan multitude, representing twenty nations, are abroad will see for himself the elements which have brought upon certain districts the character of places to be shunned even in daytime. Yesterday, at 4 o'clock, the throng in the neighbourhood of the murder numbered thousands. Every one of the heavy forbidding by-streets leading to the spot was packed with the curious and idle – a repulsive gathering it must be owned, for the vast majority represented the human types whose ways and works have earned for this part of the great Babylon its evil fame. These natural denizens were mingled with a better class – working men evidently wasting their Saturday half-holiday in the gratification of a morbid curiosity, with not a few horror hunters who might be carriage folk. Everybody was talking of one thing, and it was interesting to note how excited all seemed to be.

Even the Cockney, callous through familiarity with the daily tragedies of one kind or another, are fairly shocked and scared by deeds more monstrous and terrible than this generation has known. The East Ender is more apt to be staid than respectful over even such subjects as the loss of life by murder, but there was none of this yesterday; the hard and villainous faces which were numerous enough showed something like pity and indignation and while the assassin, if he was among us, would not have looked peculiar in such a gathering it is certain that if the worst of us – burglar, bully, wife-beater, pickpocket, highwayman or worse still though we might be – had our hands upon him we would have lynched him there and then in an honest impulse of avenging justice.

The air was filled with murder. It was the talk, there was nothing else to hear. Men, women and children all chattering at once, with deep oaths, and shrill feminine denunciations. The crowd had its nerves strong and its blood up. It was evidently raging in a blind way to go for somebody or something. It did partly indulge this mood, for the evening papers printed an interview with an inmate of the dingy lane called Hanbury street, who had described a male acquaintance of the murdered woman as of Jewish appearance. The tribe have been in very bad odour here, especially since the revelations of the sweating system. In fact there is a sort of "Judenhetze" afoot, and the natives, swift to condemn the Israelite on the ground that if he did not murder the woman he is taking the bread of Christian mouths, soon began to exclaim against the chosen people, and to threaten those present. Those were a considerable fraction of the throng, and being a congruous and choleric race, the whole evening onwards was enlivened with a series of free fights and single combats between Jew and Gentile. All the time there was a steady movement from every approach upon the scene of the tragedy. This was a very small and grimy yard, occupied by half a dozen stalwart constables who prevented the mob from swamping the place. The sergeant in charge could do nothing to hinder the inmates of the house from turning an honest penny out of the murder. This they did by charging that sum for a peep at the corner where the deed was done and the body lay. The pennies were paid as fast as they could be taken. The entry purchased you fell into single file with the procession of sightseers before and behind, passed two or three feet into the yard, saw some broken cases, a pair of steps and other things, and then in a corner a large irregular dark stain on the ground. Before you had well set eyes on it you found yourself quietly elbowed outside, for the coppers were moving too fast and time was too short to allow you more than a glance for your copper.

Naturally the newspapermen equally swamped the area, each looking for the story or the scoop of the day. Anyone and everyone was interviewed, and the rumours flew thick and fast. Some of the early editions of the English newspapers carried the story of a second murder at the rear of the London Hospital which turned out to be entirely fictional. The *Ballinrobe Chronicle* of September 15th carried an interview with Mrs Davis, the wife of the discoverer of the body:

> The bell was ringing for six o'clock, and that is how I know the time that my husband went downstairs. He went down, but did not return, as he tells me that when he saw the deceased, and the shocking state in which she was, he at once ran off for the police. We never heard any screams, either in the night or this morning. I went down myself shortly after, and nearly fainted away at what I saw. The poor woman's throat was cut and the inside of her body was lying beside her. Someone beside me then remarked that the murder was just like the one committed in Buck's-row. The other one could not have been such a dreadful sight as this, for the poor woman found this morning was quite ripped open. She was lying in a corner of the yard, on her back, with her legs drawn up. It was just in such a spot that no one could see from the outside, and thus the dead creature might have been lying there for some time.

Meanwhile the *Irish Times* of September 10th had obtained a statement from Elizabeth Bell, a resident of No. 31, the house next door to the murder site:

I have been living here some time and I wish I had never come. Such a terrible sight is enough to shock any woman with the hardest heart. The house is open all night next door, and this poor creature was taken into the yard, and butchered, no doubt by the same man who committed the others. We were all roused at six o'clock this morning by Adam Osborne calling out, "For God's sake get up; here's a woman murdered." We all got up and huddled on our clothes, and on going into the yard saw the poor creature lying by the steps in the next yard with her clothes torn and her body gashed in a dreadful manner. The people in the house next door were all asleep, I believe and knew nothing of the matter until the police came and roused them up. I cannot be sure if anybody in the house knew of the murder or took part in it, but I believe not. The passage is open all night, and anyone can get in, and no doubt that is what happened.

The house itself was occupied by a Mrs Amelia Richardson who rented the property and sub-let the rooms to various lodgers. Davis and his family lived in the front room on the top floor, the back room being occupied by an elderly woman named Sarah Cox whom Mrs Richardson kept out of charity. The second floor front room was let to a Mr Thompson and his wife, together with an adopted daughter, and the back room to two girls who were the last to go to bed the night before, having been talking with their men friends in the passage until half past midnight. Mrs Richardson herself occupied the first floor front with her grandson, and the back room on that floor was let to a Mr Walker and his son, who was said to be "feeble-minded but inoffensive." On the ground floor the front room was the home of a Mrs Hardiman and her son who ran a cat's meat shop from the room. The back room was a kitchen and parlour, used by Mrs Richardson for prayer-meetings, and locked at other times.

From the basement of the property Mrs Richardson ran a packing-case business together with her son, John, and a man named John Tyler. Mrs Richardson was interviewed by the press on the day of the murder, and this interview was carried in the *Ballinrobe Chronicle* of September 15th:

I have lived at this house 15 years, and my lodgers are poor but hard-working people. Some have lodged with me as long as 12 years. They mostly work at the fish market or the Spitalfields market. Some of the carmen in the fish market go out to work as early as one a.m., while others go out at four and five, so that the place is open all night, and any one can get in. It is certain the deceased came voluntarily into the yard, as if there had been any struggle it must have been heard. Several lodgers sleep at the back of the house, and some had their windows open, but no noise was heard from the yard. One of my lodgers, a carman named Thompson, employed at

Goodson's, in Brick-lane, went out at four o'clock in the morning. He did not go into the yard, but he did not notice anything particular in the passage as he went out. My son John came in at ten minutes to five, and he gave a look round before he went to market. He went through the yard, but no one was there then, and everything was right. Just before six o'clock, when Mr. Davis, another of my lodgers, came down, he found the deceased lying in the corner of the yard, close to the house, and by the side of the step. The lower part of her body was uncovered. There was not the slightest sign of a struggle, and the pool of blood which flowed from her throat after it was cut, was close to the step where she lay. She does not appear to have moved an inch after the fiend struck her with the knife. She must have died instantly. The murderer must have gone away from the spot covered with blood. There was an earthenware pan containing water in the yard; but this was not discoloured, and could not, therefore, have been used by the murderer. The only possible clue that I can think of is that Mr. Thompson's wife met a man about a month ago lying on the stairs. This was about four o'clock in the morning. He looked like a Jew, and spoke with a foreign accent. When asked what he was doing there, he replied that he was waiting to do a "doss" before the market opened. He slept on the stairs that night, and I believe he has slept on the stairs on other nights. Mrs. Thompson is certain she could recognise the man again, both by his personal appearance and his peculiar voice. The police have taken a full and careful description of this man.

John Richardson had in fact not gone into the yard when he arrived at ten to five. He had come to check that the cellar door was locked, a custom he had started to perform daily after they had had some tools stolen a few weeks earlier. He only opened the back door of the yard and descended a couple of the steps. He then sat down on the steps to trim some leather from one of his boots, using a kitchen knife he kept in his pocket to cut carrots for his pet rabbit. At that time in the morning on that day dawn was beginning to break, and although the yard would not be in daylight, it would not have been in total darkness either. Richardson would have been sitting almost right next to the body, and though the open door might have obscured his view somewhat it is difficult to see how he could have missed its presence if it had been there at that time.

In fact there was some confusion about just how long the body had lain there. Dr. Phillips estimated that Annie had been dead some two hours by the time he examined the body at half past six, but that would mean that Richardson had been mistaken about the body not being there when he sat on the steps. Meanwhile a next-door neighbour, Albert Cadosch, stated that shortly after quarter past five he heard a scuffle through the fence while he was in the yard, and then heard a female voice say, "No," and something fall against the fence. A Mrs Elizabeth Long, on her way to work at Spitalfields Market, however, identified the body as being a woman she had seen standing in front of 29 Hanbury Street talking with a man when she passed at half past five. The man had said the words, "Will you?" and the woman had replied, "Yes."

The testimony of Cadosch and Long seems at first glance to conflict. However, Mrs Long had taken her timing from hearing the clock on Truman's Brewery in Brick Lane chime for the half hour, whereas Cadosch had seen the time on the clock of Spitalfields Church when he left his house for work a few minutes later. If we accept that Mrs Long might have been mistaken, and that the clock may have been chiming the quarter hour rather than the half hour, then the two reports support each other almost exactly. This would place the time of death at around twenty or twenty five past five, by which time the sun had already risen, and the killing must have occurred in broad daylight.

Whether we take this as the time of death or we accept Dr Phillips' earlier estimate, and it should be pointed out that he later admitted that the coldness of the morning and the loss of blood in the body could have thrown his estimate out, the problem remains of finding out exactly what Annie Chapman's movements had been between the last time she was seen alive by John Evans and the time of her murder. There were rumours of a sighting at a public house early that morning, and this was reported in the *Dublin Evening Mail* of September 8th:

> At the Bell-Inn in Brick-lane, where, as gossip goes, "Dark Annie" was seen with the man supposed to be her murderer, the barmaid says she opened the place at five o'clock, as is customary on Saturday morning, as Spitalfields Market is in the near vicinity. She was too busy almost to notice whom she served. She might have served the woman – indeed, she had been told by those who knew her that she had, but she had no recollection of it, and certainly could not say whether the unfortunate creature was accompanied by a man.

This sighting does not appear to have been taken seriously by police. However, another incident that morning in a public house certainly was. The sighting of a man supposed to have been a possible suspect was widely reported, and the police files show that a concerted effort to find this individual was made. This report is from the same newspaper as the above:

> Mrs Fiddymont, wife of the landlord of the Prince Albert publichouse states that at seven o'clock this morning she was standing in the bar with another woman when there came in a man whose rough appearance

frightened her. His hat was over his eyes, and he asked for half-a-pint of ale. As soon as he saw the woman in the other compartment watching him he turned his back. Mrs Fiddymont then noticed that there was blood spots on the back of his right hand. She also noticed that his shirt was torn. As soon as he had drunk the ale, which he swallowed at a gulp, he went out. The story of Mrs Mary Chappell, who lives at 28 Stewart-street, near by, corroborated Mrs Fiddymont's. When the man came in, the expression of his eyes caught their attention, his look was so startling and terrifying. There was a narrow streak of blood under his right ear, and also dried blood between the fingers of his hand. When he went out she slipped out and watched him, and he went towards Bishopsgate-street. He had a nervous and frightened way about him.

None of this information, of course, brought the police one step closer to capturing the assailant, and with this second murder in just over a week both the British and Irish press were quick to criticise. Reporting the murder on the morning of Monday, September 10th, the *Cork Examiner* roundly criticised the metropolitan forces, particularly those in charge:

> In this as in the previous cases the murderer has for the time escaped, and there seems but little grounds for hoping for his speedy capture, as the police seem to be altogether without a clue. A man has been taken into custody for this latest crime, but it is not known that he can be connected with it in any way. It is little wonder, then, that intense excitement and alarm should prevail in the thickly populated and poverty-stricken locality in which those horrors have taken place, and the belief that the crimes are the work of a murderous semi-maniac is in no wise calculated to diminish the terror that exists. That belief is founded on the circumstance that there is a good deal of similarity in the surroundings of those three latter murders. In each case the victim is a woman of the "unfortunate" class, each murder was perpetrated in the early hours of the morning, and the cutting of the throat and hacking of the body are common features of all three crimes. There is, therefore, ground for supposing that they are all the work of the same hand, and they prove with appalling clearness what havoc a single wretch may make, notwithstanding all the safeguards of Society. The police system of London does not show to much advantage in reference to those crimes when the skill of the whole detective force is unable to effect the arrest of the perpetrator – believed by the police themselves to be a madman. No such real alarm has prevailed for many years in London as that which at present exists in consequence of this series of crimes, and the fact that such deeds could

be perpetrated in open daylight in a densely populated district affords justification for alarm. There is nothing whatever mysterious about those murders; they are all open butcheries, committed apparently with little regard for the safety of the perpetrator. But the murderer or murderers defy the arm of justice and seem to be quite reckless as to police interference. But if such crimes be committed with impunity people will begin to ask whether the detective power of the English police is as signally absent as that of their Irish brethren, and whether the sole use of Sir CHARLES WARREN'S army of constables is to disperse crowds in Trafalgar Square.

Sir Charles himself, as reported by many newspapers, had not in fact even been in London at the time of this killing. He had been in the South of France enjoying a vacation after what had been a difficult time within the administration of the force. However, this murder facilitated his speedy return, as reported in the *Irish Times* of September 11th:

> Sir Charles Warren has suddenly re-appeared at his office from the Continent, where he was spending a holiday which had not run half its course. Such a proceeding on the part of the Chief Commissioner of Police is explained in two ways. It is supposed that his hasty return is due to the fourth murder of a sanguinary series, all evidently the work of the same perpetrator, all committed in the same neighbourhood and within brief intervals from each other, but all, so far, most eloquent testimony to the feebleness in some vital respects of the Metropolitan Police system. Sir Charles is blamed among other things for having recently transferred the whole detective force of East London to the West, the effect of the change being to import total strangers where a personal knowledge of the criminal classes is a first essential of success in dealing with them. It is held on the other hand that the Chief Commissioner has not abandoned his holiday so much for the purpose of stimulating the search for the "man monster" as in order to adopt precautions against the threatened renewal of Socialist demonstrations, with their probabilities of consequent disturbances.

However, the *Freeman's Journal* of the same day indicated another rumour had been current with regard to this swift re-appearance:

> It was rumoured yesterday that Sir Charles Warren had resigned the Chief Commissionership of Metropolitan Police. He returned to London yesterday after a holiday on the Continent, and his unexpected

re-appearance in Scotland Yard gave rise to the report that in consequence of recent events connected with the police force under his charge he had tendered his resignation to the Home Secretary. Inquiry at Scotland Yard, however, elicited from Sir Charles Warren a prompt denial of the report. He does not intend to resign, nor does he intend to accept any other appointment.

The truth of the matter is that with Dr Robert Anderson having, almost immediately on taking office as head of the CID, taken a leave of absence to travel to Switzerland for health reasons on the advice of his doctor, there was a feeling that the whole Metropolitan force was rudderless, and the presence of its leader was therefore required. The task they were faced with was not an easy one. The *Belfast Morning News* London Correspondent made this point in his column on September 11th:

> The whole of the police force available has been concentrated on the work of trying to unravel the mystery and hunt down the criminal or criminals. We must search the pages of fiction to find in the tales of the Thugs of India or the "Gibbonainosay" of the Far West, who slaughtered the Redskins in revenge for the murder of his family, to find a parallel to the case of the savage of Whitechapel. I was speaking to an officer of Scotland Yard yesterday who has great experience, and he informed me that this case was one of the most difficult class that the police have to deal with. If the crimes are committed by a single individual, who works alone, it is always much more difficult to detect than if a whole gang were concerned. The difficulties are increased in this case, as everything seems to point to the criminal being a debased, morose, taciturn, and half-crazy creature, with considerable cunning and daring.

Police activity was naturally intense. It is well known by today's police that in any murder investigation of this nature, the first forty-eight hours are the most hectic period during which information, only a small proportion of which will prove useful, floods in and must be carefully sifted and recorded. It was much the same in the Ripper case, as this *Freeman's Journal* report of September 10th indicates:

> The inhabitants of the East end appear to have all their attention absorbed in the loathsome details of the murder, knots of people having stood about until a late hour this evening discussing every point of the tragedy. The people are in a terrible condition of terror and fear. "God knows," said an official to our reporter, "but we may have another to-

night, though we have men patrolling the whole region of Whitechapel and Spitalfields." That the police are putting forth every possible effort there can be no doubt. To-night there is a large force on duty. One-third of all the men are in plain clothes, and even those entitled to leave on absence are retained. That the public are anxious to second their efforts is testified by the presence on the record at Commercial street of no less than fifty personal statements made with the object of assisting in the work of identification. One officer has been occupied many consecutive hours in writing these statements, and up to nine o'clock to-night they were being supplemented by others.

It was plain that there would be considerable pressure on the police to produce a quick result, and the first task was to find the man who had become the prime suspect.

CHAPTER THREE ENDNOTES

1   Some writers have suggested that Amelia Farmer is the same woman as Annie Farmer who was attacked in a Ripper related incident on November 20th. There is no evidence one way or the other.

2   Mr Joseph Nolan, Member of Parliament for North Louth. Monro had brought his name up on October 26th, 1887 at the inquest on the death of an American gentleman named Joseph Cohen. Nolan had earlier that year showed two associates of Cohen calling themselves Joseph Melville and Mr McTin around the House of Commons. The men were in fact John J Moroney and Michael Harkins, and they had been provided with a letter of introduction to Nolan by General Frank Millen. The three were all involved in what became known as the Jubilee Plot to assassinate Queen Victoria in a dynamite attack on Westminster Abbey. Nolan eventually was forced to give evidence at the trial of Melville and Harkins, and Monro ensured that the implication was that Nolan was himself somehow involved in the plot. No charges were ever levied against him however.

CHAPTER FOUR

Leather Apron and other Short Stories

AFTER THE MURDER of Annie Chapman the public clamour for the police to arrest "Leather Apron" became intense. Still considered, by the newspapers at least, to be the number one suspect, stories continued to abound of this "beast in human form." The *Derry Journal* of September 12th printed an interview with a local resident:

I live not many minutes' walk from the place of the Buck's-row murder, and I thought probably an incident which I witnessed on Sunday between half-past four and a quarter past five p.m. would throw a little light on it. Coming from school at the time above stated, I was just about to turn into Albert street, by Cohen's sugar refinery, when a woman rushed across the street and cried out, "There goes Leather Apron, the Whitechapel murderer," to the policeman standing at the corner of the turning. "Run after him," she shouted; "now you have a chance of catching him. There he goes," pointing to a man. The constable then ran after the man, who seemed to be in a hurry. After about four hundred yards run he caught the man, whereupon two other constables put in their appearance, and inquired what was the matter. The woman who had run with the policeman up to the man at once began to accuse him of being the person the police were looking for – "Leather Apron." This she repeated about twenty times. She said she knew the man well by sight. This the man denied by saying he had never seen the woman before, but later on he said to one of the other constables that this woman was constantly annoying him like this; she should be careful what she was saying. She thereupon said she knew two women, and could bring them, who saw him pacing up and down Baker's-row with the murdered woman about two hours before the murder took place. She further accused him of cruelly ill using two unfortunates in a common lodging house in City

Road one night lately; and further, she said that among the unfortunates of Whitechapel he was well known as a cruel wretch. These accusations the man simply met with a sneer, and said she did not know what she was talking about. The policeman let the man go.

Detective Sergeant William Thick[1] was a career detective with over twenty years experience in the force in 1888, most of it spent in H Division. He was a well-known figure in the area, and had a good knowledge of, and rapport with, the cadre of East End villains operating in the area. He was nicknamed "Johnny Upright" among them, partly because of a peculiarly erect gait that he affected, and partly to suggest an incorruptible nature. Thick would become something of a celebrity, at one point being accused himself of being the Ripper. In his 1904 book *People of the Abyss,* the American author Jack London interviewed Thick, who arranged lodgings for him and gave him some information about some of the lower Whitechapel haunts.

When the stories of the monstrous "Leather Apron" came to the attention of the police, it was Sergeant Thick who put a name to the epithet. "Leather Apron", he said, was one John Piser, a man he had known for many years, a boot-finisher who wore the eponymous apron for his trade, and generally wore it much of the rest of the time also.

Piser must have seemed a good bet for the murders to the police. He had a history of violence and a criminal record. In July 1887 he had attacked and stabbed a fellow boot-finisher named James Willis, who he had accused of stealing work from him. For this assault he was sentenced to six months hard labour. More recently, on August 4th, he had been charged at Thames Magistrates Court with indecent assault, but the case had been dismissed due to lack of evidence. Even using today's methods it is likely that such a man's name would have flagged itself to the police, and he would at least have been questioned. Serial killers seldom emerge from nowhere, the majority have a history of lesser offences.

The problem was that when Sergeant Thick went to arrest Piser, he was missing. However, when the second murder in just over a week occurred, finding and arresting Piser would have become a priority, and from that time his home was staked out. On the morning of Monday, September 10th, Sergeant Thick called at a house at 22 Mulberry Street where Piser's step-mother and brother lived, and there he finally effected the arrest. The *Cork Examiner* of September 11th described the scene:

> When the detective called at the house Piser opened the door and the detective remarking "Just the man I wanted," charged him on suspicion of being concerned with the murder of the woman Siffey[2]. By trade

> Piser is a boot finisher, and has been living at Mulberry-street with his step-mother, Mrs Piser, and a married brother, a cabinetmaker. Piser's relatives say he came home at half-past ten on Thursday night and had not left home since; they also say he is in delicate health, and that he left the Convalescent Home six weeks ago. He is thirty-five years of age, and has been brought up from infancy by Mrs Piser. At the Leman street Police Station, where Piser was taken, a large force of police were kept in readiness with drawn staves. The arrest was effected so quietly that the fact was not generally known. The authorities refuse to give any information, and say no such arrest has taken place. This is untrue, as the relatives admit it.

Most of the newspapers of September 11th carried two stories, both received from the Press Association, the first stating that Piser had been released on inquiries into his movements proving satisfactory, the second retracting this statement. It seems that the police, realising the strength of public feeling against this character, had attempted a little subterfuge to prevent any riotous show of this feeling. In fact the suspect remained in custody until the following day. The *Irish Times* of September 12th provided some details of the inquiries:

> Throughout the day Detective Sergeant Thicke has been continuing his inquiries as to the movements and antecedents of Piser. This afternoon a number of men who were hanging about Leman street police station were asked to come inside, and they were glad to satisfy their curiosity by doing so. Piser was then brought from the room in which he is confined and placed among them. A man was then brought into the station yard and asked if he could identify "the man." He immediately picked out Piser, who appeared to be much dejected on being so readily selected. It is understood that this witness says he saw Piser threatening a woman in Hanbury street at an early hour on the morning of the murder.

The man who identified Piser was named Emmanuel Violenia. A man of mulatto appearance, possibly of Spanish or Bulgarian origin (accounts vary), he had been lodging in Hanbury Street on September 8th and claimed to have seen a woman arguing with two men, one of whom he said had threatened to attack her with a knife. However, when Violenia failed to identify Annie Chapman's body, the police became suspicious of his motives, believing that he had concocted the story in order to avail himself of any reward which might be forthcoming. It later transpired that, working in the same trade, Violenia and Piser knew each other by sight, explaining the ease with which he had made the identification in the Leman Street yard.

Meanwhile Piser's family and friends protested his innocence, stating that he had never been known by the name of "Leather Apron" and had not left the house that weekend. However, in the end, it was the fire in the London docks which finally proved him not to be the man sought. On the night of Polly Nichols' murder, Piser had been staying at a common lodging house in the Holloway Road, in Highgate, North London, several miles from the murder site, and with the sky turned red from the flames of the dock fires, he had inquired of a policeman in the Seven Sisters Road the location of the fire. The policeman remembered the incident, thus proving that Piser had indeed been where he claimed, and he was also remembered by others in the lodging house as returning at a quarter to two in the morning, almost two hours before the time that Polly was killed.

Piser was released on the Tuesday evening of September 11th and the following day appeared at Annie Chapman's inquest in order to clear his name fully. After describing his movements of the period of the crimes, the coroner stated, "I think it only fair to say that these statements by witness have been corroborated in every particular," thus putting an end to the matter. An interview with Piser, given at the 22 Mulberry Street address, appeared in the *Belfast Morning News* on September 13th:

Whatever particulars the world at large and the police authorities wish to know as to where I was staying when these atrocious and horrible crimes were committed I am quite willing to give. I came into this house at a quarter to eleven on Thursday night. I knocked, and my sister opened the door. My sister's young man was present, and we had a conversation about work. My sister first went to bed and put the belt in the latch, so that anyone going out afterwards could not get in again. From Thursday until I was arrested

I never left the House,

except to go into the yard. I was seen several times in the yard by a neighbour. On Monday morning Sergeant Thicke came. I opened the door. He said I was wanted, and I asked what for. He replied, "You know what for you will have to come with me." I said, "Very well; I will go with the greatest pleasure." The officer said, "You know you are 'Leather Apron'" or words to that effect. Up to that moment I did not know I was called by that name. I have been in the habit of

Wearing an Apron from my Employment

but not recently. When I arrived at the police station I was searched. They took everything from me, according to custom, as I suppose. They found nothing that could incriminate me, thank God, or connect me with the crime that I have been unfortunately suspected of. I know of no crime, and my character will bear the strictest investigation. I am generally here, but occasionally at a lodginghouse, but not one in Dorset street. Before coming here on Thursday I was at Holloway. Last Sunday week I was accosted in Church street by two females, unknown to me. One of them asked me if I was the man, referring presumably to the Bucks-row murder. I said "God forbid, my good woman." A man then asked me to treat him to beer. I walked on. I do not know Mrs Fiddyman's [*sic*] public-house, and was

Ignorant of Such a Name as Mrs. Siffy

until it was published. I don't know the woman. Yesterday a man came to Leman-street station, and at the request of the police I went out into the yard. A stalwart man, of negro cast, whom I know to be a boot finisher, placed his hands upon my shoulder. I said, "I don't know you, you are mistaken." His statement that he saw me threaten a woman in Hanbury-street is false. I can give

A Full Account of My Whereabouts.

I shall see if I cannot legally proceed against those who have made statements about me. The charges against me have quite broken my spirits, and I fear I shall have to place myself under medical treatment.

The question of whether or not Piser was "Leather Apron," or whether Sergeant Thick had simply arrested a man he believed to go by that name, has never been answered. His name first appears in the police files on September 7th, so it is certain at least that even before the murder of Annie Chapman, the police had already connected his name to the title. Piser later successfully sued several of the newspapers that had slandered his name. Meanwhile the epithet of "Leather Apron" continued to be connected to the murderer until it was replaced by the name by which he is better known today.

Tales of arrests filled the newspapers from day one. Reports constantly appeared of random strangers who had been taken into custody because "their movements aroused suspicion," or because they had been drunkenly talking about the murders in some public house and had appeared to know more than they should. One arrest which seems to have caused quite a scene occurred on the very day of the Hanbury Street killing. It was reported in *The Irish Times* on September 10th:

The terror and excitement were somewhat abating when, at 11.15, the people who had congregated in Commercial street were thrown into a fresh state of alarm. It was rumoured that about a quarter of an hour previously the man who was supposed to be the murderer, or connected with the murder, had been seen in the locality, but this statement, owing to the want of previous success in detecting the perpetrators of the other murders was received with incredulity. A short time afterwards, however, a young man apparently about 25 years of age, was seen running down Commercial street at full speed, followed by a large body of policemen with drawn batons, and a large crowd of persons. The man was gradually gaining on his pursuers but owing to the cries of policemen a large body of men and women blocked the street. The man at once grasped the situation and rushed down a side street. The excitement at this time became intense, as it was thought that the man, who was supposed to be the murderer, would escape. After an interval of about two minutes however a cheer was raised, and shortly afterwards the man was seen between five or six policemen. It would be almost impossible to describe his appearance; he was the picture of terror, the colour of his face being between a ghastly white and yellow. He is about the medium height, and was fairly dressed. When the police arrived in Commercial street the people crowded round in order to look at the captured man, but they were kept at a distance by a body of policemen.

In fact, when the truth became known, this man was simply a petty criminal who had accosted a woman in Spitalfields Market and resisted a policeman who had attempted to arrest him, and who simply had the misfortune to flee in the exact direction where this unruly mob awaited baying for blood. The London Correspondent of the *Dublin Evening Mail* commented on the incident on the same day:

> One could not help in a measure pitying the poor wretch who was yesterday captured and "run in" in Whitechapel for an assault on a woman. Just at the moment the indignation of the people in the neighbourhood was at its full height, consequent on the discovery of a fresh murder, and when the man was being chased by the police, and then captured, the word went round that the perpetrator of the latest terrible crime had been arrested. The excitement was so intense that there was an immediate rush for the prisoner, and had he not been surrounded by a body of stalwart officers, he would probably have been killed outright. As it was, he had the narrowest escape. I never saw a man look so terror-stricken. He became white with fear, and then turned positively yellow, while his flesh quivered, and his eyes protruded from his head. On reaching the police station he almost fainted.

We know from our own modern perspective that a serial murder case sells newspapers, and that one of the first things the press will do in any such case is try to find a catchy name for the killer. The press seem to have already learned these lessons by the time of the Whitechapel case, and the *Star* seem to have cottoned on quickest of all that their lurid tales of the monstrous "Leather Apron" prowling the streets with his wicked malevolent grin were a way to keep the story going and the sales figures high. The *Kerry Evening Post* of September 15th commented on the phenomenon of press interest:

> The London press has, with one or two honourable exceptions, gone with and not against the panic of excitement which the Whitechapel murders have excited among the large mass of the inarticulate class, to whom the *Police News* is almost their only daily *pabulum*. It is only what we should expect that the hunt after Leather Apron, whoever he is, should have developed into a sort of general arrest and detention of all sorts of suspicious persons without however lighting upon the true Miscreant, Monster or Maniac, whichever of the three big M's we like to employ. What we most dread is the mushroom growth which this will give to a fresh dung heap of penny dreadfuls, and already we find the penny gaffs and gin saloons are reaping a harvest in sensational songs on the subject.

Reporters descended on the area in droves, including most of the London Correspondents of the Irish newspapers, to present their own views of life on the streets of Whitechapel. The *Derry Standard* of September 12th printed a story of the state of the area on the Monday night after the murder of Annie Chapman had taken place:

> The scare which the discovery of the fourth and most horrible of the murders occasioned in the district has considerably subsided. People having become familiar with the details of the tragedy, and being calmed by the knowledge of the active measures adopted for their protection by the police, are returning to their normal condition of mind. This is fairly evidenced by the aspect which Whitechapel-road presented last night, and up to an early hour of the morning. A very different one from that of the corresponding period of the previous day. On Sunday night the pavements were almost deserted, but twenty-four hours later groups of men and women chatted, joked, and boisterously laughed upon the flagstones until long after St. Mary's clock struck one. In passing through the groups of people
>
> *the words most frequently heard*
>
> in their conversation were "Leather Apron." The term has already become a by-word of the pavement and gutter, and one more often hears

it accompanied by a vacant guffaw than whispered in a tone which would indicate any fear of the mysterious individual who is supposed to live under that soubriquet. Whilst a large number of persons, including many members of the police, firmly believe in the existence and almost certain guilt of the aproned one, the talk of the footways convinces the passers-by that a large number of other inhabitants of the East End are sceptical as to his personality. So it may be said with truth that the thoroughfares last night assented their customary appearance. There was the usual per-centage of gaudily-dressed loud-mouthed and vulgar women strutting or standing at the brightly-lighted crossways, and the still larger proportion of miserable, half-fed, dejected creatures of the same sex, upon whom hard life, unhealthy habits, and bad spirits have too plainly set their stamp. Soon after one o'clock the better dressed members of the motley company

disappeared by ones and twos,

and the poor, poverty-stricken arabs, to whom it would appear fortune is less kind, crawled about from lamp to lamp, or from one dark alley's mouth to another until faint signs of dawn appeared. Off the main road in such thoroughfares as Commercial-street and Brick-lane there was lit-tle to attract attention. Constables passed silently by the knots of home-less vagabonds huddled in the recess of some big doorway; other con-stables whose "plain clothes" cannot prevent their stalwart well-drilled figures from betraying their calling, paraded in couples, now and again emerging from some dimly-lighted lane and passing their uniformed comrades with an air of profound ignorance; and timid, ill-fed cats crouched in the gutters, or preyed upon some offal rejected by their hard-ly more fortunate human owners. The streets inclusively referred to by the constables on beat duty in the main thoroughfare and "round the back" presented a dismal appearance indeed, the dim yellow flames of the not too numerous public lamps only rendering

the darkness of night more gloomy.

Such passages as Edward-street, connecting Hanbury and Princess-streets, Flower and Dean-street, between Brick-lane and Commercial-street, which in daylight only strike one as very unwholesome and dirty thoroughfares, appear utterly forlorn and dismal in the darkness of the night. From an alley in one of these leading to an uninviting recess, a mis-erable specimen of a man, hollow-chested, haggard, and dirty, shuffled hurriedly into the wider street, and, crossing to the opposite pavement, dived into another recess, and was instantly lost to view. No constable would have thought of interfering with him had he met him, nor would there have been any excuse for accosting him, and yet his ragged clothes of some dark hue might have been saturated with the blood of a murdered victim, which would not have been visible in the depressing yellow shade of the flickering gas jets. In almost any one of these dark and filthy passages a human being's life might be every night sacrificed, were the blows dealt with the same terrible suddenness and precision which characterised those of the two last homicides, and a police force of double the strength of that now employed, and organised under the best possible conditions, might well be baffled in its efforts to capture the slayers. In the immediate neighbourhood of St. Mary's Church a wide entry presented

a deep cavern of stygian blackness,

into which no lamp shone, and whether, for aught a passer-by at that hour could discover, a corpse might lie, and from which – such is its position – a murderer might, if possessed of coolness, easily pass unnoticed. In a squalid thoroughfare between Hanbury-street and Whitechapel-road some houses have apparently been pulled down, the space being now waste ground, enclosed by wooden palings. This un-illuminated spot is separated by a house or two from an alley, which, at a point some yards from the street, turns at right angles apparently towards the unoccupied space mentioned. Into the mouth of this passage a slatternly woman, her face half-hidden in her shawl, which was her only headdress, thrust her head, and in a shrill and angry voice shrieked the word "Tuppy." The cry was answered in a few seconds by the appearance of

an evil-looking man, with a ragged black beard,

who, in reply to an impatient question of "Where is she?" muttered, in a surly voice, "Round there," at the same time jerking his thumb backwards towards the alley. "Well, come 'long 'ome, then. I aint agoin' to wait for she," replied the woman, who, with the dark man limping after her, soon disappeared round the corner of the street. There was no subsequent indication of the presence of a third person. The light from the street was so dim that there was no possibility of recognising the features of the man or woman, and certainly either might have borne traces of crime, which would have attracted no attention. Such occurrences as the above are, the police say, quite usual, and they neither have nor wish to have authority to question any individual whose conduct may attract attention without exciting suspicion.

The *Irish Times* man in London also commented, at rather less length, on the state of the streets, on September 11th:

There is apparently little abatement of the panic and excitement caused by the murder of Saturday. Crowds numbering many thousands gathered all day about the scene of the crime. The reported capture of "Leather Apron" produced a remarkable demonstration, for the news flying like wildfire through the throngs of people dispersed over a score of streets, lanes and alleys. A wild outburst of cheering was kept up for half an hour, and was succeeded by a monster chorus of "We'll hang 'Leather Apron' on a high gallows tree." There is a tendency among classes claiming to be more logical than the multitude to regard "Leather Apron" as the murderer, but the conclusion is considered premature, to say the least of it, although appearances and antecedents alike are decidedly against the man of mystery now in the hands of the police. A remarkable result of the crime has been the organisation of a number of vigilance committees throughout Whitechapel district. The movement has been taken up with so much zeal that some of these volunteer police societies started with a hundred members, whose duty it is to contribute from their numbers ten men per night to the work of patrolling the streets.

Meanwhile the man from the *Dublin Evening Mail,* who seems to have had an inside track on a lot of things, printed on September 12th an interview he had obtained with a representative of the police on duty in the area:

I was in conversation this evening with one of the detectives engaged on the case, and whose view of the matter was decidedly interesting. "I do not," he remarked, "for a moment believe in the maniac theory; neither do I think it at all probable that the murders have been committed by a 'High Rip' gang. My view of the case is that it is the work of a man who thirsts for revenge. Either he has been robbed or otherwise badly treated by a woman of the class to which the deceased women belonged. He swears to be avenged, and he lies in wait for the woman he says has wronged him. Whether sure of her identity I cannot say. It may be that he is so embittered against the class of women as a whole, that he is reckless upon which one the avenging hand shall fall.

"Having at length fixed upon his victim, he has not had a very difficult task. Loose women, accustomed to prowl about Whitechapel during the early hours of the morning, know almost as much about the movements of the police as do the police themselves. The man would have no occasion to lure his victim to a secluded spot. The woman herself would unwittingly give him every assistance in arranging for the safe commission of his crime. When at length the quiet spot has been found, the work of butchery has been as quick as it has been ghastly.

"The police are being taken to task because the murderer has not yet been found. As a matter of fact, the case is not the simple one some people try to make out. The idea that the murderer must have left the spot 'covered with blood' is to my mind ridiculous. Evidently the knife was not used until the women were lying on the ground. Then the throat was cut before there was time for a cry to be uttered. The other fiendish work would be accomplished with equal rapidity, and all, no doubt, in perfect silence. The blood would not 'spurt' over the murderer, as has been conjectured. The blood would flow internally, or on to the ground underneath and surrounding the woman's body. It may be safe to assume that the assassin's hands were covered with blood, but with equal safety it may be said that he might easily have cleansed them without arousing suspicion. Altogether," concluded the detective, "the case is far more complicated than many people may reasonably suppose at a first glance. There is nothing to work on at present but pure supposition, though I hope in the course of a few days to have a clue that will enable some of us to put our hands on the right man."

Ironically, it had been in the same column only two days earlier that the suggestion of the "spurting blood" had been exercised:

Whoever and whatever the man may be, the manner in which he has managed to escape after perpetrating his diabolical deeds is truly remarkable. In the last case so terrible was the mutilation of the woman's body that the murderer must needs have been literally stained with his victim's blood before the horrible work he undertook was completed. Blood had spurted from the body in great streams, staining the ground and even the walls around. The internal organs had evidently been torn from the body by the murderers hands, which must have been steeped in gore. The question consequently arises, how the assassin could not only have escaped from the locality, but could have cleansed himself of the terrible traces of his crime without exciting suspicion.

The reticence of the police to talk to the press was a subject of frequent comment. From our point of view today this does cause several problems, due to the incompleteness of the police files which have been depleted over the years partly through officers taking documents away as souvenirs, partly due to files being destroyed to free up space in the archives. What we are left with, where it tallies with the newspaper reports, gives us a reasonable idea of the manner in which the investigation was conducted, but many of the more confused and uncorroborated press reports resulted in some of the wilder theories of the last century. The *Dublin Evening Mail* on September 11th was among the newspapers bemoaning their lack of access to the official investigation:

> Intense excitement continues to be visible in Whitechapel. Thousands of loungers hang about street corners, and nothing is spoken of but the latest tragedy and the probabilities of its perpetrator being brought to the scaffold. The conflicting reports that have been flying about all day to-day have been quite embarrassing. To make matters worse, the police have rigidly held their tongues, so that the newspaper representatives have had a sea of obstacles to oppose in their endeavours to obtain the latest information. Naturally, the police are very indignant at the way in which they have been attacked in certain newspapers, and the order went forth from headquarters on Saturday that no one was to be supplied with even the barest details. The result has been a perfect flood of contradictory reports.

The *Belfast News-Letter* of September 13th, meanwhile, pointed out the assistance that might sometimes be forthcoming from a more informative attitude by the police:

> "Leather Apron" retired from the coroner's court this afternoon cleared of all suspicion of having murdered the unfortunate woman Chapman. It is a way they have at Scotland Yard when a big crime is committed. They seize hold of the wrong man or two, and, after wasting several precious days, in which they nigh exhaust their detective skill and energy upon a false scent, they let the captured ones go free. The real culprit gets a good start of the officers of the law, who become disheartened in consequence of their first failure, and, if he be astute and keep a close mouth, he may escape detection altogether. At the present moment the police are just where they were when the murder of Saturday morning was reported to them. If they have got any clue at all, which I very much doubt, they keep it a secret from the public. Over and again law-breakers and criminals have been run down through certain simple facts being made known. Dr. Lamson, the poisoner, was brought to justice in consequence of a paragraph which got into the newspapers. The chemist who supplied him with the aconite, the poison with which he did for his afflicted brother-in-law, on seeing the account of the murder in the papers tendered his evidence at once at Scotland Yard, and Lamson, who was on the Continent, came back to London and offered to explain that his connection with the crime was perfectly innocent.[3] Yet, will it be believed that the police officer who gave the information to the Press was severely reprimanded for doing so? The traditions of Scotland Yard are

not easily thrown aside. Hence, the people in the East End consider it their duty to institute vigilance committees for their protection and private citizens offer large rewards in order to stimulate the detection of the wicked monster who so deeply dyed his hands in blood.

Criticism of the police was, of course, rife in the newspapers as well as on the streets. The *Dublin Evening Mail* commented on September 10th:

> The feeling against the police for being unable to trace the murderer is very strong. In the neighbourhood of the murder, a constable scarcely dare perambulate the streets alone. Even when in couples, two or three officers have been somewhat violently handled. Individually, of course, the police are not much to blame, but there is a growing opinion, even in the highest quarters, that the system generally is not what it should be. One fact that is very severely criticised is that the constables stationed in the Whitechapel district are not permitted to make any inquiries in connection with the murder. The work is left entirely to a band of detectives sent specially from Scotland Yard. These men may, it is admitted, be superior in intelligence and tact to the ordinary constable, but they labour under the great disadvantage of not being thoroughly familiar with the criminals of the district and their various haunts.

The blame was variously apportioned by the newspapers, although Sir Charles Warren came in for the lion's share of the criticism. The Home Secretary, Henry Matthews, however, did not escape lightly. Matthews, who was privately considered a very personable man, and a witty and charming raconteur with a fine legal brain, was himself an Irish Catholic and the first Cabinet minister of that religious persuasion to have been appointed since the reign of Queen Elizabeth I. He was, however, very un-statesmanlike, and was said to be the weakest link in the Government chain. Notwithstanding this he remained in office throughout the six years of Tory Government. The *Cork Examiner* of September 11th made complaint of his shortcomings in the Whitechapel case:

> The East End murders are having the salutary effect of opening the eyes of Londoners to the mischief of entrusting the police to a man like Home Secretary Matthews, whose one endeavour has been to turn this body into a political force to serve the ends of the Tories. Under the regime of Matthews murder and outrage have grown to an alarming extent in the Metropolis, owing to the police having been withdrawn from their proper duties to guard Trafalgar Square, to superintend political meetings. The police have arrested a number of persons but it is by

no means clear that any of them have any connection with the murders. The indignation at the incompetence of the police is, however, so great that they are bound to make some show of activity.

The same newspaper returned to the subject three days later:

> The police have utterly failed to detect any trace of the Whitechapel murderer or murderers, in fact Scotland Yard has in recent years, under the direction of Home Secretary Matthews, been so busy in political matters that it has had no time nor taste to attend to its proper work – the prevention and detection of crime. It is very probable that within a short time we shall hear of renewed conflicts between the police of the metropolis and the people, as the unemployed have already begun what has now become an annual series of demonstrations. The number of vagrants is larger at this time of year than it has been ever before, so that not alone in Ireland but in England the authorities may be on the look out for a bitter winter.

The *Freeman's Journal*, on September 13th, meanwhile, warmed to the same subject with a vengeance:

> The cry of "Down with the Home Secretary" was raised afresh yesterday by the *Daily Telegraph*. The fact that so influential a Ministerial journal should consider itself justified in making a ferocious attack upon Mr. Matthews at the present juncture, when the Government has trouble enough upon its hands, would seem to indicate that the Home Secretary's position has again become precarious. Mr. Matthews has survived many trials, and he may survive this one, but it is quite patent that he is considered by some of his colleagues as well as the majority of Ministerial supporters as a source of weakness to the Government. He is especially blamed for the mismanagement of Scotland Yard, and there can be no doubt that he was privy all along to Mr. Munro's extraordinary proceedings for the implication of Mr. Nolan in the dynamite plots. He has not got on well with Sir Charles Warren, who is too independent for him, and it is reported that the fresh mess he has got into lately is entirely owing to the quarrels he has had with the Chief Commissioner, and the improbability of establishing harmonious relations between them.

More generalised criticism of the police appeared in several newspapers, both the national dailies and the local press. This report from the *Ballymena Advertiser* of September 15th is fairly representative:

The excitement incident upon the published reports of this latest atrocity, and the indignation because the guilty party or parties have so long evaded discovery and punishment, have been intense. Nothing in blood-curdling melodrama or fiction is more horrible than these tragedies which are shocking London and the rest of the land. It is to be earnestly hoped that the police will not only be able to bring to justice any person in any way responsible for the fiendish slaughter of the poor outcasts of the East-end of London, but that they will also succeed in taking such steps as will prevent the repetition of outrages which would put a naked savage to the blush. Changes have taken place just now in the Criminal Investigation and Detective Department at Scotland-yard, and the re-organisation of these important branches of the Metropolitan Police ought to lead to greater vigilance and higher efficiency among the officials responsible for ferreting out evil-doers. There is at present a long and sadly unsatisfactory list of undiscovered London murders[4] and each addition thereto goes to give a further shaking to the public confidence in the skill of the guardians of life and property.

Another article of the same date, this one from a London Correspondent shared by the *Bray Herald,* the *Ballinrobe Chronicle* and the *Enniscorthy News,* was more understanding of the kinds of problems faced by the police in the discovery of crime:

London has not for many a year received so great a shock as it has done within the past few days by what has seemed the culmination of a series of ruthless and purposeless murders in the East-end. The terrible details of these tragedies have already been fully described by a variety of pens, and it will suffice here to chronicle the state of panic fear into which they have reduced the people of a large section of the metropolis. Recollections of "Williams the Monster"[5] and of other violent and bloodthirsty desperadoes, whose crimes have from time to time within this century filled London with horror, have naturally been abundant since the series of Whitechapel horrors began; but it may be doubted whether any of the crimes perpetrated by those men have been worse in character or degree than those with which we have recently been startled. Readers of the more morbid of the works of Poe will well remember his sketch of "The Murders in the Rue Morgue," a tale which was not merely thrilling in its essence, but so precise in its details that many were persuaded of its truth, but were disappointed when they looked for the street named among the thoroughfares of Paris; and to such as those there will appear to have been no recent parallel to those imaginary horrors more exact than the very real horrors to which we have just been subjected in London.

Naturally, as a consequence of these crimes, popular attention has been directed even more closely than it otherwise would have been to the change which has recently taken place in the headship of the Criminal Investigation Department of the Metropolitan police, or, in more common phrase, the detective section at Scotland-yard. Mr. Monro, who had filled that position for some years, has been transferred to a post of great difficulty and confidence at the Home Office; and his successor, Mr. Anderson, more fortunate than many men similarly circumstanced, has immediately had placed in his hands an excellent opportunity for proving his capacity for his new position. Of late there has been a very large development among novel writers of what is technically known as the detective story, and nothing has ensured a more ready sale than tales of extremely mysterious but ultimately discovered crime. The detective of real life, however, is not quite the figure to which we are accustomed in fiction; and it is obviously one thing for an author to construct in his study a puzzle of which he himself has the key, and quite another of a police officer to have to deal with a crime towards the elucidation of which scarcely even the faintest clue can be obtained.

The London Correspondent of the *Dublin Evening Mail* equally gave some support to the police efforts at this early stage in the September 11th edition:

The police keenly feel that they are on their trial. Upward of a hundred detectives from Scotland Yard have been engaged in scouring the neighbourhood of Whitechapel with a view to obtain clues. They are strictly ordered to keep any information they may obtain a close secret. At a late hour on Sunday night I perambulated the streets in the vicinity of the murder, and I found constables stationed at every few yards, and all of them thoroughly on the *qui rive*. If another assassination is attempted the perpetrator stands a poor chance of getting away unobserved from the scene of horror.

However, it should be mentioned that detective activity had not confined itself to the arrest of Piser. A second arrest, and one which, although it eventually went nowhere, must at the time have seemed a highly promising one, had occurred almost simultaneously. The man's name was William Henry Pigott, and the same September 11th edition of the *Dublin Evening Mail* commented on the arrest:

A good deal of attention is focussed on the peculiar circumstances attending the arrest of the man Pigott at Gravesend, and the action of the police in regard to him is being eagerly discussed. There are certainly some remarkable circumstances attached to the man's arrest and appearance. In the first place, he admits having been in Whitechapel on Saturday night. His story is that a woman fell down in a fit and bit him severely. Presuming the statement to be true, people naturally ask why he should hurriedly leave London immediately afterwards and proceed to Gravesend? His clothes were stained all over with blood, and it is difficult to see how this state of things could have resulted from a bite, however severe. The man, too, is declared to be insane – a fact which rather intensifies the notion that he may have been connected with the tragedy, seeing that, by many people, the horrible butchery associated with it is thought to be only compatible with the fierce brutality of a maniac.

Although the arrest of Pigott was reported extensively in the newspapers both in England and Ireland, nothing remains in the police files to confirm the accuracy of these reports. Pigott, it seems, was arrested in the Pope's Head public house in West Street, Gravesend, on the evening of Sunday September 9th, after he had aroused the suspicion of the landlady by talking about the murders and expressing his hatred of women. Word was sent to Superintendent Berry of the Gravesend Police who sent a Sergeant Vellensworth to arrest the man. On being brought to the station Pigott was found to have an injury to his hand, which he explained by stating that on Saturday morning, at approximately the time of the murder, he had been in Brick Lane, Whitechapel, when a woman fell down in a fit near him, and that when he had tried to help her she had bitten him on the hand. He stated that he had then punched her, and on seeing a policeman approach as a consequence had run away. He later stated that the incident had taken place at the back of a lodging house, which tended to strengthen suspicion against him.

On news of the arrest reaching Inspector Abberline, he had immediately recognised that here was a very good suspect, and had personally travelled to Gravesend to bring the man back to Leman Street station for further investigation. In the meantime the Police Surgeon of Gravesend had found stains of blood on two shirts carried by the Pigott, and also signs that his boots had recently been wiped clean of blood.

On arrival in the East End, Mrs Fiddymont, Mrs Chappell and Joseph Taylor were sent for to see if they could identify Pigott as the man who had come into the Prince Albert public house on the morning of the murder, but they stated that he was not the man. Without police records it is not clear exactly what happened to Pigott after his arrest. Reports state that due to his general demeanour

Dr Phillips was sent for, and that he certified the man to be insane, whereupon he was taken to Whitechapel workhouse infirmary for treatment for Delerium Tremens. He was found to have been a man who in former years had been a successful publican, but had recently fallen on hard times, and the police were apparently satisfied that he was not the murderer. The Admissions and Discharge book of the Whitechapel workhouse indicates that he was not released until October 9th, by which time the next murders in the series had already occurred.

In the absence of any other likely suspects,[6] investigations continued amid an increasingly critical and speculative press. At the same time, suggestions flooded in to both police and press from the general public whose appetite for catching the killer had been whetted by the barrage of press coverage and the continual suggestions that a reward might be offered. The *Belfast News-Letter* of September 12th reported on this trend:

> One officer informs me that the detective department has already been delayed with suggestions how to track the murderer. "Why not employ bloodhounds?" writes one correspondent, who forgets that Whitechapel is not Wormwood Scrubs. "Search all the lodging-houses from the Borough Road to Stepney," is the suggestion of another citizen, who entirely considers that those cheap institutions are patronised solely by the criminal class. "Our great difficulty," said the officer to me, "is this; when detectives go forth into the bye-ways and alleys and slums of the East End they see there a large criminal class – people whose wretchedness and misery might lead them into any crime. It is like looking for a needle in a bundle of straw, unless by some fortunate accident a detective might happen to drop upon the veritable criminal." From these words and other observations that fell from the police officer, I gathered that the police do not welcome, much less invite, suggestions from the public as to the detection of crime. What they want is "information," not suggestions how to entrap the fugitive from justice and the law.

In Ireland another trend was observable in the press, both national and local, and this was the way in which the crimes were used as a lead in to discussions of the "Irish Question." While the Ripper case in itself was undoubtedly a huge story for some of the Irish press, particularly the national dailies, often the more radical local press reported only on those aspects of the case which they felt directly affected them. For both the Nationalist and Unionist factions of the press, the main usefulness of coverage of events in Whitechapel was as a big stick to beat each other up with.

CHAPTER FOUR ENDNOTES

1   This is the correct spelling of Sergeant Thick's name. It appears in various newspaper reports as Thicke.

2   Annie Chapman's nickname was variously reported as Siffey, Sivvey, Sivvy and various other permutations.

3   This account is fairly accurate. On December 3rd, 1881, Bournemouth doctor George Henry Lamson murdered his disabled brother-in-law before he reached his majority so that his share of a large inheritance would pass to Lamson's wife. The murder was achieved with a poisoned slice of Dundee cake.

4   See Appendix One for an article relating to undiscovered crime in London.

5   It is not entirely clear whether this refers to Renwick Williams, known as "The Monster", whose crimes were from the previous century, or John Williams the Ratcliffe Highway murderer. See Appendix One for more details of both.

6   Police records indicate that one Joseph Isenschmid was also strongly suspected at this time, but only brief reports of his arrest, not mentioning him by name, appeared in Ireland.

CHAPTER FIVE

The Irish Question

The *Freeman's Journal* was one of Ireland's oldest newspapers, having been published in Dublin since 1763. In the early part of the nineteenth century the paper had had close connections with Dublin Castle, but after falling into a dispute with the Chief Secretary for Ireland at the beginning of the second decade of the century, it slowly changed its allegiance such that by the time of the Ripper crimes it was one of the most popular voices of Nationalist opinion in the country. On September 12th the *Freeman* printed a leader column which used the murders as a means of heaping criticism against English attitudes to Ireland:

> As any reader of the newspapers can see, an epidemic of crime is raging in England. Every day brings its own budget of dreadful deeds; horror succeeds horror; and the most hardened student of the gruesome literature of murder pauses involuntarily to ask how such atrocities are possible in communities that are not accounted barbarous. The English people are certainly to be commiserated with. A fierce light has been cast into the obscure noisome places of their civilisation, and the world, according to its custom, regards the ghastly sights that are disclosed as the shame, not of localities nor of a class, but of the entire nation. So the English people have regarded Irish crime in the past; they cannot complain if others apply to them the system of reasoning which they never hesitate to apply to the Irish. We have always protested against the assumption that, because half-a-dozen Irishmen in the course of a year commit as many murders, all Irishmen are to be considered and treated as murderers; our English friends will now appreciate the force of our protest.

Before the day had passed the accusation had been repudiated at great length by the *Freeman's* local rival, the *Dublin Evening Mail*, a newspaper whose hard-line Unionist politics tended to permeate its every word:

The Whitechapel murders are made the peg from which the *Freeman* hangs up to-day one of its frequent dissertations on the rampancy of crime in England. "The most hardened student," we read, "of the gruesome literature of murder pauses involuntarily to ask how such atrocities are possible in communities that are not accounted barbarous." Ireland, on the contrary, is a "crimeless country," according to our contemporary, and it is, of course, a shocking inversion of the natural order of things that a forced union should be kept up between the crimeless country and the barbarous, and still more shocking, that the crimeless should be outvoted by the barbarous in the common Parliament and not allowed to manage, at least, its own affairs. We are glad to find our Popular Instructor recognising the principle that on the whole it is well that decent and crimeless people should not be placed at the mercy of ruffians, and, we suppose, we may add, of cheats and swindlers; and that the decent people have some sort of a right, if not to rule, at least to manage their own affairs and go about their lawful business free from molestation and intimidation by those who are morally their inferiors. That is a sound principle, and its general recognition by the Irish masses is of so much importance, both to themselves and others, that we do not care to cavil at the road by which our contemporary arrived at it. But as the *Freeman* seems to be seriously puzzled, not to say flabbergasted, at the prevalence of crime in England, we feel it a charity to offer some explanation of the mystery. The explanation is indeed an exceedingly simple and obvious one, but, somehow, facts that are obvious and simple enough do frequently escape the acumen of the Irish Popular Instructor. The English criminal statistics do not contain any indication of the nationality of the criminal. One may guess from the name given in the newspaper reports whether a particular criminal be a Pole, or an Italian, or a Frenchman, or a Russian, or an Irishman, but it would be an endless, and, perhaps, quite an impossible task to collect from these scattered and uncertain data any trustworthy idea that the percentages of "crime in England" to be laid at the door of any particular nation. The difficulty is greatest in respect of Irish and Scottish criminals, since many surnames are common to the three countries. Take, for instance, the "Savage assault upon a policeman," recorded in the papers of yesterday. "Two men," we read, "named MICHAEL ROBINSON and JAMES QUIN, were charged at Manchester with a cruel assault on a police constable. The policeman had a woman in custody on Saturday night when these two men attacked him and savagely beat him with the buckle ends of their belts. His eye was knocked from its socket and hung upon his cheek. Prisoners were remanded."

Who is to tell the country of origin of these savages? There are plenty of ROBINSONS, and QUIN is not an exclusively Irish name. The senseless antipathy to the police is also a feeling common to the criminals of all countries, though perhaps Ireland and Hayti are the only two in which it pervades the populace at large. But while little is known for certain as to the nationality of the so-called English criminals, we do know that there are few countries in the world that harbour so large a proportion of foreigners – including Irishmen in that term – in the chief centres of its wealth and industrial activity. New York and a few other American cities may rival the English centres in this particular, and we think it will be found that in them, too, the criminal statistics are as formidable as in England. We have been informed on good authority that half a dozen dead bodies are not unfrequently fished up out of the docks and rivers of New York in a single morning, some of them, doubtless, cases of suicide, but most of them bearing the marks of murder. "We have always protested," says the *Freeman*, "against the assumption that because half-a-dozen Irishmen in the course of a year commit as many murders, all Irishmen are to be considered and treated as murderers; our English friends will now appreciate the force of our protest." The *Freeman's* English friends have not needed, we think, the *Freeman's* protest against a view which nobody in his senses ever entertained. It is not on account of the actual murderers, be they a few or many, in any parts of the United Kingdom that the special enactments which go by the generic title of Coercion Acts are necessary. What makes this legislation necessary, or, on the other hand, superfluous, is the attitude of the populace at large towards the criminal. Do they think the crime advantageous to themselves, do they wink at it, do they supply him with the needful intelligence where he may surprise his intended victim, do they keep all counteracting intelligence from the victim himself, and from the police, do they frustrate the detection of crime and swear false *alibi's* and obstinately refuse to assist the authorities in unravelling a piece of wickedness, do they execrate such authorities as Star Chamber tyrants, do they terrorise the relatives of the deceased into a silent acquiescence in their wrongs, do the popular newspapers apologise for crime and blacken the character of every honest witness or honest judge and jury who seek to give effect to the law? These are the questions which a statesman must ask himself when he is determining whether a Coercion Act is necessary, or whether the ordinary law may be left to take its course. It is the question Mr. GLADSTONE asked himself until he was bribed by eighty-five Parliamentary votes, to throw in his lot with the abettors and instigators of Irish crime, and represent that the responsibility for crime lay at the door, not of the criminal, but of the laws that refused to give the criminal his way. If the Irish people – Sir GEORGE TREVELYAN'S Ireland, No. 2 – object to Coercion Acts, they have the remedy in their own hands. Let them cease to sympathise with crime, to foster it, to screen it, to pay for it. And let them do this for some better motive than that which they now profess to be their only one, namely, that they hope, by Mr GLADSTONE'S aid, to compass all their dishonest ends by means that stop short of murder. A Government, worthy of the name of Government, will not tolerate murder. Both crimes are deadly to a community, though of course, the Irish populace have not the sense to know it. They have natural intelligence enough, but it is blinded by their greed and hocussed by the false teachings they receive and swallow. The actual lull in Irish crime is not to be relied on. So their own orators tell us. They threaten a recurrence of "unconstitutional methods" if their lawless and absurd demands are not granted them. But the orators' threats are as little to be feared as the enforced good behaviour of the rank and file is to be trusted. A steady and sensible Government will know how to deal with both.

In spite of its comparative brevity, it must be said that the *Freeman* view is the more persuasive. In response to the accusation of hypocrisy that England treats all Irishmen as criminal because some Irishmen are criminal, but applies no such standard to itself, the *Evening Mail* appears only to be able to say, "Ah, but we don't know if all the criminals in England are English, so it doesn't count," and then go on to re-assert that Ireland needs special laws because the natural tendency of the Irish is to support crime!

However, it is not the remit of this book to comment on the rights and wrongs of any particular political ideology. The exchange above is a highly enlightening example of similar exchanges of comment that had been going on either openly or in private throughout the island long before the Whitechapel murders had commenced, and which would continue long afterwards. For this three-month period, the events in the East End of London simply provided a bright floodlight under which such opinions could be given prominence. The late 1880s was a difficult period for Nationalist politics, with a Tory Government in St James's Palace which allied itself very closely with the Unionist Party which had been instrumental in its gaining office through its support in defeating Gladstone's Home Rule Bill of 1886.

While the "Autumn of Terror" was occurring in Whitechapel, Ireland itself was in a state of turmoil, and during that brief period a considerable number of important incidents and developments would occur, the most high profile of which was, naturally, the opening of the Parnell Commission.

The previous year the Prime Minister, Lord Salisbury, had appointed his nephew Arthur Balfour as Chief Secretary for Ireland in succession to Sir Michael Hicks-Beach. Balfour took office while Ireland was in the grip of a Nationalist insurgency going under the name of the Plan of Campaign. The basis of this plan was to secure a reduction in rent for tenant farmers suffering from a depression in dairy produce and cattle prices which had left many in serious arrears. The operation of the scheme was that the tenants were to offer their landlords a reduced rent, and if this were not accepted then they were to pay no rent at all, but rather to pay the reduced amount into a fund administered by the campaign which would then be used to assist evicted tenants.

The plan was conceived by Timothy Healy, Member of Parliament for Longford North and former secretary to Charles Stewart Parnell who had first bestowed on his mentor the title of "Uncrowned King of Ireland." He was assisted in the administration of the plan by three fellow members of Parliament for the Irish Party: William O'Brien, John Dillon, and Tim Harrington. O'Brien, as editor of the *United Ireland*, was able to use that publication as the voice of the campaign, which was first announced in its pages in an article written by Harrington.

In taking office, Balfour had been given a remit by his uncle to smash the Plan of Campaign, and accordingly one of the first actions taken in office was to secure the Criminal Law (Amendment) Act, popularly known as the Perpetual Coercion Act, granting wide-ranging powers to the agents of the Lord Lieutenant to combat the actions of the National League, which on August 19th, 1887 was proclaimed an illegal organisation under the act, thus also rendering *United Ireland*, as its mouthpiece, an illegal publication. Notwithstanding, that newspaper continued production, despite the fact that its sale was legally prohibited, and on September 15th, 1888 contributed its own comments on the events in East London:

> The air around us these days reeks of blood. The fourth horrible murder of a woman within a short space of time has just been committed in Whitechapel, and while I write there comes a rumour of another similar outrage in Pimlico.[I] All these are murders the perpetrators of which have so far not been discovered. A mystery enwraps them like the mystery of the "Murders of the Rue Morgue." The whole series appear to have been the work of the one man, a maniac poisoned by a frenzy similar to that described in that horrible book by the Marquis DE SADE, against which MIRABEAU wrote his equally horrible "Anti-Junstine." But this is the only reason why they are remarkable. Undetected murders are nothing uncommon in the East of London. Murders and attempts at murder are constantly taking place in that lamentable territory. The

police, too busy at Trafalgar-square, are powerless, and the murderers escape securely through the labyrinth of crooked and foetid streets. The present excitement serves but to throw a lurid light on the condition in which a vast population in London lives cheek-by-jowl with all its wealth and magnificence. It is a condition of absolute savagery compared with which the life of a tribe of cannibals is wholesome. What it will end in when some day these savages of the age of steam feel their power is a thought to cause a shudder. But what strikes me most, I confess, in all their gory panic is the strangeness of the notion of these people setting up next week in their Law Courts a Commission to draw up an indictment of crime against the Irish Nation! The *Times* this very morning contains no less than half-a-dozen paragraphs, apart altogether from those relating to the Whitechapel affair, about murders and outrages in other parts of England. Every day the papers teem with accounts of murders of women, murders of servant girls, patricides, fratricides, infanticides. And the *Times* is employing GEORGE BOLTON and PETER O'BRIEN and spending fabulous sums at the present moment to work up a case to prove that Ireland is a nation of murderers!

Oh! but, it is said, in England crime is punished, but in Ireland it is almost impossible to bring the perpetrators to justice, owing to terrorism, and the depraved sympathy of the people. The *Star*[2] has brought to light some very suggestive, not to say startling figures on this head. Taking an average year, 1886, it shows that 177 verdicts of murder were recorded by coroners' juries in England alone. Out of these only 72 charges of murder arose. That is to say, that in 105 cases not only was the murderer undetected but no one was even charged on suspicion! One hundred and five men and women who committed murder in that one year are still at large. But even of the 72 cases in which there was a charge, in only 35 was the full guilt brought home to the accused. Whether it be "terrorism" or the "depraved sympathy of the people," or whatever the cause be, this is a percentage of undetected capital crime at which Ireland may hang its head. Calculating the average for the past ten years there are now one thousand murderers going about England unpunished and undetected! It is a sorry work measuring the character of a people by their criminal classes, and I am only tempted to think of this comparison by the coincidence of such an epidemic of English crime with the preliminary sitting of the PARNELL Commission. We know what that typical British Pharisee, Mr. W.H. SMITH expects of the PARNELL Commission – to raise such a reek of the doings of Ireland's criminal classes that the whole character of the Irish people and their cause will be hopelessly befouled in British eyes by the association.

The Parnell Commission had been convened as a result of a series of articles published in the *Times* newspaper beginning on March 7th, 1887 under the title of "Parnellism and Crime." A full explanation of how this came about will be provided in Chapter Nine, I will only provide the salient points here. On May 6th, 1882, the Chief Secretary of Ireland, Lord Frederick Cavendish, who had been in office only four days, and his Under-Secretary Thomas Henry Burke had been murdered in the Phoenix Park outside the Viceregal Lodge by a Fenian splinter group known as the Invincibles. On April 18th, 1887, in the "Parnellism and Crime" series, the *Times* printed a facsimile of a letter purported to have been written by Charles Stewart Parnell:

> *Dear Sir,*
> *I am not surprised at your friend's anger but he and you should have known that to denounce the murders was the only course open to us. To do that promptly was plainly our best policy. But you can tell him and all others concerned that though I regret the accident of Lord Cavendish's death, I cannot refuse to admit that Burke got no more than his just deserts. You are at liberty to show him this, and others whom you can trust also, but let not my address be known. He can write to the House of Commons.*
> *Yours very truly,*
> *Chas. S. Parnell.*

Parnell immediately went before the House of Commons and denounced the letter as a forgery, pointing out that the signature did not resemble his own. He later demanded a House of Commons select committee be appointed to investigate the charges made against him. The demand was rejected, and instead the special commission was announced which would investigate not only the *Times* accusations, but the conduct of the whole of the Irish Party under Parnell's leadership. Referred to variously in the Irish press as the Parnell Commission, the Special Commission and the Times Forgeries Commission, the judicial hearing sat for over a year from the time the preliminary hearings began on September 17th, 1888, competing with the Ripper crimes for space on the pages of the daily newspapers.

On September 11th, the *Limerick Reporter and Tipperary Vindicator* was moved to publish the following leader column by this close confluence in time between the two important stories:

> The unprecedented murders of no less than four females in one of the most populous district of London, and amid a state of civilization said to be unparalleled on the face of the earth, has electrified the world, and thrown the organs of public opinion in the great Metropolis into a state

of confusion and bewilderment, whilst it has set the 13,000 policemen, who watch and ward a population of nearly five millions of souls into utter doubt as to their capacity to cope with an evil apparently of unequalled magnitude in any direction. The cry is, what use are the police for which we are taxed to the utmost? What the services of those who are to be seen at all hours, day and night, in every part, from the West to the East-end, from the North to the South? Where shall we obtain protection from the recurrences of horrors such as throw the imaginings of fable mongers into insignificance, and make the tenements and houses of the poor and the palaces of the proud and noble unsafe from the burglar, the murderer, the repetition of horrors which beat the revelations of the Newgate Calendar hollow. It is a curious commentary on the ravings and libels of the infamous *Times,* which is day after day exhibiting "Parnellism and Crime" in Ireland where there is actually no crime whatsoever, where butcheries of women have never been heard of, to find that within a short distance of Printing House Square deeds are committed which have no peer in atrocity, in the hellish deliberation and scientific ease with which they are perpetrated. There is scarcely a day that passes over our heads that, within the radius of London, crimes are not committed appalling to humanity. Every day drowning, suicides from one bridge or the other, poisonings which fill the mind with a sense of dreadful apprehension, murders of childhood, murders of the aged and weakly, murders of fathers by sons, of sons by fathers – every conceivable iniquity in the long catalogue of human guilt, not to speak of the hidden condition of unspeakable crime within that enormous centre. It is true that every succeeding day does not reveal Whitechapel tragedies, but every succeeding day drags to light deeds of blood congenial to those which have at length shaken faith in the police system, and made the stoutest hearted shudder not only in Whitechapel, Shoreditch, and those notorious parts of the capital, but in the neighbourhood of the loftiest mansions, and to a certain extent the most inaccessible seats of aristocracy and royalty. To inquire into the causes of this state of things to afford some clue to the agency which these inconceivably frightful deeds fill the columns of every newspaper that comes across the Channel, would puzzle the ingenuity of the most profound thinkers and philosophers. The Statute Book bristles with pains and penalties against the guilty, or those who are found guilty. Courts of law, on the architectural effects of which hundreds of thousands of the public money are wasted in fruitless vanities. Yet the crimes go ahead; and the *Times,* which we repeat, has little other stock-in-trade than virulent abuse and hatred to Ireland, little to deploy columns upon columns of foul and acrid and scandalous vituperation on "Parnellism and Crime," only wakens up to the state of things round and about it when such almost unheard of iniquities fill the mind with doubt that the hand of man is formed to commit them, and which show that the gigantic police force on which millions are expended, are but straws on the surface in sight of such a state of indescribable and inconceivable iniquity.

Here in Ireland there is actually no crime that merits the name, except that which the steel-and-flint genius of BALFOUR has begotten in the fell but feeble Crimes Act. It is a poor triumph of legislative action to empower the imprisonment under bolt and bar, within white stone walls, of men who entertain a feeling of revulsion of crime in any shape. Yet our gaols are crowded with the victims of this fell and feeble system, which, deeply iniquitous, is at the same moment of no avail, for the punishment which it is intended to deter, has no such influence, and the victim with his experience of plank bed, starving fare, and treatment authorised by the Crimes Act which wastes the system and takes the vital essence from the constitution of some men, kills, as in the case of Mr. MANDEVILLE and others, and robs of weight and marrow week after week of such men as Mr. HALPIN, of whom little or nothing is said, but who lost 2st. in weight during his incarceration in Limerick District Prison. The moment the "criminal" is beyond the threshold of the prison he is met by the multitude, who greet him as a martyr, who accompany him with bands and banners, with every emblem of jubilation; and he, on his part, when he opens his mouth to speak, is defiance again to the whole Balfourian system, and declares his unaltered and unalterable determination to move in the path for which his liberty was torn from him for any length of time. Fell and feeble is the description applicable to the system, and Mr. BALFOUR may rack his inventive ingenuity to try the thumbscrew, the scavenger's daughter, any instrument of torture, before he can make Irishmen believe that the course which he is pursuing is based on the eternal principles of justice, has right or reason to recommend it. The police of this country – the Royal Irish Constabulary – are never engaged as they are in London in pursuit of inhuman savages who gloat in the sacrifice of the lives of women. No! It is to be regretted that they have been converted to purposes for which in their initiation they never were intended. They are now become part and parcel of the crowbar and battering-ram battalion which levels to the ground the houses of the tenant who cannot pay an impossible rent. As under the aegis of Lord CLANRICARDE[3], and lately in Clare under other agencies, they have become the uprooters of the foundations of the humble homes of the distressed and distraught farmer who is unable to meet the exaction of agents or the pressure of landlords who have no hearts of flesh. Years have passed since anything in the shape of deliberate crime has startled this country or set the police force on foot to discover the guilty. Crime at any time was the offspring of discordant relations between landlord and tenant, the unnatural course of things which endeavours to make that possible which is impossible, and supply the extravagance and waste of the absentee by the outcome of a soil which yields no return to the husbandman. In the midst of the historic dreadful famine years of 1847–'8–'9, there were more homesteads annihilated and families sent adrift to perish of cholera in unprovided sheds thrown up to shelter them, or at sea in the hold or on the deck of ships not sufficient to carry them across the Atlantic, or on some inhospitable shore which if they lived to reach, refused them succour in their unheard of misery. Let the cry of "PARNELLISM and Crime" cease, let the dreadful savagery of a persistent course of wholesale clearance of the population, become a thing of the past, let some new life be infused into stoney hearts of legislators, let those scenes which Mr. DAVITT[4] has so graphically pictured in one of his most recent public pronouncements for which he apprehends the plank bed is preparing for him, or another taste of Millbank or Pentonville, let something be done to give self-Government to Ireland and we shall cease to look upon those scenes which crowd around the soul like the dreams of the foremost poet of Italy in the Inferno.

The general argument which prevailed in Ireland with regard to crime was one of what exactly constituted a crime. To the Nationalists, a tenant farmer resisting eviction did not constitute an illegal action, it was simply a matter of his protecting his homestead and livelihood. The tenant was seen as the victim, and such support as could be given him would so be given. This was where the coercion acts came in, a series of legislations providing emergency powers to the Lord Lieutenant in times of unrest, of which the Perpetual Coercion Act was merely the most recent of over fifty such acts passed during the nineteenth century. Interpretations of the coercion acts were often somewhat loose, and although it is difficult to believe today, people found themselves imprisoned quite literally for an action as seemingly harmless as looking at a policeman in a way he did not approve of.

Many of the Irish Party MP's found themselves imprisoned at various times under the auspices of coercion, including Charles Stewart Parnell himself who, in 1882, was incarcerated in Kilmainham Jail for publishing what was considered a seditious article about the then Prime Minister William Gladstone in the *United Ireland*. William O'Brien and John Dillon both spent periods imprisoned under coercion as well. Dillon was charged in May 1888, the charges being that "on the 8th April at Tullyallen, in the petty sessions district, he did take part in an illegal conspiracy, namely the Plan of Campaign; the second, that he did incite persons to join that conspiracy; and third, that he did take part in an unlawful assembly."[5] He remained in prison until the middle of September.

In the case of William O'Brien, the Member of Parliament for North-East Cork was indicted for organising a rent strike on the Kingston estate near Mitchelstown, Co. Cork, together with local politician John Mandeville. The pair were served with a magistrate's order to appear at court in the town on September 9th, 1887 on a charge of using seditious language. They announced that they would not appear, but on the day some eight thousand protesters turned up at the courthouse. The Royal Irish Constabulary attempted to clear what was considered an illegal gathering, at which John Dillon was speaking. Finding themselves unable to reach the platform the police began to use their batons, whereupon a riot ensued and the crowd beat the police back to their barracks in Upper Cork Street which was quickly surrounded. Without any warning, a policeman opened fire on the crowd from an upper window of the barracks, killing three men, John Casey, Michael Lonergan, and John Shinnock. The incident became known as the Mitchelstown Massacre and would become a chief *cause celebre* of the Nationalist movement. For many years the cry of "Remember Mitchelstown" would be heard at rallies across the country. The Chief Secretary, who was held responsible for the actions of the police, earned the pseudonym of "Bloody Balfour" as a result of the events of that day.

Convictions against O'Brien and Mandeville were eventually obtained, and they were imprisoned in Tullamore Jail on November 2nd, 1887, O'Brien for three months and Mandeville for two. As had become a custom among Nationalists imprisoned under the auspices of coercion, they immediately declared themselves political prisoners and therefore refused to wear prison issue clothes, as they insisted was their right. Arthur Balfour, meanwhile, issued an order that they were not to wear their own clothes, and as a result the two men were left with nothing but a sheet to cover themselves, although O'Brien later obtained clothing which had been smuggled into his cell for him. Mandeville became seriously ill as a result of the treatment, and died in July 1888, seven months after his release. An inquest on his body recorded a verdict of death caused by "brutal and unjustifiable treatment" received in the prison, a verdict which amounted to a charge of murder against the state. Dr George Ridley, the prison doctor who had certified him fit to undergo the regime, committed suicide at the time of the inquest.

These, however, were simply the high profile cases, there were countless other examples of ill treatment under the conditions of the Coercion Act involving lesser personages, as the new Chief Secretary and the Resident Magistrates, or Removables as they were known, attempted to use the act in a heavy-handed manner to subdue the population from their course of insurrection. The leader columns of the more militantly Nationalist of the Irish newspapers cited coercion again and again as they commented on the events occurring across the Irish Sea in East London. Wicklow newspaper *The People* had this to say on October 3rd:

> What wretched hypocrites our Tory moralists and rulers are! They never tire of denouncing Irish lawlessness, and of prescribing Coercion in drenching doses as the remedy for the same. With smug satisfaction they proclaim to the world that their policy has no other end but to make the Irish people as law-abiding as Englishmen. They profess that but for them Ireland would be weltering in crime, and that Coercion is needed to restrain the criminal propensities of the people. And all the time, in the very heart of their own metropolis, in the most densely-populated district of London, murders are being committed which would make an African savage sick with horror. They are not ordinary murders, such as are committed daily by the superior British citizen who kicks or hacks or burns to death his wife or her paramour; not such murders as are briefly chronicled in the morning newspapers as every-day incidents of life in "merrie England." The Whitechapel atrocities, with all their ghastly surroundings of sordid vice and fiendish callousness, are the results of sheer bloodthirstiness. They are crimes which, thank God, are impossible in this country, where, even amongst the lowest of the low, human nature still distinguishes men and women from wild beasts. On reading of the horrors that are perpetrated under the shadow of St. Paul's, one experiences a sensation of sickness. It is like breathing the air of a charnel-house. Miserable women butchered and cut up by some unknown British citizen with a morbid craving for slaughter are now amongst the ordinary discoveries of the policemen who patrol the slums of the great city.

The same article, after a description of the murder of another woman by her husband in the West of London, continues:

> These criminals choose the rulers of Ireland, and arm them with powers to repress "lawlessness and disorder" here. They yell in holy horror in their denunciations of the Irish people whenever a maddened peasant reddens his hands with blood of the man who has doomed him and his family to a fate worse than death – herding in exile with the scum of humanity, that the seething cauldron of English vice and misery throws off. They are piously shocked if Irish tenants do not bow down and worship every Emergency blackguard and vile land-grabber that swaggers or

sneaks amongst us. Prating of "law and order," they applaud when Irishmen of pure lives and untainted honour are flung into prison as criminals – their crime being that they resist wrong-doing. Really it is not a cause for wonder that the two nations have been unable to strike up a friendship, for – judging the two races by their genuine criminals – and that is the test that the Tories apply to Ireland – there could be no community of feeling between them. Even Yahoos would scorn to submit to the role of such monsters. But it will be said that it is preposterous to judge Englishmen as a nation by the Whitechapel monster and by their ordinary murderers. That is not the Tory doctrine, which requires that the Irish people are to be judged by the latest perpetrators of a moonlight outrage, and that the Irish nation must be held accountable for every deed of wickedness committed within the four shores of Ireland. Applying that principle to our neighbours at the other side of the Channel, we could not form a very high opinion of them. Perhaps such of them as reflect upon the matter will admit now that the Tory doctrine is not always to be taken as true.

A similar example was to be found in the *Westmeath Examiner* of October 6th:

MURDER of late has become a familiar figure in the streets of London. No woman can move about after dark, even in the heart of the city, but the grim shadow of the assassin stealthily treads behind her. Perhaps in the whole history of murder in every civilised country in a civilised time no such atrocious crimes have been committed as the ones known as the Whitechapel tragedies, murders which have shaken the English capital to its very heart, which have thrown the people into a state of panic and which have fixed the attention of the world upon the state of society in the British capital. There can be no doubt that the people of London live in daily and hourly expectation of hearing of another terrible murder in their very midst and under the noses, so to speak, of the Scotland Yard authorities and their hosts of detectives, whose once vaunted smartness is now spoken of as non-existent. The duty they were supposed to do was to watch criminals and prevent or punish crime. But they were taken from their legitimate business and set as spies upon men who differed in politics with the powers that be. Tracking Irish members to their residences and arresting a few of them were their principal business. Now when a criminal who seems to be something of a fiend in addition, is pursuing his dreadful career of murder and mutilation, when several unsuspecting women have fallen victims to his thirst for blood, the authorities are absolutely paralysed in [the] face of his daring. There has been no

clue by which he can be found. How different would the course of proceedings be if the tragedies occurred in Ireland. We would within a short
time of the murders have Crimes Acts, Arms Acts, Coercion Acts, and all
the other etceteras with which misrule has made us so familiar. Yet our
Christianity-canting Chief Secretary does not as much as hint at
Coercion for London, while the Home Secretary refused to offer a
reward for information. If there be the slightest grounds for thinking that
any popular man in Ireland can be run into jail, bribery by policeman, as
has been often proved, is largely availed of to secure the object. Not so
however in England in the case of a murderer. The action of the
Government in reference to these terrible murders shows to the English
people and all others what truth there is in the statement so often made
that we have equal laws with England.

The *United Ireland*, foremost among the Irish Nationalist newspapers, founded
by Charles Stewart Parnell in 1881 and described by its editor, the aforemen-
tioned William O'Brien, as an "insurrection in print", was never slow to score
political points from any situation. A brief article in the September 29th issue
decried:

> Supposing the Whitechapel assassinations had taken place in Kerry what
> a universal outcry there would be about the inate [sic] depravity and bru-
> tality of the Irish race. There has been nothing in Kerry, with all the fierce
> provocation to which the wretched inhabitants are subjected, a hundred-
> part as brutal as these purposeless crimes. There would be no loss for a
> motive in Ireland. The assassinations, it would be taken for granted, were
> committed at "the secret orders" of a savage, irresponsible tribunal, and
> the failure of the police to discover a clue would be explained by the
> secret sympathy of the inhabitants with the criminals. A very neat pam-
> phlet would be published on the text to prove that the Irish people are a
> race of degraded assassins utterly unfit for self-government. How would
> the English people like the argument pressed home to themselves?

Meanwhile the Nationalist elements of the more mainstream daily press, while
using less inflammatory language, made similar points on a regular basis, as, for
example, indicated by this article from the *Cork Examiner* of September 12th:

> WHAT possesses all the features of a murder epidemic appears to prevail
> in some parts of England. Our columns day after day give details of
> cruel, vile, and most wicked murders committed within the past few
> weeks in various districts of that country. In London atrocity has excelled

itself, and a murderer, or gang of murderers, has done deeds the horror of which makes men grow pale. And the murderers are at large. If it should be proved that the two men in custody, or one of them, committed the Whitechapel murders, which seems rather unlikely by the way, the argument which may be based on the circumstances is not shaken by that fact. A vast amount of capital has been made by some English journals over undetected crime in Ireland, and it has been asserted over and over again by the *Times* and newspapers that take their light and leading from that organ, that those murders must have been known to a great number of people. Not a murder has been committed of recent years in this country that that shameless and baseless falsehood was not published all over the Three Kingdoms, and disseminated in some form through the world. If the Irish people set their faces against crime, said those public instructors, if the National League only gave a direction to the criminals of the country, all would be peace. A fouler slander than that imputed to the Irish people and the National League was never uttered. But the English people, it is to be feared, were largely prejudiced against the Irish cause by such statements. The dreadful crimes committed at their own doors within the past few weeks must make them aware of the absurdity and the falsity of the charges levelled against the whole Irish people. In spite of the exertions of the whole police force of London and of England, murderers have escaped. Many of those crimes, like those London murders, have been committed in populous districts, and yet the police are without a clue by which to detect the perpetrators. We do not seek to make any capital out of the circumstance, but it certainly should lead Englishmen to consider, with more discrimination, the position of the Irish people in reference to crime committed in their midst. Irishmen do not, it must at once be admitted constitute themselves a police when a great crime has been committed; the circumstances under which they live leave them no option; the police regarding the people hostile, as they are, to their ordinary work, discountenance all aid from the people in the detection of serious crime. There is no inducement, no reason whatever, why the Irish people should go out of their way to help the officials of the Government in catching criminals. It should not be so, but so it is. Deprived of every civic privilege that the English Government can deprive them of, and ruled by a police force, the main object of which is to defeat and baton them on all occasions, the natural desire of the people to aid the agents of the law in bringing criminals to justice is considerably diminished. When honest men and true patriots are made "criminals" by Mr BALFOUR, the Irish people are not over-zealous in aiding the police to bring real criminals to justice. But all the same, the Irish people hate crime, and ever have hated it, and those who have alleged the contrary have perpetrated a gross libel on them. But so long as England employs her police to baton them for political purposes, to break up their lawful meetings, and obstruct them in every way, it is not to be wondered at that they do not heartily co-operate with the Force in catching criminals. With a Parliament in College Green and a Police force ruled in sympathy with the people things could be vastly different. But the criminals and the police have it all between them in this country just now.

If the majority of these reports put the Nationalist point of view, this is for two reasons. Firstly, obviously the majority of the press, like the majority of the public, took either the Nationalist or a neutral point of view. Secondly, while there certainly were a number of papers with staunchly Unionist views, such as the *Belfast News-Letter*, the *Dublin Evening Mail*, and bizarrely the *Kerry Evening Post* (one wonders how many of the population of the Kingdom were keen to obtain their daily dose of effusive praise for Bloody Balfour and his Removables!), on this particular issue they were very much put on the defensive. There was little answer to be given in the accusations of the Nationalists. The Unionists could argue in favour of coercion as long and as loud as they liked, but the "what's sauce for the goose" argument is always a difficult one to argue against. One must give the *Dublin Evening Mail* credit then for a subtle but quite brilliant response in kind in its leader column of September 11th. Its conception of a killer who believes himself to be fighting a moral wrong takes a long time to come to the point, but when it does so it puts forward the Unionist view quite succinctly:

> There is a very precious political lesson to be gathered from the shocking series of Whitechapel murders. It is now pretty clear that the four murders have been perpetrated by the one man, and that his motive was not any of the ordinary ones – viz, plunder, or personal spite, or the dread of the consequences of some previous offence. Moreover, the fact that the women whom he butchered all belonged to a single miserable class of the community, leads strongly to the conviction that his motive was one which to his own morbid consciousness appeared a highly moral one. He thought to extirpate or to check a certain form of vice by killing off a certain number of "unfortunates" and terrorising the rest. If he could have got the laws to do this for him, he probably would have much preferred to leave the task to them, and not to imbrue his own hands in blood, and risk his neck. But finding the laws ineffective or apathetic, he took the bull by the horns and set up as administrator of his own ethical system. The fact that he has so long escaped detection, notwithstanding the army of

detectives on his trail, and the keenness with which half a million of civilian neighbours are eagerly on the watch for him, suggests the strong presumption that he is a person of outwardly respectable and regular life. Nobody suspects him, because there is nothing suspicious in his appearance, or in his ordinary avocations, or in his daily associates. Possibly he is a good son, or father, or husband, and gives entire satisfaction to his employers, if he be a wage earner, or to his customers, if he be a shopkeeper. We should not be surprised to learn that he was a regular attendant at divine worship, though he turns a deaf ear to those parts of the decalogue or of the pulpit exhortations addressed to him which come into collision with his peculiar views of duty, moral, religious, and political. On no other hypothesis, indeed, can we account for the immunity he has hitherto enjoyed. Our own hypothesis is quite consistent with his being a BAYARD and a *preux chevalier* in every relation of life other than that which he has chosen with respect to the "unfortunates" of Whitechapel. But whether he be a model citizen or not, it is almost certain that he is a monomaniac, and commits murder under a perverted moral sentiment. Some twenty years ago, there was a monk executed in Germany for a far longer series of murders by poison having been administered with the most benevolent intentions. The monk thought that life without good health was a horrible affliction, and in pure mercy to a number of people whom he regarded as hopeless invalids, he relieved them of their troubles by the skilful use of poison. When his practices were discovered there was no hesitation on the part of the German Government in putting him on trial for murder, and the German people cordially assented to his execution. So will the English people to the execution of the Whitechapel murderer, in case of his detection. They will stand no shilly-shalley nonsense about the excellence of his motive, or his desire to defend the virtuous homes of the people from the inroads of vice, or about the social advantages to be derived from terrorising moral outcasts into decent behaviour. They will acknowledge, *apropos* of this particular criminal, that crime must be punished under whatever high sounding pretences of benevolence or public spirit it may commend itself to indulgence or to sympathy. But we do not expect that they will generalise this truth. It is a truth we have often insisted on in these columns, pointing out that some of the very worst scourges of humanity were persons who were dominated, to all appearances, by excellent ideas and intentions. We illustrated our contention with the cases of ROBESPIERRE "the Incorruptible," by that honest fellow MARAT, who thought that France could be made happy for ever at the trifling cost of 100,000 aristocratic heads; by TORQUEMADA and other Grand

Inquisitors, who had nothing so much at heart as the salvation of souls, even the souls of the wretched heretics whom they sent to the stake. There is not a pin's point of difference in principle between these historic monsters and the German monk of twenty years ago, and the Whitechapel murderer of the present day. They differ only in the scale of their operations and in the fact, perfectly irrelevant from the ethical point of view, that one set of miscreants had a large number of backers, and were therefore able to go to work openly, while the other set had to practice secrecy for want of that backing. From the point of view of the moralist we say the difference is nothing; but to the politician it is everything. MARAT'S 100,000 victims possessed among them a goodly amount of property, and the guillotine would divide, it was hoped, that property among the *sans-culottes* patriots. Thus, the "Friend of the People" had a numerous following, and could scream out his insane and sanguinary ideas in perfect safety till CHARLOTTE CORDAY, at the cost of her own life, cut them short. There is nobody nowadays to say a word for TORQUEMADA, nor for his obscure imitator in Whitechapel, but only fancy what could be said for either of them if motives were to be taken into account; and what could be said for them if they commanded votes enough to return a batch of members to Parliament. Should we not hear a statesman declaring that the true responsibility for the Whitechapel murders lay at the door, not of the actual murderer, but of his laws and Constitution that tolerated the iniquities against which he protested in vain. The present fierce hunt after him would be described as a Star-Chamber iniquity, and the most brutal form of Coercion. If he were put on his trial, a demand would be made for a fair trial by his peers, and the most violent outcry would be raised if other murderers, or persons known to sympathise with murder, were excluded from the jury. The Home Secretary would be described as worse than King BOMBA and Sir CHARLES WARREN as the minion of barbarous and ferocious despotism. Would it not be said that the Whitechapel hero was defending the virtuous homes of the English people? But not a word of these apologies will be heard for him. There are no votes to be got by it. He cannot muster up votes, for he is not able to point to ten million sterling of yearly rents to be divided among his followers and associates. If caught, the voiceless wretch will be sent to his doom, and not one political meteorologist will wring out a tear over his grave, or bid the English people "Remember Whitechapel."

CHAPTER FIVE ENDNOTES

1   A woman's arm was fished out of the River Thames at Pimlico on September 11th. This arm was later found to be part of a body discovered in Whitehall, the story of which will be told in a later chapter.

2   *The Star*, not the same newspaper as published under that name today, was another radical London evening newspaper, and, like the *Pall Mall Gazette,* was sympathetic to the Home Rule cause.

3   Hubert George de Burgh-Canning, second Marquess and fifteenth Earl of Clanricarde, a notorious absentee landlord whose eviction of 186 tenants from his estate in Woodford, Co. Galway, during 1885, had been the prime motivation for the formation of the Plan of Campaign. Even the most ardent Unionist press could not find a good word to say about this particular individual.

4   Michael Davitt, co-founder with Charles Stewart Parnell, of the Land League, the precursor to the National League. Davitt would become effectively Parnell's co-defendant in the Special Commission, and acted as his intelligence chief, travelling to Paris in summer 1888 in order to assemble evidence to use in their defence. His notes from that trip, entitled "Notes of an Amateur Detective", are available to view at Trinity College, Dublin. Davitt later fell out with Parnell, feeling him to be too moderate.

5   *Irish Times*, May 10th. Dillon's release will be discussed in detail in Chapter Nine.

CHAPTER SIX

The Waiting Game

B Y SATURDAY, SEPTEMBER 15TH, the whole of the city of London was on tenterhooks. After two murders on consecutive weekends, it was almost expected that another atrocity would be discovered in the East End district at any moment. The same expectation affected both public and police, and extra patrols were ordered into the district for the weekend nights, supplemented by the plain-clothes detectives and the "amateurs". The scene was described on the Monday morning, September 17th, by the London Correspondent of the *Dublin Evening Mail*:

On Saturday night I leisurely strolled through the squalid thoroughfares immediately adjacent to the scenes of the recent crimes, and I was really astounded at the attitude assumed by the residents. They seem determined to take all the work out of the hands of the police. The number of "vigilance committees" that have been formed is remarkable. The duties mapped out for them will be no sinecure. They will consist in patrolling the streets, noting the various beats, watching how the constables work them, seeing that the police pay due attention to suspicious characters, calls for help, &c; and in case of neglect, reporting to headquarters, so that a formal communication may be made to the police authorities on the subject. This applies to the private constables, but a similar watch in a somewhat modified degree will also be kept on the superior officers, who will be liable to be reported at the direction of the Vigilance Committee.

The "Vigilants" say they "mean business," and evidently they do. They are all providing themselves with whistles and truncheons, or other weapons, and it will be their duty to patrol the beats of the police between times, so that at no time of the night shall a beat be unprotected. In case of suspicion, a row, robbery, &c, they will detain the culprits until the arrival of the police and in case of resistance they will sound their whistles for assistance. For further protection a reserve force of four members will be stationed at different points, but all within earshot of each other, who, on hearing the signal, will at once proceed to the spot, and assist their fellow members. These rules, it has been declared at large and enthusiastic meetings, will be rigidly attended to and enforced.

The Whitechapel Vigilance Committee had been formed after a suggestion in the *Star* newspaper by a meeting held at The Crown public house in the Mile End Road on September 10th. Under the chairmanship of a local builder named George Lusk, they organised street patrols at night to supplement the regular beat policemen, campaigned the Home Office to offer a reward and a free pardon for any accomplice turning states evidence, and set up a subscription scheme to offer a reward of their own. That their efforts were resisted at first by the regular police is evident from this interview obtained by the London Correspondent of *The Irish Times* and printed on September 17th:

> The mooted Vigilance Committee is at present engrossing the minds of residents in the East End of London, but it is a scheme fraught with danger and difficulties. Amateur detectives and amateur constables hardly meet with the support of the general public in cases of this serious magnitude, and the opinion of a police officer with a long experience of street work in the East End of London is worth giving. With regard to the proposed Vigilance Committee's prospects he remarks, "It won't last a month. They'll get little help – at least no more help than anyone else – from our chaps: and if they get interfering with respectable people our men will 'run them in' as a caution for future behaviour. With regard to the roughs, well all I can say is 'they will have a high old time of it' and to the benefit of our men. They can, to use their own words, 'smell a fly copper' – i.e. plain clothes man; and when they get hold of an 'amateur' or two, God help the amateurs! Kicking a regular policeman is a pleasure at any time not lightly to be spoken of, but the chances of 'booting' the head or ribs of an amateur 'slop' will afford a new and indescribable pleasure, and one to be indulged in on every possible occasion. These 'vigilants' will be looked upon as 'copper's noses' or 'copper's narks' – i.e. police informers – and to use the roughs own words, 'a copper' is bad enough, but his 'nark!' – well, kill him, and that is about what he will get, or something very near it. They have forgotten one thing in their outfit, and that is an 'ambulance' – that will be wanted oftener than truncheons. At least I think so."

The campaign for a reward was one of the most contentious issues in the case. The question had been aired in the newspapers almost from the beginning of the murders, and Home Office records show that the matter was brought up with them on August 31st, immediately after the Polly Nichols murder, in a letter from local traders Messrs Walter and Son, of Church Street, Spitalfields. Mr B. Harris, the secretary of the Whitechapel Vigilance Committee, first wrote to the Home Secretary on their behalf urging the granting of a reward on September 16th. The response, issued by E. Leigh Pemberton, was the same in both cases, stating that "the practice of offering rewards for the discovery of criminals has for some time been discontinued."[1]

Notwithstanding, Samuel Montagu, the Member of Parliament for Whitechapel, wrote to Sir Charles Warren, via Inspector West of H Division, on September 10th authorising the publicising of a reward of £100 at his own personal expense. The Chief Commissioner sought advice from the Home Office with the same response, this time pointing out that the policy of not offering rewards had been instituted by former Home Secretary Sir William Harcourt as a result of the opinion that such offers did more harm than good. However, by the time Sir Charles replied to Mr Montagu on September 15th his offer had already been made public, and he responded, "it is too late to withdraw my offer and in case information is received, leading to conviction of the murderer or murderers, I must pay the £100 to the person entitled to receive it."[2] It should be stated that £100 was a considerable sum of money in an age when the average wage for a working man was just a few pounds a week.

The *Belfast News-Letter* commented on the situation regarding rewards on September 21st:

> The Home Secretary's latest action shows he is wanting in tact, if not in discretion. His letter, declining to offer a reward in connection with the East End tragedies, has given great offence in Whitechapel, where leading residents have decided to offer a preliminary reward of £50. The Home Office decided some time since to discontinue the practice of offering rewards for the detection of undiscovered criminals, and this fact Mr. Matthews referred to in his latest communication. He, however, did not content himself by recounting the previous decisions, but directed his secretary to write – "The Secretary of State is satisfied that there is nothing in the circumstances of the present case to justify a departure from the rule." Thus a controversial element was needlessly introduced in Mr Matthews' refusal to comply with a pretty general request. The answer he has received from the East End of London is the starting of a fund so that a large and tempting reward may be offered. Nothing may come of it, still, considering the anomalous character of the atrocities there is no knowing how their author or authors may be made amendable to the law. Every possible means that may suggest themselves as like-

ly to throw light upon the horrible crimes ought to be adopted in the interest of the whole community. The legal mind of the Home Secretary, however, predisposes him to see things through the dim spectacles of precedent.

The *Ballymena Advertiser*, on September 29th, meanwhile, agreed with the Home Secretary's position, stating the following reason:

> The expectation in such cases of a Government reward being offered is apt to cause information likely to lead to detection to be held back till the murderer has secured time to effect his escape. It has a demoralising effect, also to induce in people a belief that they are entitled to pecuniary reward for furthering the ends of justice.

This item is of course naïve in the extreme. The practice of offering money to loosen the tongues of informants has been followed since time immemorial and continues to this day. Whether or not the reward be legal, every law enforcement officer in the world is aware that the quickest way to get a reluctant witness to open up is to make it to their benefit to do so. This practice was never more prevalent than in Ireland at the time of the Land Wars, where a few pounds in the right pocket could provide far more comprehensive results than a month of ordinary enquiries. *The Nation*, one of the radical Republican newspapers, commented on September 29th:

> Is informer-hiring to be a thing of the past? The Home Secretary, following the English practice, has refused to offer a reward for the discovery of the Whitechapel murderer. The *Spectator* supports, with long and weighty argument, the decision of Mr. Mathews. It says, among other wise things, "one of the first effects of a reward is to make a number of people speak out who might more profitably have been paid to keep silent. Where a man has been charged on a genuine suspicion, a prospective reward may lead witnesses to exaggerate their evidence against him, and even to supply missing links in the chain of proof. Wherever a miscarriage of justice has been caused in this way by the police, it has almost invariably been due to an exaggerated desire to make a case, and prevent the guilty slipping through their hands, rather than to any set purpose to convict the innocent. The danger is greater, both with them and with other witnesses, when a reward is to follow on conviction, and instances in which it has been felt are not unknown." This is all excellent theory; but will it be adopted in practice by the Dublin Castle felon-setter? Or will the half-notes and whiskey, that are inevitable agents in the making

up of a case for the Irish courts, be still continued? We shall probably be witnesses of the same process as heretofore in Ireland, and if Irish juries apply the principles of the *Spectator* to the police evidence, they will, in all likelihood, be denounced as perjurors by that impartial organ of Disunionist opinion.

On September 27th, six days after the article in the same newspaper printed above, the *Belfast News-Letter* commented on rewards again, but in something of a different tone:

> When the East End horrors, following in close succession upon each other, excited the coolest citizen in our midst, the first cry was, "What are the police doing?" For weeks past Sir Charles Warren, the Home Secretary, and the metropolitan police force have been held up to public ridicule as incompetent all round. There was a general demand for a scapegoat, but the Home Office made no sign in that direction. Mr. Matthews, with that tenacity of purpose which never deserts him, whether he be in the right or not, declined to offer a reward, tempting or otherwise. His predecessor and the combined wisdom of Scotland Yard agreed in holding that "rewards" offered in cases of great crime were worthless, in that they never brought guilty persons to justice. The Home Secretary had in consequence of his decision to run the gauntlet of an indignation meeting or two in the city, and for the present the storm of unpopularity, if not indignation, which for a couple of weeks had been raging about Scotland Yard and the Home Office, has subsided all at once, almost as suddenly as it rose. It is not that the people believe that the Whitechapel malefactor has gone on a sanguinary excursion into the provinces; it is simply a fresh illustration of the fact that the public mind cannot fix attention for longer than the usual nine or ten days in a certain direction, even when it is very angry with somebody. After all the writing in the Press on the ghastly subject, the second thought of the public seems to be that everybody is to blame for the atrocities, because they are the outcome of "crime," the offspring of human neglect.

The history of the case shows that there is a certain truth in this comment regarding the attention span of the public, but during the month of September interest was generally kept up by a steady stream of new revelations in the case.

On September 12th it was revealed that a young girl had found bloodstains in the yard of No. 25 Hanbury Street, two doors away from the murder scene. This discovery of the day before, a full three days after the murder, which was said to consist of stains not only on the fence but of a trail of blood leading to the back door and a large smudge on the wall where the killer was said to have beaten his coat, would indicate an extreme lack of observational skills on the part of the residents of that house who must have walked past them on their way back and forwards to the outhouse for those several days. In fact investigation proved the stains to be not blood at all, but urine.

Stories of strange incidents in the streets abounded. There was a tale of a man who accosted the caretaker of the Tower walkway asking if the murderers had been caught yet, and, being answered in the negative, produced a large knife and with a cry of, "this'll see to 'em," took off on his heels. Another involved a man named Charles Ludwig, who had attempted to stab a youth named Alexander Finsburg at a coffee stall in Commercial Street in an argument over the price of a cup of coffee. This incident, the like of which would most likely have been a fairly regular occurrence in Whitechapel, was given significance when it was found that the man had had a run-in with the police previously that night. The *Irish Times* of September 19th reported:

> Constable John Johnson, 886, stated that early that morning he was on duty in the Minories, when he heard loud screams of "Murder" proceeding from a court. The court led to some railway arches, and was well known as a dangerous locality. On going into the court he found the prisoner with a woman. The former appeared to be under the influence of drink. He (witness) asked what he was doing there when he replied, "Nothing." The woman, who appeared to be in a very agitated state, said "Oh, policeman, do take me out of this." The woman was so frightened that she could give no further explanation. The witness got her and the accused out of the court and sent the latter off. He walked with the woman to the end of his beat, when she said, "Dear me, he frightened me very much when he pulled a big knife out." The witness said, "Why didn't you tell me that at the time?" and she said, "I was much too frightened."

Although in this case there could be said to be some justification for connecting Ludwig as a possible suspect in the murders, such was usually not the case, and it seemed for a while that every crime which occurred anywhere in London was immediately connected to the Whitechapel case. The *Belfast News-Letter* commented on this on September 20th:

> One bad effect of the East End tragedies is the prevalent tendency to exaggerate every crime of violence as it becomes known. What was merely a violent assault on a woman of a certain class in Piccadilly early this morning not far from Devonshire House, was described in the

evening papers as another horrible outrage. The public, however, so long as the recent atrocities go unpunished, will continue for a considerable time apprehensive of further crimes being committed in their midst.

In fact no crime even needed to be committed, as the papers were full of stories of men given into custody as the murderer for scaring women simply by behaving in a strange manner or looking at them in what they considered to be a threatening way. The London Correspondent of *The Irish Times* gave his opinion on September 26th:

> Now again to-day Dr. Forbes Winslow[3] keeps the ball rolling by a graphic description – second hand, by the way, from his sister-in-law and her daughter – of a man at Brighton who, according to the testimony of the ladies, procured a large bowie knife, and proceeded to sharpen it in their presence. The affrighted ladies immediately took refuge in their own house, the man beat a retreat, and so the story ends. The facts, we think, hardly warrant their appearance in print. Most women's nerves are affected by reading the ghastly details of the recent brutalities, and the mere fact of a man sharpening a knife on the public highway ought not to brand him a suspicious person. If all these strange coincidences, witnessed in most cases by women with highly strung nerves, continue to be chronicled, the result may prove anything but pleasant for the community at large.

By the morning of Monday, September 24th it was believed that another weekend had passed without incident, although again the district, both public and police, had been in a state of high vigilance with the expectation of further horrors. Whitechapel was an area where, in general, life happened on the streets, but many of the newspapers noted that since the murders had begun this was tending to be less and less the case. The *Dublin Evening Mail* on that Monday commented:

> One striking effect of the recent Whitechapel tragedies has been to materially reduce the number of disorderly women in the neighbourhood. Before the murders, certain of the East End thoroughfares swarmed after dark with women of the most degraded type, and the scenes witnessed after the publichouses closed were disgraceful in the extreme. To a large extent, this state of things has been altered since the commission of the recent crimes. The streets are quieter, and in every respect more orderly. A large proportion even of the most abandoned of females have been so terrified by the atrocious nature of the murders, that they have expressed

the intention never again to lead the old form of life. Others not quite so scared still stick to their former haunts; but most of them are armed with formidable weapons, and manifest far greater discrimination in selecting companions, than formerly. All things considered, it may once more be truly said, that out of evil ariseth good.

By the following day, however, news was beginning to leak out that the week-end may not have been as uneventful as had hoped. Rather, the killer had simply moved his base of operations, not merely to another part of the city, but to completely the other end of the country. The *Cork Examiner* on September 26th reported:

> Gateshead has been the scene of a Whitechapel murder. The victim is a young woman named Jane Beatmoor, 26 years of age. She was in delicate health, and on Saturday went to the Gateshead Dispensary for medicine. After returning home she went out again to purchase some sweets to take with her medicine. She called at several farms while she was out, and at half-past seven at night left the house of an acquaintance named Mrs Newell, evidently with the intention of returning home. She had not arrived at 11 o'clock, and her mother and step-father went to look for her without success, and concluded that she must have spent the night with some neighbour. Early on Monday morning a miner named John Fish, going to work, found the body of the deceased at the bottom of the railway embankment horribly mutilated. The county police were communicated with, and Superintendent Harrison and Sergeant Hutchinson, of Birtley, were soon on the spot. The affair has caused quite a panic in the district, the resemblance to the Whitechapel tragedies encouraging the idea that the maniac who has been at work in London has travelled down to the north of England to pursue his fiendish vocation. The unfortunate woman is stabbed in three places; once in the bowels and twice in the face. The wound in the stomach is very deep, the knife having knocked a piece off the vertebral column. The body was found only a few hundred yards from the Girls' Home, by the side of the colliery railway. There were no marks of a struggle where she was found, and no trace of footsteps. The police are completely baffled, as the murderer has left not the slightest clue. On Monday thousands of persons visited the spot.

Before the end of that Monday Dr George Bagster Phillips, the doctor who had attended the scene and performed the post mortem on Annie Chapman, was travelling to Gateshead in the company of Inspector Thomas Roots of the CID to investigate whether the case was connected. Both came quickly to the conclusion that it was not, but the fact that they had been despatched to the area shows how seriously the suggestion was taken by the police authorities. In fact it was quickly suspected that the girl had been murdered by a former boyfriend, William Waddell, who had vanished from the area immediately after the murder. For a while there was a suggestion that he had committed suicide by jumping into one of the many disused pit shafts in the area, but slowly reports began to reach the authorities of sightings of the man near the Scottish borders, and in early October he was arrested in Yetholm, Roxburghshire, and confessed to the crime. He was executed by hanging at Durham Gaol on December 19th.

On September 26th, the *Cork Examiner* took the case as the initial basis for an editorial on the harmful effects of some of the reporting of the recent atrocities:

> The murder and mutilation of a woman near Gateshead, in the North of England, under circumstances shockingly similar to the recent Whitechapel murders, have given rise to the opinion that the wretch who perpetrated these latter outrages has also committed the terrible crime in the North. Another suggestion, however, which is largely accepted, is that it is "a crime of imitation" committed by some debased person who had read and studied the whole of the details of the ghastly Whitechapel tragedies. Some very competent persons, indeed, advanced the same theory in reference to the NICHOLS and CHAPMAN murders – that they were the work of persons of a low order of intellect, corrupted, and absolutely driven on to crime by reading the details of the previous murder. If such a theory were in any degree borne out by the facts in the future, it would certainly lead to the inquiry whether something could not be done to check the actions of the Press in reference to such matters. The arguments in favour of the fullest publicity of the details of such crimes are of course very great. It very frequently leads to the detection of criminals who have utterly baffled the agents of the law; and this is of course a fact of immense weight. There is besides the consideration that any cloaking or suppression of facts or evidence would only tend to the circulation of statements and rumours probably far more sensational and more deleterious to public morals than the bare truth. But it must be confessed that those matters seem to have but a secondary influence on the action of a considerable number of newspapers, and that a great deal of revolting matter is published which might in the interests of decency be suppressed. The medical and surgical evidence given in the inquiries into those recent Whitechapel murders, for instance, can hardly be considered, except to one or two general facts, likely to lead to the detection of the murderers. Yet in the latest inquest, the Coroner, notwithstanding the protest of the doctor under

examination, insisted on having the whole of the coarse and obscene details stated fully in open court, and they were published over the length and breadth of the Three Kingdoms by certain newspapers. Such a proceeding as this is undoubtedly calculated to do a vast amount of mischief, and any legislation that would go towards minimising the evil or preventing it altogether would meet the approval of all decent people. Subsequent to a certain notorious trial a couple of years ago, there was much clamour raised on this subject, and a document signed by numbers of the most distinguished personages in the country was forwarded to every important newspaper in England, Ireland, and Scotland, representing the ill effects likely to follow from the publication of offensive and indecent details. That well-intentioned circular does not seem to have had much effect; and there really is little worth in appealing to people who chose to publish garbage. And on the other hand, it is not clear that interference by Legislature would have a beneficial result. Enterprising journals would find additional zest in publishing such matters when their publication was absolutely illegal. Experience of the ways of Transatlantic journalism in such or similar matters is not very reassuring. The Legislature of New York, with a fine regard for a sensitive public, has decided that hanging shall be abolished in the State, and that in future its murderers will be killed by electricity. Further, it has decreed with the very commendable view of suppressing sensational and hurtful reports, that it shall be unlawful to publish anything whatever concerning the execution beyond the mere fact of its occurrence. And a leading New York journal has announced that on the occasion of the first execution by electricity in the State it will publish the fullest available details on the subject. And there is no reason to doubt the complete fulfilment of its promise. Many English journals would follow a similar course if the occasion arose, and it might turn out that the attempted cure would only aggravate the original complaint. The Press of this country, it is well known, has, with hardly an exception, displayed great prudence and good, decent, taste in dealing with such matters; but, undoubtedly, the respectable public has a very decided grievance against the English Press as a body. It is, however, much easier to make a complaint than to suggest a remedy at all adequate to the necessities of the case.

That very same day, however, the coroner who had presided over the inquests of both victims, was stating a very different opinion regarding the outcome of his insistence on full disclosure of the medical details. The *Dublin Evening Mail* London Correspondent had already intimated as much in his column two days earlier:

The statement that an important clue has been obtained in connection with the perpetration of the Whitechapel murders created intense excitement in the East end of London on Saturday night, and was also much commented on in higher social circles. The announcement made was to the effect that Mr Baxter had received a communication from a person of good standing in the medical world which afforded an important clue to the murderer's probable motive. This statement impressed the coroner so much that he personally attended at Scotland Yard in order to confer with the heads of the detective department.

In the following day's column he commented once again on the issue:

I hear that a fresh consignment of Scotland Yard detectives have been deputed to track the Whitechapel murderer, but that at present no satisfactory clue has been obtained. The facts put before the police authorities by the Coroner of the district – to which I referred yesterday – have been duly chronicled and discussed, but whether the heads of the Detective Department attach any importance to them, it is impossible to say, for the police remain dumb to all interrogations however seductively put.

In the meantime a large number of indignant letters have passed through the post on the subject of the coroner's course of procedure in compelling the medical man to make the disclosures he did in regard to the missing portion of the woman Chapman's body. His action, it is urged, though probably prompted by the best of intentions, may have had the effect of putting the assassin all the more on his guard against the vigilance of the police. It will generally be admitted, I think, that the coroner did not exercise the discretion that he might have done in the matter, and that all through the inquest proceedings there has been too much "talkee-talkee."

The information in question was finally revealed by the coroner in his summing up at the inquest on Annie Chapman, and was widely reported in all of the following day's newspapers. This verbatim account is taken from *Freeman's Journal*:

The organ has been taken away by one who knew where to find it, what difficulties he would have to contend against, and how he should use his knife so as to abstract the organ without injury to it. No unskilled person could have known where to find it or have recognised it when it was found. For instance, no mere slaughterer of animals could have carried out these operations; it must have been someone accustomed to the *post-*

mortem room. The desire to posses the missing organ seems overwhelming. If the object were robbery, the injuries to the viscera were meaningless, for death had previously resulted from loss of blood at the neck. There was difficulty in believing that the purpose of the murderer was the possession of the uterus. It is unnatural and abhorrent to our feelings to conclude that a life should be taken for so slight an object; but when rightly considered the reasons for most murders are altogether out of proportion to the guilt. It has been suggested that the criminal is a lunatic with morbid feelings. This may or may not be the case, but the object of the murderer appears palpably shown by facts, and it is not necessary to assume lunacy, for it is clear that there is a market for the missing organ. To show you this I must mention a fact which at the same time proves the assistance which publicity and the newspaper Press afford in the detection of crime. Within a few hours of the issue of the morning papers containing the medical evidence given at the last sitting of the court I received a communication from an officer of one of our great schools that they had information which might or might not have bearing upon our inquiry. I attended at the first opportunity, and was informed by the sub-curator of the Pathological Museum that some months ago an American had called on him and asked him to procure a number of specimens of the organ that was missing in the deceased. He stated his willingness to give £20 for each specimen, and said his object was to issue an actual specimen with each copy of a publication on which he was then engaged. He was told that his request was impossible to be complied with, but he still urged his request. He wished them preserved, not in spirits of wine, the usual medium, but in glycerine, in order to preserve them in a flaccid condition, and he wished them sent to America direct. It is known that this request was repeated to another institution of a similar character. Now is it not possible that knowledge of this demand incited some abandoned wretch to possess himself of specimens?

The revelation caused a sensation in the newspapers, and no doubt within the district itself. The crimes, which had previously been considered motiveless, were suddenly possibly the work of an iniquitous profit-seeker. The very idea that life could be regarded as so cheap in any portion of the world, let alone in the heart of the capital city of the British Empire, horrified all who considered it. The editorial in the *Limerick Reporter* of September 28th gave their opinion of the matter:

A new and lurid light is shed on the atrocious Whitechapel murders which shocked and thrilled the world not only of London, but of Europe,

America, &c, a few weeks ago in the most densely populated districts of the great Metropolis. "Leather Apron," who may have been the creation of the brain of an imaginative purveyor of the daily Press, was described to the letter. He was shown in all directions as a Jew of Jews, as if it were impossible that there are not within the circle of London more hideous and revolting criminals than the most abandoned of the Hebrew race. "Leather Apron" was at long length discovered and brought before the courts of preliminary inquiry; but it was evident that the individual who was found to don that article of apparel was other than a bloody monster. It was shown, indeed, that he was not only innocent of the fierce assassination of ANNIE CHAPMAN and her companion, but, though living in the midst of Shoreditch, he had heard nothing whatever of the mysterious crimes which set nearly the whole population in terror. Others were pounced upon and arrested, but with the same result. The police were then attacked in every direction for not achieving what now turns up to have been an impossibility. Science is progressing with giant speed, and the discoveries of one day are outrun and eclipsed by those of the day after; but though the coroner's jury have discovered all that baffled the police and caused a shudder through the heart of humanity, we find that these appalling horrors have been perpetrated in the instance of science, that the wounds were made by no common, untutored hand, that the picture presented by the racked and ensanguined bodies of the victims was the result of no ordinary artist. It would appear that the deeds of BURKE and HARE in Scotland over sixty years ago, and by BISHOP afterwards, are now in the last quarter of the nineteenth century revived, not by men in the rank of BURKE and HARE and BISHOP, who, having imbued their guilty hands in the blood of their victims, or smothered them until they could not breathe more, brought the bodies to Surgeons' Hall, where they were purchased for a certain sum; but the Whitechapel deeds by persons of knowledge and education well acquainted with the dissecting table, who do not care to pay others for work they can indulge in without apparent fear of detection. After carefully reviewing the evidence concerning the injuries on CHAPMAN, the coroner pronounces his deliberate judgement that a "mere slaughterer of animals could not have done these operations. It must have been some one accustomed to the *post mortem* room." It is a singular fact, too, we are told, "that the murderer had some special knowledge of the method of suddenly arresting consciousness in his victim, that not one single cry was heard to escape CHAPMAN by the sixteen persons who were sleeping within a few yards of her. The same thing is to be noted of the woman NICHOLLS." In one case and the other some process more scientific than the coarse and ready one of placing a handkerchief around the mouth of the victims, as BURKE and HARE made their "subjects" ready for the pounds, shillings and pence of the dissecting hall, was adopted by the cruel executioner of those two unfortunate women who very likely used some or other of those narcotics which are at hand in every apothecary's shop, and which it is not difficult now-a-days to manufacture. To this it has come in the big heart of the greatest city in the world, and amid a degree of civilization which was not surpassed by ancient Rome. What the issue is likely to be it is impossible to foretell. The authorities now will withdraw the army of detectives from Scotland Yard; but we are assured on the other hand, "that the whole civilized world is concerned in bringing the murderer to justice, and it cannot afford to be beaten in the attempt. The police will be expected to follow up with the keenest vigilance the valuable clue elicited through the Coroner's inquest, since the lines of their investigation are plainly chalked out by information which they themselves failed to collect, it will be a signal disgrace if they do not succeed." So says the *Times,* and the words of that journal are echoed far and wide.

Meanwhile in the *Dublin Evening Mail,* where the information had first been intimated, the London Correspondent on September 27th described the effect the information was having on both police and public, together with a brief boast at his exclusive:

The statement made by the Coroner to-day in summing up the evidence given in connection with the murder of Annie Chapman in Whitechapel has created quite a sensation in London. The statements made are so extraordinary that in spite of their delicate nature they are being commented on in all circles of society. The requests said to have been made by an American at certain of the metropolitan hospitals is of a kind unparalleled, so far, at least, as the knowledge of the general public is concerned.

Whether these particular requests have anything to do with the Whitechapel atrocities, is, of course, pure conjecture. The coroner evidently thinks they have, and he may be right. Other people, however, argue that the information conveyed to the hospital authorities could scarcely have become disseminated throughout the East End; and supposing this to be true, there is no possibility of any class of individuals or even a single individual entertaining the horrible notion suggested by the coroner.

The police, so far as I can gather, are more than ever inclined to the notion that the murderer may be a crazy medical student of morbid tastes. Supposing this hypothesis to be the correct one, it is easy to understand how his knowledge of a certain desire was obtained. Yet all inquiries made at the different institutions in the Metropolis have so far failed to furnish a clue that might in any way lead to elucidate the mystery.

To-day's evidence has revived the Whitechapel tragedy in a manner truly remarkable. To-night the East End is again filled with gloom and horror, and women venture forth from their homes in fear and trembling The Durham tragedy is declared by the London experts – if so they may be termed – to have no possible connection with the crimes committed in Whitechapel. I may add that the disclosures made by the coroner to-day bear out the statement that I was able to furnish you with on Monday last, and which, I believe, appeared in no other paper.

With regard to the American previously referred to, I hear that the police are making elaborate inquiries with a view to discover his whereabouts. Up to the hour of writing, however, no information whatever of a satisfactory nature has been obtained.

The *Kerry Evening Post* of October 3rd noted a fact regarding the revelation which appeared to have escaped the notice of all the other newspapers who had commented upon it:

> Mr. Wynne Baxter, the ablest perhaps of the coroners, evidently "wound himself up" for his charge to the jury in the Whitechapel murder case. His address was carefully prepared, and of very high merit from a literary point of view. In one respect he laid himself open to criticism. His "startling revelation," as the papers called it, was based upon personal information. It was doubly improper, according to technical rules, for it was evidence given by himself not under oath, and it was "hearsay" evidence. The persons from whom he derived his information ought in strictness to have been called before the jury.

The *Belfast Morning News* of October 2nd, meanwhile, exploded Baxter's theory entirely with the following short article:

> The *Pall Mall Gazette* says the only practical thing to be done is to keep a sharp look out, and dismiss once for all the Coroner's theory as to the motives of the murder. The Coroner seems to have been made the innocent victim of a somewhat stupid hoax. The *Gazette* sets forth the prices paid by the Pathological Museum for subjects which includes £3 as the

price of a complete corpse. The organ removed by Chapman's murderer could be had for asking at any *post-mortem* room twelve hours after death.

It should be said that the whole theory seems bizarre from a modern standpoint. It is undoubtedly the case that £20 would have been an excessive price for anyone to pay for any portion of the body, and especially one wonders what price the scientific publication of this mysterious American would have had to retail for in order to cover such high expenses. The *Freeman's Journal* of October 1st carried a letter from a Dublin man relating to the subject:

TO THE EDITOR OF THE FREEMAN
80 Lower Gardiner-street
SIR – The observations of the coroner at the inquest on the body of Annie Chapman, one of the Whitechapel victims, are so peculiar, and I think, so likely to mislead public opinion and create a prejudice against men engaged in the study of tissue changes in unhealthy organs, that I ask your permission to place some facts and deductions from them that will, I think, invalidate the coroner's conclusions.

The fact that the womb was removed from the body of each victim is taken to imply that the organ was the sole object of the murder, and that the crime was committed to obtain it. Every anatomist must know that a large percentage of the dead bodies brought to the anatomy rooms are those of the unfortunate class, and that human wombs are plentiful in the rooms; and, from considerable experience as an anatomy lecturer, I can say I never know of any demand for them as pathological specimens that was not easily met.

To excise the womb in its entirety does require some anatomical knowledge, but not more than any anatomy porter possesses. As for the crime, we find it carried out with a reckless devilry worthy of a monomaniac, but not to be found associated with the cool villainy that characterises the criminal for pecuniary gain.

As any person familiar with the working of the Anatomy Act knows perfectly well that no specimen of any portion of the human body could be offered for sale without the seller being subjected to searching examination into all the details of the case, and he would run the risk, if his statements were not satisfactory, of being handed over to the police.

The Whitechapel murder silenced his victim by a method of choking, or pressing the lower jaw up against the upper one, the method of a bully but not such as a skilful anatomist would adopt, who of necessity should know that a fine cut with a small knife would deprive the person of all power of sound.

The victim's throats were cut, allowing the large vessels of the neck to pour out blood to the risk of besmearing the criminal – a danger which he need not have incurred had he known, as an anatomist would have, how to destroy life; but is not the fact important in pointing out the ruthless determination and fierce rage of the deep-dyed ruffian who has thus dared to carry on his crimes with an apparent contempt for all laws human and divine! – I am, sir, yours,
GEORGE FOX

The coroner's statement revived excitement in the case briefly, but as the month of September drifted to a close the spark had gone out of the public interest with no fresh horrors to salivate over. With two murder-free weekends behind them, most of the public were likely not anticipating that the final weekend of the month would bring any great change in the case. They would be mistaken, and the final day of the month would be the day that all hell broke loose.

CHAPTER SIX ENDNOTES
1   Ref. HO 144/220/A49301, f16, National Archives.
2   Ref. HO 144/220/A49301B, ff172–3, National Archives.
3   Dr Lyttleton Stewart Forbes Winslow was considered one of the foremost experts in mental disorders of the period. He involved himself in the case on a number of occasions, offering his services to Scotland Yard and providing his opinions in the press. He later insisted that he had identified the Ripper as one G. Wentworth Bell Smith, and claimed that the murders ceased because he had scared the killer off. The details can be found in his autobiography, *Recollections of Forty Years*.

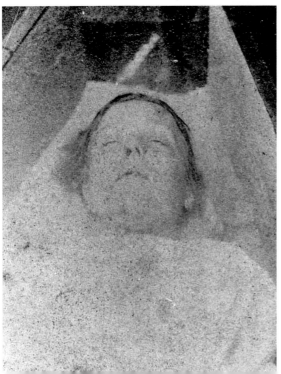

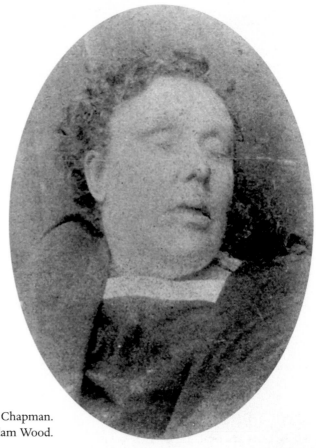

Above:
The back yard of No 29,
Hanbury Street, where the
body of Annie Chapman
was discovered.
Courtesy of the Evans
Skinner Crime Archive.

Mortuary photograph of Annie Chapman.
Courtesy of Adam Wood.

Berner Street. The entrance beneath the large cart wheel is Dutfield's Yard, where the body of Elizabeth Stride was discovered. Courtesy of the Evans Skinner Crime Archive.

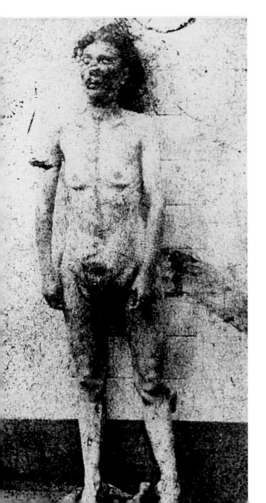

Mortuary photographs of Catherine Eddowes (left) and Liz Stride (below).
Courtesy of Adam Wood.

Jack the Ripper letter postmarked November 2, 1888, (MEPO 3/142, ff. 496-8), Metropolitan Police/National Archive, photo courtesy of The Evans Skinner Crime Archive.

Crime Scene photograph of Mary Jane Kelly. Courtesy of Adam Wood.

Left:
Sir Charles Warren, Cheif Commissioner of the Metropolitan Police until his resignation in November 1888

Below left:
James Monro, resigned as head of the CID just prior to the Ripper investigation, but remained in charge of Irish affairs at the Home Office. Appointed Chief Commissioner of the Metropolitan Police to succeed Sir Charles Warren.

Below right:
Henry Matthews, the Home Secretary was heavily criticised for failing to offer a reward for the capture of the Ripper.
All pictures courtesy of Adam Wood.

Dr. Robert Anderson, a native of Dublin and head
of the CID during the Ripper investigation.
Courtesy of Adam Wood.

Calling card of Major Henri Le Caron found
among some of Dr Robert Anderson's papers.
Courtesy of The Evans Skinner Crime Archive

Envelope from a letter recieved by Dr Robert Anderson
from the Home Office during his time working in the
anti-Fenian office at Dublin Castle.
Courtesy of The Evans Skinner
Crime Archive

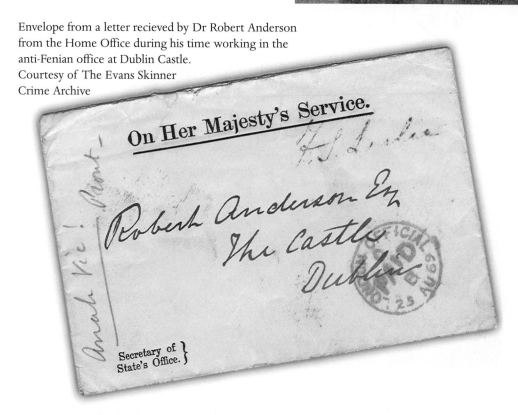

THE FENIAN-PEST.

Left:
Cartoon from *Punch*, March 3rd, 1866,
regarding Fenian activity.
Courtesy of Adam Wood.

Below:
Drawing of the Bloody Sunday riot in
Trafalgar Square, November 13th, 1887.
Courtesy of Adam Wood.

Drawing of the murder of Lord Frederick Cavendish and Thomas Henry Burke in Phoenix Park, May 6th, 1882. Courtesy of Adam Wood.

Left:
Charles Stewart Parnell, Nationalist MP - "The Uncrowned King of Ireland". Courtesy of Adam Wood.

Below:
The main protagonists in the Parnell Commission.
Courtesy of The Evans Skinner Crime Archive

MR. JUSTICE DAY

MR. JUSTICE A.L. SMITH.

THE Rt. HON. SIR JAMES HANNEN.

MR. WALTER PROPRIETOR OF "THE TIMES"

MR. PARNELL, M.P.

ɪᴇ just impartiality of our English
dges, who honour the land that gave
ᴇm birth, was notably exemplified
t Monday. All shades of politicians had
ᴜꜱon to be satisfied with the fair rulings of
ꞓ James Hannen—speaking for Mr. Justice
ꞓy, Mr. Justice A. L. Smith, and himself—in
dicially opening the Commission appointed by Parliament
ᵢ inquire into the terrible charges and allegations brought
ainst Mr. Parnell, M.P., and his colleagues by the *Times*
ᴡspaper. What those rulings were will be found set
ᴡn on another page of this Number. Suffice it here to
d that the opening proceedings in Sir James Hannen's
ᴜrt must have satisfied everyone that this grave State trial
ll, on its resumption in October, be conducted in a perfectly just and open

Arthur Balfour, Chief Secretary for Ireland and nephew to the Prime Minister, Lord Salisbury. Courtesy of The Evans Skinner Crime Archive

Lord Salisbury, Conservative Prime Minister during the time of the Ripper murders. Courtesy of Adam Wood.

William Gladstone, former Liberal Prime Minister and a supporter of the Home Rule cause. Courtesy of Adam Wood.

William O'Brien, Nationalist MP for North East Cork and editor of the *United Ireland*. One of the organisers of the Plan of Campaign, his refusal to wear prison clothes during incarceration in Tullamore Jail led to the Bloody Sunday riot in Trafalgar Square. Courtesy of Adam Wood.

John Dillon, Nationalist MP for East Mayo and one of the organisers of the Plan of Campaign, he was present at the Michelstown massacre and was in Dundalk Prison under the Coercion Act at the time the Ripper murders began. Courtesy of Adam Wood.

Engraving of General Frank Millen from *The Sphere* magazine, used as a mugshot after he was accused of masterminding the Jubilee plot to assassinate Queen Victoria. Courtesy of The Evans Skinner Crime Archive

Michael Davitt, co-founder with Charles Stewart Parnell of the Land League, who acted as a private detective to assemble evidence for the Nationalists at the Parnell Commission. Courtesy of Adam Wood.

Frank Hugh O'Donnell, Nationalist MP - his spurious lawsuit against the *Times* led to the Parnell Commission. Courtesy of Adam Wood.

CHAPTER SEVEN

The Night of the Double Event

As SATURDAY, SEPTEMBER 29TH slipped into Sunday the 30th, few of the people of London's East End, as they huddled out of the rain in the pubs and clubs, the gin palaces and music halls, could have anticipated that before dawn broke the bodies of two more unfortunates would be lying on the mortuary slab, and that London's two police forces would have joined forces in the largest manhunt in the history of that city up to that point.

The events of that night began on the return home of Louis Diemschütz, the steward of the International Workingmen's Educational Club, a Jewish Socialist club situated at 40 Berner Street, just south of Commercial Road. The building occupied one side of a narrow yard known as Dutfield's Yard because it had formerly housed the business premises of a cart builder named Arthur Dutfield. At the rear of the building were the printing offices of a Yiddish journal, *Der Arbeter Fraint (The Worker's Friend)*, and opposite were a few small artisan's cottages. The *Irish Times* of October 1st contained Diemschütz's own account of events:

> I went yesterday to Weston Hill market, a place I usually visit on Saturdays, and I got back about one o'clock this morning. I drove home in my own trap. My pony is rather shy, and as I turned into the yard it struck me that he bore too much to the left hand side against the wall. I bent my head to see what it was that he was shying at, and I noticed that the ground was not level. I saw a little heap which I thought might perhaps be some mud swept together. I touched the heap with the handle of my whip, and then I found that it was not mud. I jumped off the trap and struck a match, when I saw that it was the body of a woman. I did not wait to see whether she was drunk or dead, but went indoors, and asked whether my wife was there. I did this because I knew my wife had rather

a weak constitution, and anything of that kind shocks her. I saw my wife was sitting downstairs, and I at once informed the members that something had happened in the yard. I did not tell them whether the woman was murdered or drunk because I did not then know. A member named Isaacs went down into the yard with me, and we struck a match. We saw blood right from the gate up the yard. Then we both went for the police, but unfortunately it was several minutes before we could find a constable. At last another member of the club named Eagle, who ran out after us and went in a different direction, found one in Commercial road.

In the following day's edition he added:

I passed several streets without seeing a constable, and I returned without one. The men with me shouted as loud as they could for the police, but we could not make one hear. When I returned to the club a man whom we met in Grove street and told about the murder lifted up the woman's head, and then for the first time I saw the wound in the throat.

At this point the yard was filled with members of the club who had come out to see what was happening. However, being a Jewish club, and the Jewish faith having strict rules regarding the touching of a dead body, nobody until this point had approached the body any closer than absolutely necessary.

After Diemschütz had informed the members in the front room of the club of his discovery, a member by the name of Gilleman[1] went to the upstairs room where a group of twenty or thirty members were engaged in singing songs in the Russian language, as was the custom of the club on Saturday nights after their evening debate was finished. Gilleman informed them of the discovery, and Morris Eagle was the first to respond. He tells his story in the October 2nd *Irish Times*:

I went out, and striking a match found a woman lying with her feet six feet from the gate, near the club wall, with her head to the yard. Others came with me, but seemed frightened to go near. Assuming it was a drunken and not a dead woman before lighting the match I said "get up." There being no reply I then lighted the match and was fearfully upset by seeing a woman lying in a lot of blood. I immediately ran away for a policeman and found two. When we reached the yard again there were some members and some strangers who had been attracted by the cries for the police. One of the constables turned his lantern upon the deceased, while I went for the inspector.

The entrance to Dutfield's Yard was about nine feet wide, with a pair of tall gates in one of which was a small wicket gate for access when they were closed. On the night in question, however, they were wide open, and in the hour preceding the discovery at least two club members, one of them Eagle, had passed through the yard without seeing anything suspicious. There was, however, no lamp in the yard, nor in Berner Street in such a position as to cast light into it, and for eighteen feet back from the street blind wall bordered the entrance throwing it into almost total darkness, so that both men stated that the body might have been there without their seeing it. The only light in the yard came from the windows of the cottages and the club. At the time of the discovery only the upstairs lights in the club were on, casting their light on the cottages opposite, and this was said to have only accentuated the darkness of the entrance.

The man who returned to the yard with Diemschütz was Edward Spooner. His inquest testimony was reported in *The Irish Times* on October 3rd:

> He was outside the Beehive public house, at the corner of Christian street and Fairclough street with a young woman. They had been standing there about 25 minutes when two Jews came along shouting out "Murder, Police." They ran as far as Grove street, and turned back. The witness stopped them, and asked what was the matter. They replied, "There is a woman murdered," and the witness then returned with them into the yard in Berner street. He saw the deceased lying just inside the gate, and about 15 people in the yard, all standing around the body. A match was struck, but he saw the woman before that was done. He lifted the deceased's chin with his hand. He saw the wound in her throat, from which blood was flowing on to her breast. The deceased had a piece of paper in her hand folded up. So many people came "flocking" in that witness could not see whether anyone went out of the yard. He noticed that deceased's legs were drawn up. When Police Constable Lamb arrived he, with the aid of witness, fastened the gates.

The same newspaper reported PC Henry Lamb's testimony:

> On Sunday morning about 1 o'clock, he was in Commercial road when two men came to him, running and shouting. They said, as he moved towards them, "Come on; there's been another murder." He asked "Where?" And as they got to the corner of Berner street they pointed up the street and said, "There." He ran to the spot indicated, and, entering the gateway of 40 Berner street, he saw something dark on the right hand

side, close to the gate. He turned his light on and found it was a woman with her throat cut, and apparently dead. He sent to the office for another constable. There were a number of people in the yard when he arrived – perhaps twenty or thirty, but there was no one touching the body or near it. As he turned the light on the crowd gathered round the body. He begged them to stand back lest they might get some blood on themselves and thus get into trouble. He felt the face and arm of the deceased and found they were slightly warm. He then blew his whistle. The deceased was lying on her left side, her left arm lying by her side. Her right arm was lying across her breast. The body was about five or six inches away from the wall. The clothes were not disturbed; the boots were scarcely visible. There as no appearance of a struggle. Some of the blood on the ground was congealed, and some was still liquid. Dr. Blackwell, who was the first medical man to arrive, examined the body. He (the witness) went into the club and examined all the persons present to see if their clothes had any marks of blood, but he found no traces of blood. He also examined the cottages in the yard, and found all the inhabitants to be in bed. As he was in the yard for some time by himself it would have been quite possible for anyone to have escaped from among the people standing around while he examined the body. Still he thought it more likely that the culprit escaped before he arrived. The place was not on his beat, and therefore he had not passed the yard before during the night.

Dr William Blackwell, whose surgery was at 100 Commercial Road, was called at ten past one by a constable and hurried to the spot, arriving by his own timing six minutes later:

> My assistant, Mr. Johnston, returned with the constable and I followed. I found the woman lying on her left side, completely across the yard. Her feet were against the wall on the right side of the yard passage, her head resting in the cartwheel rut. Her feet were about three yards from the gateway. The neck and chest were quite warm, also the legs and the face, the latter slightly so. There were no rings or marks of them on her hands. The appearance of the face was quite placid. Round her neck was a check silk scarf, the bow of which was turned to the left side, and pulled very tight. There was a long incision in the neck commenced on the left side 2 inches below the angle of the jaw, and almost in a line with it.

There was no mutilation on the body of the victim, and Dr Blackwell estimated that she had been dead no more than twenty minutes when he arrived, suggesting that her murder had taken place within minutes of Louis Diemschütz discovering the body. The theory therefore was adopted that the killer had been disturbed before he could set about the second part of his usual task, and might easily have been hiding behind the gate as the discovery was made, making his getaway when Diemschütz entered the club.

Having done so he made his way west, possibly along Commercial Road, more likely through the maze of narrow streets, alleys and courts between Berner Street and Leman Street. At some point he found himself in the district of Aldgate where, with his blood lust unsatisfied, he quickly located a second potential victim.

The Metropolitan Police force was the main body of police for the London Metropolitan area, but the boundaries of the City of London itself had, and still has, its own separate force. Where the Metropolitan force came under the control of the Home Office, the City Police was the responsibility of the City Corporation, whose chief magistrate was the Lord Mayor. Although essentially adjacent to, and a part of, the East End districts, the two main streets of Aldgate and the Minories were City police territory.

Constable Edward Watkins had been a member of that force for seventeen years, was said to be a most reliable man, and had a good knowledge of his beat, which ran along Duke Street, through Creechurch Lane and back along Leadenhall Street, from there to Mitre Street and then through St James's Place back to Duke Street. The beat took him around fourteen minutes to traverse, and as part of it his duty was to check a dingy court named Mitre Square which led off Mitre Street. He had passed around this square at 1.30, shining his lamp into all the doorways and down the two alleys which led away from the northeast and north-west corners.

At 1.44, as he made his next pass, a shock awaited him. As he entered the square through the wide main entrance and turned to his right, his lantern shone across what can only be described as a bloody mess lying on the pavement. From the light of the lantern, which hung from his belt, it was quickly evident that what he was looking at was the body of a woman, horribly mangled. Without touching the body he crossed the square quickly to the warehouse of Kearley and Tonge's, tea merchants, where he knew a watchman who was a former Metropolitan police constable was on duty.

George James Morris heard the banging on the door and opened it quickly to the wild-eyed policeman. The *Bray Herald* of October 6th printed his own account of what happened next:

> When he replied, the constable said, "For God's sake, man, come out and assist me; another woman has been ripped open!" He said, "All right; keep yourself cool while I light a lamp. Having done so, he accompanied the constable to the south-west corner of the square, where he saw a

woman lying stretched upon the pavement, with her throat cut and horribly mutilated. He then left the constable and proceeded into Aldgate, where he blew his whistle, and other police-officers soon made their appearance. The whole shape of the woman was marked out in blood upon the pavement. In addition to her throat being cut, there were two slashes across the face, one of the cuts almost completely severing the nose. The woman's face was so mutilated that he could not describe what she was like. She wore a dark skirt and a black bonnet, and her appearance was exceedingly shabby. The strangest part of the whole thing was that he did not hear the slightest sound. As a rule he could hear the footsteps of the policeman as he passed on his beat every quarter of an hour, so that it appeared impossible that the woman could have uttered any sound without his detecting it. It was only on the night that he remarked to some policemen that he wished the "butcher" would come round Mitre-square and he would give him a doing; yet the "butcher" had come and he was perfectly ignorant of it.

As at Berner Street, the square was soon swarming with officials. The first to arrive were Constables Holland and Harvey, both having beats nearby. Detective Constable Daniel Halse, a City detective who had been in Aldgate with two colleagues arrived next and took charge of the scene until a more senior officer arrived, quickly organising a search of the local area and ordering anyone seen to be stopped and questioned. Next came Dr George Sequeira, whose surgery was nearby at 34 Jewry Street, who made a brief examination of the body and gave the declaration of death.

Inspector Edward Collard was the officer in charge of Bishopsgate Police Station, the closest station to the scene of the crime. He received news of the discovery at five to two, and, after despatching a constable to fetch the official surgeon and telegraphing the news to headquarters, he hurried to the scene to take over charge of the investigation from DC Halse, who then left the square to carry out investigations himself, travelling through Middlesex Street to Wentworth Street, returning by way of Goulston Street which he passed through at approximately twenty minutes past two.

Dr Gordon Brown, the City Police surgeon, arrived at around twenty past two and made a close examination of the body. As none of the Irish newspapers carried full details of Dr Brown's inquest testimony, the following account of his examination of the body is taken from the inquest report at the Corporation of London Record Office:

The body was on its back – the head turned to the left shoulder – the arms by the side of the body as if they had fallen there, both palms upwards – the fingers slightly bent, a thimble was lying off the finger on the right side. The clothes drawn up above the abdomen, the thighs were naked, left leg extended in a line with the body, the abdomen was exposed, right leg bent at the thigh and knee. The bonnet was at the back of the head – great disfigurement of face, the throat cut across, below the cut was a neckerchief. The upper part of the dress was pulled open a little way. The abdomen was all exposed. The intestines were drawn out to a large extent and placed over the right shoulder – they were smeared with some feculent matter. A piece of about 2 feet was quite detached from the body and placed between the body and the left arm, apparently by design. The lobe and auricle of the right ear was cut obliquely through. There was a quantity of clotted blood on the pavement on the left side of the neck, round the shoulder and upper part of the arm, and fluid blood coloured serum which had flowed under the neck to the right shoulder – the pavement sloping in that direction. Body was quite warm – no death stiffening had taken place. She must have been dead most likely within the half hour.

By now, there were two major murder investigations occurring within a mile of each other, being carried out by two different police forces. However, the night's discoveries were not yet complete, and the final discovery involved both forces and resulted in one of the most controversial actions of the entire investigation.

Constable Alfred Long was a policeman from A Division (Westminster) who had been drafted into Whitechapel just that night to supplement the H Division company, and was patrolling a beat which took him along Goulston Street. He had passed through that street at around twenty past two, approximately the same time that DC Halse had also been in the area, and neither man had seen anything unusual at that time. At five to three, however, as Long passed along the street, his eye was drawn to something lying in a passage leading to the stairway of a model dwelling house. Closer inspection showed it to be a portion of a woman's apron, smeared with blood and faecal matter. According to Long some of the blood was still wet. Dr Brown later matched the cut section to the portion of the apron still on the body of the Mitre Square victim and found it to be an exact match. On the brickwork of the doorway above where the apron lay, someone had chalked some words on the wall:

The Juwes are The men that Will not be Blamed for nothing.[2]

Long's first action was to search the staircases of all the local buildings for traces of blood or recent footprints, then summoning a fixed-point constable to take over the beat and take special notice of anyone entering or leaving the buildings, he proceeded to Leman Street station with the apron to report what he had found. Superintendent Arnold, the commanding officer of H Division, was summoned to the spot and found there DC Halse of the City police who had returned to the street on hearing of the discovery. Halse suggested that the writing should be photographed, and sent for a photographer. The area, however, was part of Arnold's H Division jurisdiction, and being the man responsible for keeping order in the area, he expressed his concern that if the writing remained in place once daylight had arrived it could cause a riot against the Jewish population of the area. Arnold therefore summoned an officer to bring a bucket and sponge to the doorway in readiness to wipe away the writing.

Arnold communicated his decision to Scotland Yard, where Sir Charles Warren, realising the importance of the decision, decided that he should be the one to make the call. He therefore hurried to the spot, and, in his own words:

> A discussion took place whether the writing could be left covered up or otherwise or whether any portion of it could be left for an hour until it could be photographed, but after taking into consideration the excited state of the population in London generally at the time the strong feeling which had been excited against the Jews, and the fact that in a short time there would be a large concourse of the people in the streets and having before me the Report that if it was left there the house was likely to be wrecked (in which from my own observation I entirely concurred) I considered it desirable to obliterate the writing at once.[3]

Before proceeding it is important for me to mention that news of this discovery was not made public for a week, and that the writing was removed on Warren's direct orders did not become apparent for nearly two weeks. Therefore any reports reproduced here written prior to October 8th were written in ignorance of the above information.

An unsuspecting London awoke on the morning of Sunday, September 30th, put on their Sunday best and went about their business as they usually did on their day of rest. There was no anticipation of the news that awaited them. The *Drogheda Argus* of October 6th described the scene:

> The day was bright and balmy, in fitting close to the best month of the year. In most of the churches service was about half over, when through the open windows came the startling cries of the newsvendors – "Shocking double murder in the East End this morning!" In several of the churches in the city where the news was known early, outspoken references were made to the nature of the crimes and the state of life revealed

by them. There was at first a natural disposition to discredit the report of the murders, and when the congregation left St Paul's, a probably unprecedented scene was witnessed. A score of newsvendors began a roaring trade under the shadow of the cathedral, and the space about the steps, and Queen Anne's renovated statue was crowded with extremely well dressed people reading the reports in the special editions of the various Sunday papers. Until late in the evening the suburbs were patrolled by men selling the newspapers and, of course, yelling out the nature of the news with an emphasis on a certain adjective which seemed to come from long practice. Thus, probably, within a few hours after the crime there was not a street in the vicinity which was not resounding with the cry of murder. The criminal himself must have heard it many times.

The London Correspondent of the *Dublin Evening Mail* submitted his column that evening for publication in the following day's newspaper:

> Never, I think, have Londoners been in such a state of frantic excitement as they have been during the whole of to-day. They awoke early this morning to find themselves confronted by the intelligence of two fresh diabolical outrages perpetrated in East End, and inasmuch as the circumstances resembled in every respect the fiendish tragedies of a few weeks ago, it is easy to understand that only a few hours had elapsed before there was a genuine panic throughout the whole of the Whitechapel district and the surrounding neighbourhood.

He later continued:

> It can be imagined that two such horrible tragedies following so closely on the former ones have produced a greater panic than has existed at any time before. Aldgate, Commercial-road, and all the adjacent streets have been like a fair the whole of to-day, and special late editions of the Sunday papers have had a sale unprecedented in their history.

The *Irish Times* London Correspondent similarly gave over his column that morning to a description of the condition of the streets in the area of the two murders:

> Fresh horrors were in store for us this morning, and ere the church bells had commenced to ring the sensational news of two fresh murders in the East End had travelled to the far distant suburbs of the metropolis. The panic produced by the dreadful news was widespread and general, and later on when the ghastly details became known the effect on the

Londoner can only be likened to the sensation which prevailed in Dublin on the Sunday following the murders of Lord Frederick Cavendish and Mr Burke.

The similarity of the newly-discovered outrages with those perpetrated on the unfortunate Annie Chapman and Mary Ann Nicholls plainly indicate the fiendish handiwork of the same murderer. If anything the crimes of this morning display a far greater desperation, combined with ghoulish cunning, than either of the former murders. The neighbourhood of Aldgate and Commercial road is an exceptionally busy one on a Saturday night, and, as a rule, it is some three hours after midnight before the streets are actually quiet. Moreover, I hear that a number of extra detectives were told off on Saturday afternoon for special duty in the neighbourhood of Whitechapel in connection with the previous outrage. Yet in the face of these facts, these two additional horrors are sprung upon an already panic-stricken people.

An hour after the discovery of the murders the whole of the East End population were in the streets, thrilled once more with the strange and sickly horror, which rapidly acquired dimensions little short of genuine panic. As the day advanced thousands flocked from all quarters of London to gaze upon the scenes of the latest atrocities and pick up such scanty information as could be obtained in the locality. Detectives of course are scouring every street and alley, but up to midnight no arrests are reported, and apparently the police have no definite clue. The feeling among the inhabitants is one of intense excitement and it would be extremely difficult for the police should they make an arrest to get the prisoner safely to the station, owing to the present excited condition of the labouring classes, who form a large proportion of the residents in the locality. Great caution is therefore being taken by the authorities not to state any suspicion of a clue.

Meanwhile the *Belfast Morning News* of October 2nd commented that it was not only the public which was flocking into the district:

The news that two more awful murders had been committed at the East End has created a profound sensation. All the London dailies telegraphed early yesterday for the members of their reporting staffs, and some despatched their entire corps to the scenes of the murders. The news spread like wildfire, and enormous crowds visited the theatres of these terrible crimes from all parts of the metropolis, and gathered the shocking details, which will no doubt reach you fully from another source, with horror-stricken faces. The daring with which the foul deeds have been perpetrated, and the blood-thirsty ghoulish nature of the fiend who is spreading such terror throughout the East End has filled the populace with feelings of the wildest excitement. Indeed, so terribly have the passions of certain sections amongst the lower classes been aroused that I firmly believe had the police arrested anyone during the height of the excitement he would have inevitably been torn from his captors, unless they were a very strong force, and lynched upon the spot. These additional tragedies will be a heavy blow to the *regime* of Sir Chas Warren and the police force in general, for it must be admitted that they have completely broken down over these murders. It is at the same time but fair to admit that in this case they have had extraordinary difficulties to contend with, for they have, out of a population as large as Liverpool, Manchester, and Dublin combined, to seek out and run to earth a monster who can only be compared to the inhuman creation of Mrs Shelly in the weird, sensational romance, "Frankenstein." The murders were the all-absorbing topic of conversation at the Press Club here last evening, and the general opinion seemed to be that the police were as much at fault as ever, and that unless the murderer was absolutely caught in the act of slaughtering some poor creature he would never be discovered.

Indeed, with the news flashing around the world within hours of the discovery of the bodies, it was not merely in the East End where the panic was setting in. This article is from the *Drogheda Argus* of October 6th:

The theories that have been put forward in Dublin concerning the Whitechapel murders are scarcely less numerous or varied than those which have been put afloat in London. Some are of the opinion that the perpetrator of the foul deeds is a religious enthusiast; others that he is a medical scientist; and more again believe he is a madman who delights in the sensation created by his desperate work. It may seem strange, but many of the women of Dublin are very frightened over the murders and there are not a few females in the city who remain indoors at night oftener than was their custom. Should it so happen that a street murder was perpetrated in the city public feeling is at present so high strung over the subject that it would cause little less than a panic.

The leader columns of virtually every Irish daily that day had its own comment on the murders, with attitudes ranging from disgust at the atrocity, condemnation of the police and not a few points scored for Republican Ireland. The *Belfast News-Letter* began their October 1st editorial thus:

It is not too much to say that the entire history of crime affords no parallel to the series of tragedies that have recently taken place in Whitechapel – the latest two of which were perpetrated early yesterday morning. Indeed, it is no exaggeration to say that those writers whose morbid imagination caused them to deal with the perpetration of murder, with a view of illustrating certain psychological phenomena which may or may not have existed, never conceived of so extraordinary a series of crimes as have just been recorded in the East End of London during the past few weeks. If Edgar Allen Poe had ventured to add to the ghastly list of imaginary murders which he describes in a way that is more fascinating than revolting in the course of his weird stories, such a series as have just convulsed the country, the author of "Murders in the Rue Morgue" would have been pronounced surpassing the license which even so eccentric a genius could claim.

The Irish Times meanwhile, in condemnation of the London police, brought out the suggestion that those in Dublin Castle might have more success in the case than their counterparts in Scotland Yard:

Two more unspeakably horrible murders of women in Whitechapel on Saturday night suddenly raised the excitement in London yesterday to fury pitch. The appalling record of that dismal district now numbers up the atrocious slaughter and mutilation of six hapless creatures, the victims of a gang of miscreants, or of one maniac as some suppose; and there is no guarantee that further similar deeds may not yet be done. The motive, if it be at all comprehended, or not too shocking to admit; the treachery to the decoyed and defenceless, the coolness and suddenness of the attack; the obstinate defiance of police acumen; the fearful mastery of the means of committing unmatched savagery, accumulate to cause an indignation for which there certainly is no parallel, and the disappointing of which by non-detection would be an anguish which society could not content itself to endure. The consternation which kept the whole population up and awake throughout the night of these last outrages and has prevailed universally every hour of the interval since, gives place to a hot impatience that will not brook failure from the authorities in tracking the miscreants, and satisfying all humanity against them. Every eye in every land in both hemispheres is fixed upon the officers who have the duty of making this mystery plain, and their inability to get to the bottom of it, even for so long a disgrace, will be ruinous should it now further continue. Not to go into the particulars it is clear enough that the murders of Berner street and Mitre square are by the same pair of hands as perpetrated those that occurred before. The first stroke which took away the life was the same in every case, and by a bold and skilful miscreant. The common origin and commission of the crimes can be readily inferred, and it would thus seem that every fresh iniquity should have put the doer in greater peril and made the task easier of those that are pursuing him. The police appear to have been from the first utterly at fault. We think that they are justly blamed for want of knowledge, want of ingenuity, and want of grasp and resource. They appear to have got no clue, or if they found any they have let it slip. They have made no progress whatever, and the repetition of the acts in the same manner and in the same locality is a marked boast over the collapse of detective sagacity. Two more murders committed in a single night, in the near neighbourhood to a constable's residence, in another place where from a clubroom many men were going in and out, demonstrate that the measures taken by the police executive have been totally inadequate, ill-directed, and superficial. What is in such circumstances to be done? If the people entrusted with the task are incompetent, instantly others should have the work transferred to them. It is no time for questioning or considering the feelings of any body or person who might object to an arrangement promising better success, and we do think that it would be suitable to import into the business some of the talent which has been from time to time exhibited by Irish detectives. In conference with their English colleagues they might be able to see farther or plan more successfully. There is no reason to believe that people living in the locality are putting any difficulties in the way of the police. They are paralysed, indeed, with horror and fear, and can hardly venture to assume that worse will not still happen; but one and all are anxious to see the assassin secured and proof obtained at once of his crime, so that an end may be put to suspense and alarm. Sir CHARLES WARREN, by his action yesterday, appears at last to understand that it will be fatal to men in his position if those murders are not traced. The means which are at his command are ample. Whatever special steps he may think it necessary to adopt the public will complicity sanction. Why was not every doubtful house in Whitechapel searched long since for knives or other instruments by which the deeds were committed? In all honest places the constables would have every facility given to them, and where they were resisted suspicion would usefully arise. If also experience proves that little is to be done by offering of a reward, there are expenditures which would in such a crisis be justified, and could hardly fail to open the mouths of some whose information, though perhaps in itself slight, would start investigation.

The *Freeman's Journal* were equally ferocious in their condemnation of the police efforts, but the point made was an altogether different one:

> The awful fact that the people of East London have now to face is that within six weeks six atrocious murders have been committed in their midst in a circumscribed locality, under circumstances almost identical, and that still the murderer is at large. This fact places a terrible responsibility on the police. A whole army of detectives have been searching the East End for the past three weeks for the perpetrator of these murders. He must have been all the time under their eyes. His latest horror shows that he was in the heart of Whitechapel when they supposed he was elsewhere. The fiend seems to delight in defying them. He murdered two women on Saturday night almost within sight of a policeman. Still he walks abroad with impunity, and perhaps some other wretched creature will fall victim to his knife before his career is brought to an end. The circumstances of Saturday night's murders show clearly that the wretch must have left the scene with the signs of blood upon him. Nobody, however, has come forward to say that he saw him, and up to the time I write the police do not appear to have any substantial clue whatever either as to his identity or to his whereabouts. If six such murders as these occurred in any part of Ireland the district would have been promptly saddled with a crushing blood tax. It would have been proved to demonstration by Tory speakers that the reason of the non-discovery of the murderer was the sympathy of the people with crime. Nobody however makes that suggestion in the case of Whitechapel. Yet the grounds are more plausible than they have been in any of the cases in which Irish taxpayers have been almost ruined by compensation for crimes in which they had no more share than Adam.

The same point was apparent in the *Belfast Morning News*:

> It is sickening to think of these atrocious deeds. The most morbid appetite for sensationalism cannot but be disgusted by these hellish deeds. Who is the guilty wretch? We are as far, nay further than ever from an answer to this most important question. The police have now surely had time enough to unravel the mystery, if it ever is to be unravelled. The Press has been filled with guesses and hints and solutions, probable and improbable. But let the murderer be who he may, or what he may, there are others to whom popular opinion – popular prejudice, perhaps – will point as guilty of negligence in this matter. People will begin to ask what is the use of a force of police and detectives if they can neither detect nor prevent such hellish outrages, if almost under their very noses some dar-

ing bloodthirsty ruffian can plan and carry out with diabolical completeness his horrid intentions. Life seems to be no more secure in London than in the backwoods of America, not near as secure as is that of the evicting landlord or his agent in the most disturbed part of Kerry or Clare. We need not point out how the Unionist Press would shriek if such a state of things prevailed in Ireland, and would denounce the lawlessness of the Irish and their sympathy with crime, because no clue to the criminals could be found. We should be sorry to imitate the Unionist tactics, and accuse the people of London of complicity with these frightful deeds; but it is impossible to hide away the horrible fact that London, or at least parts of it, are cesspools of immorality – that there in a week more crime is committed than takes place in Ireland in a year.

The comments in these two newspapers, however, can be considered comparatively moderate when placed alongside those printed in the *Limerick Reporter and Tipperary Vindicator* on the morning of October 2nd:

War no doubt is the most horrible of all human calamities, and those who have experience of its tremendous teachings can never forget how the iron entered into their souls. But how little attention after all is given to the war which has been carried on for centuries in Ireland against the entire population and which rages as intensely at this moment in Clare, Galway, and in other Irish counties, as at any former period. We look with dismay at the battering ram of modern times levelling the homesteads of the poor, tearing the vitals of the tenants, showing no symptom of mercy for childhood or old age, for quality, sex, or the attachment which burns in the heart for the sacredness of home. The whole world stands aghast at the Whitechapel murders, and men drop a tear over the revelations of the deceased Emperor who built up Germany through oceans of blood; but where is the sympathy for the farmer ruthlessly bundled out of his house and home, sent with wife and children adrift on a cold, callous world, a prey to an unheard of system of intense cruelty and wrong unknown in any other part of the world? The Whitechapel murderers have sought their victims in abandoned, helpless, most miserable and outcast units of the vast population of London. A few unfortunate women fall beneath the knife of the atrocious murderer who scorns police and rejoices in immunity, and threatens to repeat the deed of utter horror at the very first convenient opportunity. This only demonstrates beyond the power of contradiction or gainsay or explanation that "there is something rotten in the state of Denmark" – something utterly, miserably, irretrievably rotten. It shows that the State is out of joint, for what benefit is the most showy and costly police force in the civilized world in the prevention or detection of crime when these murders are done openly under the very shadow of their batons? This is all very dreadful; but what shall we say of the wholesale forced emigration of millions of our population? What of the millions who have fallen under the blight of hunger, in the jaws of famine? – in scenes more shocking than the battlefield ever presented, and which go on from day to day? "I was never in Ireland before a day or two ago," said an intelligent, well-informed English gentleman to us the other day; "Where are the people? Are there no people in Ireland? I have gone several miles and have scarcely met one person. Where are the people? Within a radius of a limited space around Manchester from where I come there are more people than in the whole of Ireland. Instead of four and a half millions there should be at least ten millions of people, not paupers and beggars in this fine fertile country." "England did it all, " was our reply, "Your English laws and English jealousies, your Coercion Acts and infamous injustices, the garrison you have planted here amongst us, have been the cause; and sooner or later you will reap the fruits of a policy unknown in any other portion of Christendom. For over seven hundred years you English have been on this sacred soil of Ireland, and though you have hunted, torn, banished and murdered our people, there is a spark of life remaining which will make itself felt though you send out your legions of crowbars and battering rams and the whole machinery of enforced expatriation and death in their most hideous features. Our people came to life amid the wilderness created by your ELIZABETH. They will revive under the grey stone walls and skilly and water of your BALFOUR." The Englishman expressed a hope that it would be so, and went on to Woodford to witness the crimes perpetrated there by Lord CLANRICARDE.

CHAPTER SEVEN ENDNOTES

1 Possibly Giddleman, the spelling varies in different reports.
2 There is some argument regarding the spelling of the word Juwes. Constable Long spelled it Juews, while others have insisted it was Jewes. Also there was disagreement over the wording, DC Halse claiming it was, "The Juwes are not the men who will be blamed for nothing." The spelling and wording used above, together with the capitalisation, is as taken down by Sir Charles Warren, Ref. HO 144/221/A49301C, f183, National Archives.
3 Ref. HO 144/221/A49301C, ff 173–81, National Archives.

CHAPTER EIGHT

Liz and Kate

THE SITUATION that the London police, whether Metropolitan or City, found themselves in on the morning of September 30th was one of two bodies and no names. The first order of the day then was to identify the victims, and yet this proved no easy task in either case.

In the Berner Street case the name Elizabeth Stride was forthcoming before the end of the day. The *Irish Times* of October 1st gives the following details:

> At 11 o'clock to-night a reporter visited Elizabeth Stride's late residence, No. 22 Flower and Dean street, Spitalfields, a common lodging-house inhabited by men and women of the poorest kind. The female occupants were afraid to enter into the streets after sunset, but they were listening with eagerness to information afforded them from time to time by male occupants arriving from the streets. Inquiries made amongst these wretched people elicit the fact that the deceased woman was commonly known as "Long Liz." She left Flower and Dean street between 6 and 7 o'clock on Saturday night. She then said she was not going to meet anyone in particular. Stride is believed to be a Swedish woman from Stockholm. According to her associates she was of calm temperament, rarely quarrelling with anyone. Her occupation was that of a charwoman. She had the misfortune to lose her husband in the Princess Alice disaster on the Thames some years ago. She had lost her teeth and suffered from a throat affection. It transpired that she was identified at the mortuary this morning by John Arundell and Charles Preston, who reside at 22 Flower and Dean street.

This all seemed fairly straightforward, and would have been had it not been for a woman by the name of Mary Malcolm. Mrs Malcolm arrived at the mortuary on the Sunday stating that she believed the deceased to be her sister, Elizabeth Watts. Although unable to identify her that day, the next day she insisted that the woman was indeed her sister, whom she recognised due to the mark of an adder bite she had received as a child. Mrs Malcolm appeared at the second day of the inquest, and although throughout her appearance the coroner kept impressing on her the necessity of her being sure about her identification, she was unshakeable in her belief that the deceased was her sister. The *Dublin Evening Mail* London Correspondent commented on October 3rd:

> The evidence given to-day at the adjourned inquest on the woman Stride one of the women found murdered in Whitechapel on Sunday, has added fuel to the flames of excitement which rage in the neighbourhood. A sister stated that the deceased woman, whose real name was Watts, was the wife of one of the wealthiest and best known wine merchants in Bath, but that the latter had separated from her through his wife's misconduct. On the morning of the murder, continued the witness, she had a dream, during which she heard a heavy fall, and immediately afterwards she felt three distinct kisses imprinted on her lips. "When," added the witness, "I saw an account of the murders in the papers, I was at once convinced that one of the women was my sister." As may be imagined this evidence created a profound impression in the Coroner's Court. It was afterwards much commented on in all circles of society.

It was obvious that only one of these stories could be correct, that the woman, if she was Mrs Malcolm's sister, plainly did not hail from Sweden. On the third day of the inquest a positive parade of witnesses appeared each prepared to state on oath that the woman they had seen in the mortuary, whilst fluent in English, spoke with a distinct accent and had told them she was from Sweden. The last of these witnesses was Michael Kidney, a dock labourer who claimed that he had co-habited with the deceased for three years, and who provided for her a lengthy history.

Liz, he explained, was indeed a Swedish woman who had come to England in the service of a family and had married a ship's carpenter named Thomas Stride. She and her husband had later kept a coffee house in Poplar. The pair had both been working on the pleasure boat the Princess Alice which had sunk in the Thames in 1878. Liz had told him that her husband and two of her nine children had drowned in the tragedy, the other children now being cared for by the Swedish Church. She herself had been kicked in the face and as a result had sustained damage to the roof of her mouth. The time spent with Kidney had not been without its problems. She had left him several times, and the previous Tuesday she had not returned home. Other witnesses confirmed that she had been at the lodging house only since the middle of the week. So once again it seemed straightforward that the original identification had been correct, and

Mrs Malcolm mistaken. The *Dublin Evening Mail* man continued his musing on the subject on October 4th:

> It seems almost a pity that the pretty little story told on Tuesday by the woman who imagined herself to be the sister of the woman Stride, and who narrated how she felt the ghostly lips of the deceased on her face at the very moment that the murder took place, should be ruthlessly upset by the matter of fact statements made at the adjourned inquiry to-day. The Spiritualists had already received the story with rapturous joy and were intent upon hashing it up in a variety of forms as proof positive of the reliability of their theories. Now all that is knocked on the head! The lady who felt the kisses may, like the damsel in the ballad, have had indigestion; but it is pretty certain that her sister was not, on the eventful night, the victim of a foul and atrocious crime. Of course there is great wailing and gnashing of teeth in the Spiritualistic ranks. It is a keen disappointment to them.

Unfortunately a spanner was again thrown into the works when Dr Phillips stated that his examination had shown absolutely no damage to the roof of the victims mouth. The final confirmation came from Sven Ollson, the clerk of the Swedish Church at Prince's Square, who had known Stride for seventeen years. He identified a bible left at her lodging-house, and produced the records of her marriage. He also provided more details of her antecedents, his parish records showing that she had been born Elizabeth Gustafsdotter, the daughter of a farmer at Torslanda, near Gothenburg, Sweden, on 27th November 1843, making her forty-four years old at the time of death.

The final nail in the coffin of Mrs Malcolm's story, meanwhile, was banged in on October 23rd when Elizabeth Stokes, formerly Mrs Watts of Bath, appeared at the final sitting of the inquest to inform the world that she was certainly not dead, nor living a loose life on the streets of Whitechapel, but living in Tottenham and respectably remarried.

As far as the identification of the Mitre Square victim was concerned, there was little enough for the City police to go on. They had found near the body an old mustard tin containing two pawn tickets, one for a man's flannel shirt pledged in the name of Emily Burrell, 52 White's Row, the other for a pair of boots in the name of Jane Kelly, 6 Dorset Street. Both turned out to be blank leads. Nobody by the name of Jane Kelly was known at the Dorset Street house, while 52 White's Row turned out not to exist at all. The only other method of identification was a tattoo on the victim's left forearm, the letters T.C. picked out in blue ink.

The name Kelly, however, turned up again shortly afterwards. By Tuesday the 2nd it had been found that the deceased had spent a few hours in custody at Bishopsgate Police Station on the night of her death. She was detained at half past eight on the Saturday evening by a policeman named Louis Robinson who had been alerted to her causing a disturbance in Aldgate by drunkenly imitating a fire engine. By the time he arrived she was passed out in a drunken haze on the pavement outside No. 29. On arrival at the station she was asked her name but replied "Nothing."

PC George Hutt took charge of the cells at Bishopsgate Station at ten that evening, and at five to one in the morning he found the prisoner awake and sober, or at least relatively so, and on instructions from Sergeant Byfield he discharged her. On taking her from the cell she had asked him the time and he replied, "Too late for you to get any more drink." Before being discharged she had given the name of Mary Anne Kelly, and the address 6 Fashion Street. This too turned out to be false.

On this occasion the newspapers had every right to argue that it was publicity which obtained results. The identification came when a man named John Kelly, living at 55 Flower and Dean Street, having seen the details in the morning papers, came to Bishopsgate Station informing the officers there that he believed the victim to be his common-law wife, whose name he gave as Kate Conway. The *Freeman's Journal* on October 4th supplied the details:

> The identification of the mutilated remains of the woman murdered in Mitre-square is now complete. She has lived seven years with a man named Kelly in Flower and Dean street, Spitalfields, who yesterday fully identified the body, partly by the linen, and partly by the marks on the flesh. He says she had a husband before she came to live with him, and his name was Tom Conway, a pensioner from the Royal Artillery. She had several children by Conway, and one of them was married to a gunmaker in Bermondsey, but, having had a falling out with her husband, they separated. The initials of her husband, "T.C." were pricked in her arm. Kelly and she had been tramping about Kent last week, and on Saturday morning, when they had their last meal together at the lodging-house in Flower and Dean street, she said she would go to her daughter in Bermondsey. Kelly said he cautioned her to be back early, and not to get into the hands of the Whitechapel murderer, but she assured him she was able to take care of herself. He had no suspicion she had fallen a victim until he read in the papers a description of the pawn tickets found on her, and the marks on her arm. He then told the police, and they showed him the body, which he identified.

In fact the woman's name was Catherine Eddowes, and although she often referred to Conway as her husband, they had never actually been married. She had been born in Wolverhampton in the West Midlands, but her family had moved to Bermondsey when she was two. She later moved back to Wolverhampton where she met Tom Conway and moved in with him in Birmingham. The couple had three children, and separated in 1880. A year later she had met Kelly, who was said to be an Irishman and was certainly a Catholic, and the pair had lived together at the Flower and Dean Street address ever since. It seems to have been a stable relationship, those who knew the pair spoke of them being very happy together and rarely quarrelling. Kate was forty-six years old at the time of her death.

The difficulty of the police in identifying the bodies seems surprising from today's viewpoint, but it must be remembered that the conditions prevalent in the East End at the time were not conducive to a quick identification. Most of the lodging house dwellers went under two or three names as it suited them, and ties of family were not strong. Mrs Malcolm may have been something of an aberration, she seems to have constructed an elaborate fantasy claiming that she met her sister once a week to give her money, which turned out to be a complete fabrication, and weaving elements of Liz Stride's life into that she provided for her sister, including that she was known as "Long Liz" and had run a coffee shop with a man in Poplar. However, if this confusion was deliberate, some of the problems were just tragic, as pointed out in this item from the *Dublin Evening Mail* London Correspondent on October 12th.

> Here is a curious instance of how little the poor of London know of each other, even when related by ties of blood! I happened to be in the Coroner's Court this afternoon, and when the victim's blood-stained apron was produced, a respectable young woman in mourning commenced to cry bitterly. A sister of the deceased, on asking me who that was weeping, was surprised to find she was her own dead sister's child, and that she had grown up to be a young married woman without her aunt ever having known of her existence.

Of course, learning the identity of the victims was one thing, but it didn't move the police any closer to their ultimate objective, that of learning the identity of the killer. Not that they were short of suggestions from both press and public. From the first the suggestions as to his possible identity came thick and fast. The *Belfast News-Letter* London Correspondent on October 1st provided this suggestion:

> The absence of all understandable motive is what really baffles the police and their advisers. It is now quite evident that the theory of the previous atrocities propounded by Mr. Coroner Baxter must be abandoned as

worthless and misleading. From the first it did not commend itself to the logical-minded portion of the community. The criminal must be a person who is in a position to elude all detection through being able immediately to divest himself of all evidence of guilt. He may be, as I have heard it suggested, a night watchman or warehouse-keeper – living by himself, like another Dr. Hyde, and issuing forth in the small hours of the morning on his murderous mission. There is not a household in the whole of the metropolis which would not, during the last month, have had its attention called to any suspicious circumstances attending the absence or appearance of any of its inmates. Redhanded criminals, seeking to conceal traces of their guilt, seldom go long undetected. The whole community, so to speak, is acting as its own police, for there can be no feeling of safety so long as wanton savagery remains undetected and unpunished.

The *Dublin Evening Mail* of the same day, very reasonably, had this to say:

The two tragedies of yesterday have deepened the local impression that the police are unable to cope with the cunning of the fiend for whom they are seeking, and a positive anger, which has spread to the leading columns of the London Press, is evinced at the failure of every effort to capture the murderer. There is, of course, good reason for this irritability. It is an unpleasant consciousness for the dwellers in and around that particular district of the metropolis that something worse than a wolf in sheep's clothing is prowling about, and that his disguise cannot be penetrated by anyone. But the man has several advantages to which proper weight is hardly given. In ordinary cases of secret murder the victim is difficult to get at without discovery, and the motive generally points out the murderer. In these dreadful cases, however, the murderer is unknown to his victim, and the motive cannot be of a personal nature. It must also be kept in view that the relations between the two actors in the tragedy, during the moments preceding its consummation, are such as to insure privacy, without suspicion on the part of the woman, and every other facility for her destruction, without struggle or alarm. One important matter should now be self-evident. The assassin cannot outwardly exhibit any sign of his murderous character. The unfortunate women who are his victims are on the alert, and, before trusting themselves to the mercies of any unknown person, must, in view of what has already occurred, satisfy their own minds that *this* cannot be the individual who has taken so many lives. The man who is wanted must be suave rather than forbidding in his manner, and respectable to all appearance.

The *Freeman's Journal* published its own musings on the subject on October 2nd:

He must have been drenched with blood, yet nobody noticed him, and he reached his lair in safety. The supreme daring, the marvellous coolness, celerity, and cunning that distinguish his horrible work are not less remarkable than the scientific skill with which he accomplished the brutality that perfects the crime. He is a mystery, a revelation, an enigma amongst monsters in human shape. In all the blood-curdling literature of murder there is no prototype of him. He cannot come from the ranks of ordinary murderers; there is nothing common to him and the unhappy wretch who, to gratify avarice, anger, or any other passion, takes away life. Nor yet is it clear that he kills for the savage delight of killing. Of course, theories as to his motive are numerous, and generally absurd. In default of a better explanation it is suggested that he must be a homicidal madman – a truism, if ever there was one. No sane man, as the term is generally understood, would be capable of such deeds. What seems clear is; first, that he knows the district intimately, and that he has some place of refuge in it; secondly, that he possesses some surgical knowledge and great dexterity in the use of the surgeon's knife; thirdly, that he mutilates possibly for wantonness, but possibly for a definite purpose of an entirely different character. He may be a mad scientist, and in that case it should not be difficult to discover him amongst the population of Whitechapel, where scientists – sane or mad – do not abound, and where such a man could not, were his cunning never so great, avoid betraying himself. He may be a maniac of another sort, or he may be – though not probably – a mere wild beast of exceptional ferocity, a kind of man–wolf. Whatever he is, one certain fact is, that the police are powerless against him, and that the ingenuity of the London detectives has been employed so far vainly in ill-directed attempts to establish his identity.

On October 2nd the *Belfast News-Letter* printed the opinion of Sir James Ridson Bennett, one of the pre-eminent physicians of the day:

He says he has come to the conclusion that the criminal is under a delusion which has reference to matters of a sexual character. "The two crimes which were perpetuated yesterday morning do not," he continues, "lead me to modify my opinion that the assassin is a lunatic. Even if it should transpire that in the case of the Mitre Square victim the uterus is missing I should not be disposed to favour what I may call the American theory in the slightest degree, and I must confess that it is with considerable surprise that I noticed in certain newspapers a disposition to readily accept the theory. It has been said – and it is a very natural observation – that if the murderer were a lunatic he could not commit these crimes and escape with impunity. That is a comment which any person not fully acquainted with the peculiarities of lunatic subjects might very well make. In my view the cunning which is evinced by the homicide is a convincing proof of his insanity. No sane man could have escaped in just the same fashion as this man seems to have done; he must almost necessarily have betrayed himself. It is a matter of common knowledge, however, among "mad doctors" that lunatics display a wonderful intelligence – if it may be called so – in their criminal operations, and I have little doubt that if the murderer were other than a madman he would ere this have been captured by the police. In many instances a madman's delusion is directed to only one subject, and he is mad upon that subject alone. I think the murderer of these women is a man suffering from an acute mania, and that being so his infirmity would be obvious to almost every person with whom he came into contact – that is to say, if he were in the presence of either of us we should probably say, "Oh, he's a madman." There are many instances in which the common test is for the doctor to enter into conversation with the subject, to touch upon a variety of topics and then, as if by accident, to mention the matter in regard to which the patient has a specific delusion. Then the person's madness is manifested, although upon every other point he converses rationally. But here the disease is acute, and I should say that those persons with whom he comes into daily contact cannot regard him as a sane person. Dr. Phillips has stated that the injuries inflicted upon these women had been apparently performed by a person possessing some anatomical knowledge. That is likely enough, but would not a butcher be quite capable of treating the body in this way?

It even appeared to be the case that the murderer himself was getting in on the act, for on September 27th the Central News Agency had received through the post a letter written in red ink purporting to have been written by the perpetrator of the murders. At first they considered the letter a stupid hoax, but after the double event they realised that it might just be the real McCoy, and the letter was published in various newspapers on October 1st, giving the murderer at last the name with which he would be remembered for posterity. The letter read:

> *25th Sept. 1888*
> *Dear Boss,*
> *I keep on hearing the police have caught me but they wont fix me just yet. I have laughed when they look so clever and talk about being on the right track. That joke about Leather Apron gave me real fits. I am down on whores and I shant quit*

ripping them till I do get buckled. Grand work that last job was. I gave the lady no time to squeal. How can they catch me now. I love my work and want to start again. You will soon hear of me with my funny little games. I saved some of the proper red stuff in a ginger beer bottle over the last job to write with but it went thick like glue and I cant use it. Red ink is fit enough I hope ha. ha. The next job I do I shall clip the ladys ears off and send to the police officers just for jolly wouldnt you. Keep this letter back till I do a bit more work, then give it out straight. My knife's so nice and sharp I want to get to work right away if I get a chance. Good luck.
Yours truly
Jack the Ripper
Don't mind me giving the trade name
Wasnt good enough to post this before I got all the red ink off my hands curse it
No luck yet. They say I'm a doctor now ha ha

The comment regarding the clipping off of the ears was the item which had given the Central News men pause for thought, considering part of Kate Eddowes ear had been severed, and the police agreed, especially when on the morning of October 1st a second communication arrived from the same hand, this time in the form of a postcard smeared with bloody fingerprints.

I was not codding dear old Boss when I gave you the tip, youll hear about saucy Jackys work tomorrow double event this time number one squealed a bit couldnt finish straight off. had not time to get ears for police thanks for keeping last letter back till I got to work again.
Jack the Ripper

Opinion has been divided for the last century over whether these communications were from the real killer or not. Whoever wrote them, he was educated enough to correctly spell some fairly difficult words, and his handwriting was in the neat and regular copperplate of a person accustomed to letter writing. Certain expressions such as "Boss" and "shant quit" also suggested an author either of American origin or of long acquaintance with the speech patterns of that country. The majority of commentators in the Irish press tended to regard them as fakes, and a perusal of the police files shows that they quickly came to the same conclusion. Nonetheless they reproduced both communications in facsimile and posted them up in police stations across the district. The *Belfast Morning News* of October 12th noted the following:

Curious nobody thought of it before. Mr George R Sims noted the phenomenon that "Jack the Ripper" must be an editor or a reporter from the fact that he addressed his horrid warnings only to Press agencies, and the most obscure of them too.[1]

The *Cork Examiner* referred to the letters in a somewhat amusing editorial of September 8th, in which they summed up, with increasing exasperation, some of the suggestions that had so far been published:

Endless arrests have, of course, been made; suggestions out of number are hourly proffered, and, as always appears, a host of half crazy, or wholly drunk, individuals are confessing themselves to be the guilty parties, or by talking wildly and threatening people after the supposed manner of the murderer, are doing their best to get themselves into temporary trouble. Naturally also the papers are filled with suggestions of the most contradictory character, which are valuable merely as indications of the number of excitable souls who seize an occasion like this for ventilating their folly in print. Everybody insists that the murderer must be what in all likelihood he is not or cannot possibly be. The man who has lived all his life in the East End, is certain he is a Lascar seaman taking his vengeance on a class who have wronged him, and a sailor in New York, to which city the suggestion was telegraphed, is ready with a tale which fits in suspicion unusually with the suggestion. Then we have the supremely absurd story about the murderer being an American physician in search of material for a scientific investigation which immediately tempted some silly fellow to frighten anonymous persons in Yankee phraseology, declaring that he was the man, though, perhaps, he never expected such success for his lucubrations in red ink as to see them facsimiled for the use of the police. The theory, a favourite one with a certain class of letter writers. Accordingly, when the American doctor's is shown to be impossible, the hypothesis of a medical student, maddened by some special grievance, is put forward, and in due time an actual student, maudlin in his cups, surrenders himself as the murderer. Next, the man who has "Dr Jekyll and Mr Hyde" on the brain insists that the criminal is a highly respectable householder during the day, and an assassin at night. The Socialists, an escaped lunatic, the Jews, an unknown man who murdered negro women in Texas, a Chimpanzee, a butcher's slaughter man, and a jealous woman are all indicated as the culprits; and finally, a dark soul, who has been supping on melodrama, hints that the Whitechapel murderer will be found to be a policeman. All manner of people have been improving the occasion. Parsons have been preaching on it. Philanthropists have hastened to impress the wealthy with the fact that now is the time to do this or do that. A magistrate considers the common lodging houses to blame, while emotional ladies write from Belgravia a letter out of which one is free to gather that what Whitechapel is really in need of is a gallery of old masters and some good chamber music.

The *Kerry Evening Post* appeared equally incredulous in their London Correspondent's column of September 13th:

There are limits to sensationalism, but those limits are long since over-stepped when the *Daily Telegraph* issues a rude pastille of the supposed murderer or Minotaur, whichever we like to call him, and the result is that a nervous old gentleman in a bus collars the supposed murderer and gets himself into a kind of Pickwickian fizzle and scrape. Scarcely less absurd was the letter of a Mr. Evans, who, if his name means anything, means that he should give good advice not bad. Now our misnamed Eubrile has beaten the record of the German professor who drew out a description of a camel from his inner consciousness. He knows by second sight what hat the scoundrel wore, how he was shod, and above all that he had steel grey eyes, for it is only such eyes could do such a deed. If any of our readers chance to have eyes of this cold grey glint let them, if not too late, get goggles and go about concealed or they may get a bad quarter of an hour in the police court. On the whole, it is nonsense of this kind which is doing its best to throw the police off the clue.

The *Limerick Chronicle* on October 4th also provided a brief round up of some of the more notable suggestions which had appeared in that week's newspapers:

Amongst the hints and suggestions thrown out the following seems worthy of attention:– One correspondent, writing from St. Alban's, says: "Just about twelve months ago an inmate of the Lunatic Asylum at Leavesden, near Watford, escaped while out with others in the charge of keepers. He managed to get into the Bricket Woods, and has since evaded capture. The local paper warned females against being out at night in the neighbourhood, as this man was dangerous only to women. The question is, whether the authorities in London have had this lunatic's description, as the fearful crimes in the East-end point to such a person." This is worth attending to.[2] The following communication with the Editor of the *Daily Telegraph* is curious. The writer states that in examining the chart representing the locality of the Whitechapel murders, published in Monday's issue, "It is curious to observe that lines drawn through the spots where the murders were committed assume the exact form of a dagger, the hilt and blade of which pass through the scenes of the sixth, second, first and third murders, the extremities of the guard making the fourth and fifth. Further, the spot where the portion of the apron belonging to the victim of the Mitre-square tragedy was picked up lies in the imaginary line which forms the hilt of the dagger." He then asks, "Can this possibly afford a clue to the position of the next atrocity?" A more sensible suggestion proceeds from a correspondent who signs himself H. F. W. He says: "Since it is, at least, possible that the person signing himself 'Jack the Ripper,' who wrote the letter and post-card published yesterday, is really the murderer he claims to be, would it not be well that the Press should be enabled and requested by the police to furnish a facsimile of his handwriting. Should he indeed be identical with the assassin the detection of the latter would be rendered probable, if not certain, by such a course. Should he prove to be but an infamous buffoon, his exposure to universal contempt would surely serve the end of hindering other similar jesters from like diabolical folly."

The musings of many of the newspapers were not quite so good natured, however, and in those less enlightened times when political correctness was still a concept of the far distant future, the Jews and other foreign immigrants came in for a certain amount of abuse in the pages of a number of periodicals. In the *Belfast News-Letter* of October 2nd the following appeared:

> Englishmen would fain believe that the crimes have been committed by some miserable foreigner, because the atrocities in every way are "un-English," and perpetrated on a well-arranged plan, intended to render detection almost impossible. There is a preponderating population of Polish and Russian Jews within the radius of the tragedies; they are in most cases penniless, and a standing danger to the peace and welfare of the community. The foreign immigrants in the East End must be dealt with, all the rookeries cleared out, and the light of day let in upon the dingy slums before we can expect to hear the end of the horrors, the very contemplation of which exercise a degrading influence upon the lower strata of society, and tempts an unprincipled journalism to dish up daily revolting topics and "cooked" information to catch the coppers of the uneducated classes.

The *Irish Times* of October 1st commented:

> Strong suspicion has fallen upon Jews and other foreigners, and the Socialists who have clubs in the East End. There is no definite ground for these surmises, and it is not fair to direct public anger against a class. But

it is certainly in an especial way the duty of the Jews and Poles, and particularly of the members of the Socialist club to assist in every way in effecting a discovery. Until it has been made they cannot be perfectly free from a responsibility greater than belongs in those less connected with the spot and its lawlessness.

On October 1st the *Times* of London caused a scandal when it printed an article from its Vienna Correspondent detailing an 1884 trial of a Galacian Jew named Ritter who had been falsely accused of murder. The article intimated that a superstition existed among the Jews, expressly sanctioned by the Talmud, which allowed for them to atone for illicit sexual relations with a Christian woman by slaying and mutilating the woman in question. The weight of the entire Jewish faith swiftly descended on the head of that journal, as described in the *Belfast Morning News* of October 4th:

> Dr Hermann Adler, one of the chief Rabbis of the Jewish Church, writes to the *Times* denying in the strongest terms the existence of any superstition amongst the scattered children of the Hebrew race that under certain circumstances a Jew might be justified in slaying and mutilating a Christian woman, as was suggested yesterday by a Vienna Correspondent. This was alleged by certain persons some time back with reference to the murder near Cracow some time ago, of which a Jew named Ritter was accused. Doctor Adler, who is one of the most learned and respected members of the Jewish community in this city, declares without hesitation that in no Hebrew book is such a barbarity even hinted at. In this he is fully confirmed by M. Gaster, Ph.D., Chief Rabbi of the Spanish and Portuguese Jewish congregations in England. The dissemination of such calumnious assertions cannot be too strongly condemned, and, in the present state of public feeling, it was calculated to arouse the worst passions of the ignorant populace against some of the poorest and most wretched Jewish slaves of the "sweaters" who live near the scenes of these East-end murders. M. Gaster's eloquent refutation of these slanders will meet with the sympathy of all fair-minded and just men. The age of religious persecutions is not surely to be revived.

Of course the proximity of the Jewish club to the site of one of the murders could be said to have been some justification for a suspicion that the murderer was of that religious persuasion, but in truth the feeling against the Jews was more widespread than hinging on that one single fact, and had been from the beginning of the murders. This article had appeared in the *Derry Journal* on September 12th:

There is not any people so ridiculous in their periods of panic as the English. The English are not an excitable people; they are supposed to have the stolidity of the Teuton as distinguished from the mercurial excitability of the Celt; yet, tried severely, they are helplessness itself, or rush wildly into the most absurd extravagances. The appalling atrocity of Whitechapel shocks the world. The people, amongst whom this dreadful thing is done, crime laden, as they are known to be, are startled by the exceeding savagery of the murder. It is natural enough that they should be affrighted, and for the moment unhinged, but it ill-accords with the English claim to exceptional steadiness of head, to go on from day to day conjuring up phantoms and reasoning none at all. There is one thing, however, that curiously displays itself in the fearful tumult of thought and action – the never failing belief in their own self righteousness. Somebody else than an Englishman did the deed! There is a loud cry of "the Jew!" Some one, it is urged, not a Christian must be the criminal, and the vulgar idea of the Jew is greedily seized on and spread to the danger of a revival of the days of senseless persecution. Why London should set itself up, in Whitechapel, and look beyond its own circle for the maniac, or savage, may be understood in the metropolis of the world's wickedness, but outsiders find nothing in the history of "Babylon's" dark record to justify the idea in the least. London is simply a world in itself, with humanity in all its phases compressed within its space, and the dregs, in the order of things, settle down from generation to generation in localities such as Whitechapel. That is the great problem to be faced sometime, somehow, in the great cities; and that it is yet so formidable and not growing less formidable, is owing to this self-same smug self-righteousness with which the Britishers clothe themselves. Their mission seems to be to enlighten the universe, leaving dismal shadow behind them in their own land. They are the self constituted apostles of civilization to every clime, and the civilization, nay, the Christianity of England, reveals to us Whitechapel! The cry of "the Jew" is apiece with all this long-drawn ghastly hypocrisy – "unconscious hypocrisy," John Bright calls it. The "Christianity" whose product is Whitechapel, or say, the East End, at its best, or for that matter, the West End, in some of its disclosures, shows considerable audacity, or at least a lack of the reflective quality, in assailing a race that in many ways are at once an example and a rebuke to "Christian" pretensions. In what we might call the parade of prayer, London's voice is the loudest, heard all over the globe. But the preaching and "converting" are for the most part directed to countries remote, where the uncivilized savage roams innocent of the ingenious devilry of the "Christian" products in the dark places of London. Ship loads of English gold are poured out, with due acclaim, to save the swart sons of the land of the sun, and pious London – having secured a showy report in the Press – goes to bed in sweet and sanctified complacency, to waken up face to face with Whitechapel. This is the "Christianity" that can afford to rail at the Jew, and with a society encrusted with a very leprosy of crime, exclaim, "Somebody else did the deed."

If criticism of the police was by this point fairly widespread and embarrassing to that august body, their lot was not improved when on October 2nd horror piled upon horror in London with another hideous discovery in the city, this time in the West End, just yards from the Houses of Parliament in the heart of Whitehall and only a short distance from Scotland Yard itself. Far worse, the building in whose half-constructed basement the discovery was made was intended as a replacement headquarters for the Metropolitan Police themselves.

On Monday morning a carpenter named Frederick Wildborn, working on the site, had been in the cellars and noticed a parcel lying in a dark corner. He had not thought much about it at the time, nor that evening when he placed his tools in the cellar for safekeeping overnight. The next day, however, he detected a bad smell and alerted one of the assistant foremen to the presence of the bundle. The object was extracted from the cellar and the wrapping removed, whereupon it was found to be the dismembered trunk of a woman.

Although the incident was undoubtedly not the work of the Whitechapel killer, and in fact was one of a series of similar discoveries stretching over three years in the city, the press seized on the opportunity for further condemnation of the police. The *Freeman's Journal* of October 3rd had this to say:

> London was again appalled last evening by a fresh addition to the hideous tale of unpunished murder which has disgraced it for the past two months. The Whitehall discovery may turn out not to be precisely on all fours with those that have been made in the East End, but it is, nevertheless, another most shocking illustration of the perfect impunity with which human life can be taken in the metropolis of the British Empire. It is a remarkable, and may be a significant, fact that the place selected for the concealment of the body was in the building which is to be the new headquarters of the detective department. It appears that almost literally the most audacious crimes can be committed under the very nose of that body. It is not surprising that the people of London should have lost all sense of security, and that they should regard the police as worse than useless as at present managed. Like most events of tragic horror, these have their grimly humorous side. Everyone has become an amateur

detective here, and the favourite pastime in train, in bus, and in the streets is to endeavour to find one's ideal of the unknown miscreant. The only thing that can be said for this craze is that it is of as much practical utility as the work of the professional detectives.

The Irish Times, which had by now become one of the most vociferous critics of the London force, printed a damning condemnation in their leader column of the same day:

The details of this further abominable act are fully described in other columns to-day, and they are too painful to follow. They cannot be read without a shudder of horror, nor is it any wonder that, coming after the recital of the fiendish acts that have already astonished the community, they should intensify the panic now existing. The black records of the Newgate Calendar might be searched in vain for a parallel to this triumph of iniquity. Undetected crime has brought forth its vile progeny. The plague spreads and no means have been found to check it. All the vigilance of the detective and police forces seems powerless to track the evil to its source, and while this is the manifest experience, how can it be hoped that a period can be set to the propagation of the moral disease. All that has transpired during the past few months in the known districts of London where crime is actually taught and practised as a profession suggests the inevitable conclusion that insufficient value is rendered for the vast sums yearly paid out of the public purse for the maintenance of the police and detective forces. What have they been doing? Their duty is not merely to track a particular crime, but by exercise of highly-paid vigilance to prevent such outrages as those with which we have so frightfully been made familiar. Their industry and assiduity have broken down, and the public stand face to face with the shocking circumstance that with all their practically unlimited resources they have failed. How, under such circumstances, can it be said that panic is unjustifiable, and what excuse can be offered for the officials under the government of the HOME SECRETARY, who have failed conspicuously to satisfy the public of their absolute determination to pursue the criminal, irrespective of official precedents inapplicable in such a case, to the very end?

It is impossible to suppose that the English people will any longer tolerate this feebleness of the law. The question is of small consequence whether a series of crimes have been committed by a single individual or by a gang of miscreants. What is wanted is police activity, and not detective theory, and in tracking the villainy to its fountain-head no means should be left unemployed, whether justified by official "precedent" or not. In the pass to which things have come the public will refuse to be misled by mere phrases and red-tape processes. They want to find the criminal or criminals, and are prepared to sanction the most extreme measures that may be proposed leading to discovery. Never has such a reproach been cast upon the police and detective forces of London. Their resources of enterprise and of activity seem to be paralysed, and the acumen that they have displayed in far more complicated instances is notably at fault. We do not think that the murderous gang or the individual – if such a fiend in human shape exists – can ultimately escape the outraged laws of humanity, but the impunity that is presently enjoyed cannot be considered as other than a direct incentive to crime in the most ghastly aspects of which the public are aware.

The *Freeman's Journal* were equally forceful in their condemnation of the police, and of the personalities involved. This item appeared in the London Correspondence column of October 2nd:

The ineptitude of the police is causing the most serious misgivings in the public mind. The detective department seems to be utterly devoid of the slightest resource in attempting to meet the frightful emergency that has arisen. I am informed that it was not until yesterday that the normal strength of the force in the district where the murders were committed was increased. That it might have been supposed would have been the first step taken by Sir Charles Warren and Mr. Matthews, but only yesterday did it strike them to adopt it and send fifty additional constables to Leman street. The detectives are themselves, I hear, completely demoralised by the success with which the murderer has baulked them up to the present. All the commonplace expedients of Scotland Yard have proved utterly useless in this case, and the authorities appear to be incapable of conceiving any new plan of coping with the difficulty. The result is that the panic which has already set in with terrible intensity in the East End is rapidly spreading over London. The immunity with which these awful crimes have been committed will tempt the murderer or his imitators to extend the field of operations. The criminals may be caught in the long run, but it is feared that it will not be until a long course of uninterrupted success in their ghastly work has made them careless in the adoption of the cunning precautions which have so entirely checkmated the police up to the present.

    Opinion is still very fiercely against Mr. Matthews and Sir Charles Warren. Between them they appear to have destroyed whatever utility the London police may ever have possessed as detectives of crime. It is pretty well known that a serious conflict is raging at the present moment between the First Commissioner of Police and the Home Office, a conflict which is largely accountable for the paralysis which prevails at Scotland Yard. Mr. Matthews represents the opinions and methods of Mr. Munro, while Sir Charles Warren has his own notions and is determined to carry them out. There appears to be little doubt entertained that the upshot of the business will be the resignation of both the Home Secretary and Sir Charles Warren. But Mr. Munro is as inveterate a muddler as either of them, and he certainly should not be permitted to remain drawing a handsome salary from the public for mismanaging its business. When he controlled the Detective Department a great proportion of the officers were employed in watching Irish members instead of doing their proper duty. The people of London are paying dearly now for Mr. Munro's proceedings.

The pressure on the Home Secretary to offer a reward was once again a matter of the highest public concern, and his resistance to this course of action was put all the more in the spotlight when the Lord Mayor of London, now brought into proceedings by the fact of Mitre Square being under his jurisdiction, immediately offered up £500 for the capture of the miscreant. The London Correspondent for Dublin's *Evening Telegraph* commented on October 2nd:

> There is a general belief here that the Government must make a "Jonah" of Mr Home Secretary Matthews to appease in some degree the wrath of the public. The *Daily Telegraph's* savage attack upon him yesterday was very ominous, and to-day he comes off considerably "second best" in an encounter with Mr Harry Marks, the proprietor of the *Financial News*. I would remind your readers that when last the Home Secretary was urged to offer a reward for the apprehension of the murderer he declined on the plea that "there was no public fund available for such a purpose;"[3] but now, after Mr. Marks has forwarded him a cheque for £300 with a letter stating that he had been requested by a number of readers of the *Financial News* to ask him to offer this reward, he returns the cheque with an assurance that "had he deemed it advisable he would have offered a reward in the first instance." This certainly is a miserable change of front, and, when compared with his first excuse, a stupid inconsistency on his part. The Corporation of the City of London have offered a reward of £500 for the apprehension of the murderer, in this respect showing an example to the Government. Nor is this all. I have been informed, moreover, that a number of persons on the Stock Exchange here are getting up a fund to offer a reward of £2,000 for the same object.

Of course not all the press were so thorough in their condemnation, but it is interesting to note that even in the Unionist press, in articles which purported to give support to the London authorities, such as the following piece from the *Kilkenny Moderator* of October 6th, there is still a shrouded criticism of the Whitehall mandarins whose control over that force was implicit:

Old Horace tells us that punishment, though lame and halting, is pretty sure to overtake the criminal in the long-run. That genial optimistic poet would probably alter his opinion if he were translated into the nineteenth century and the Victorian age. It is the tendency of public opinion to excite itself over things sensational, and to ignore things just as bad but devoid of those characteristics which horrify and arouse. Mysterious disappearances, dead bodies found in nooks or floating in the Thames, and many other indications and proofs of foul play have been for a long time matters of most frequent occurrence in London. The horrible character, however, and fiendish malignity and cruelty of these late murders in the heart of the great modern Babylon, have roused public opinion upon the subject of crime and of those paid for the detection of it in a manner in which it has never been stirred up in our time. The feeling that everywhere prevails could hardly be surpassed if it were established that the Principle of Evil itself had taken human shape and form in London. Indeed we rather think that this feeling, though not expressed, is not absent from many minds at present, as they consider what London in these times is almost nightly bringing forth.

Meanwhile the Press is, we think, a little inconsiderate. The ceaseless railings at the police, because they cannot discover the criminal are rather worse than silly. One great London paper has actually raved at the police because they did not search "between the brick and mortar of the houses." Suppose half a dozen police, armed with pickaxes and shovels, were to enter the offices of the *Daily Telegraph,* the author of this wild idea, of this wild rhetoric run mad, proposing to demolish all the plaster there in consequence of the suggestion how would this effect the mind of the editor? The language, however, absurd as it is, indicates the great excitement produced in London by these horrible outrages. The police, we suppose, are doing their very best; and if they cannot do better it is the fault of those who are responsible for the organisation of the London detective force. If the *Daily Telegraph* comes out badly written and badly printed, men do not blame the ready-writers of the staff, or the poor printers and their "devils"; they blame the editor or the proprietor. The London police, we may be perfectly certain, are doing their best to hunt out this Thug, and if the Thug has left behind absolutely no traces, and given no clues, how is he to be caught? It is only in novels that we find preternaturally acute detectives.

Obviously the press generally had their own particular axes to grind, and should not be relied upon for an unbiased view. The *Cork Examiner* of October 4th printed an interview with Captain Nott Bower, the Chief Constable of the Liverpool police, whose views on the subject make interesting reading:

Captain Bower, however, requested to be excused from making any statement upon the point on which his views were more particularly requested, namely, the organisation and administration of the London police and detective forces. He explained that in the first place he had little knowledge on the subject beyond that of an outsider; and in the second place he desired to abstain from any observations in the nature of criticism, on the ground that he might thereby assume an invidious attitude which he had no wish to occupy. The opinion of the Liverpool police authorities generally appears to be much the same as now seems to be generally entertained – viz, that the murders are the work of one man, who is probably a lunatic, or at any rate suffering from homicidal mania, and that the chance of his detection is exceedingly remote. The only hope of his capture, in fact, is thought to rest upon the probability of his attempting another outrage, and his being taken red-handed before he succeeds in his murderous design. As to the failure of the London police a certain sympathy is expressed. The difficulties attending their detective work are rendered enormously great by reason of the vast size of London; and so far as the organisation of the force in the metropolis is concerned, it is not so much the system itself that is regarded by the Liverpool authorities as defective, but the fatal plan of appointing to heads of departments military men of no police training whatever and of the five chief constableships and the two assistant chief-constableships created by Sir Charles Warren, five of the posts having been allotted by Sir Charles to military officers. On the subject of the Home Secretary's refusal to offer a reward, the opinion of the Liverpool police is in support of Mr Matthews' action. A distinction is drawn between rewards for the capture of thieves who have decamped with valuable property and for the detection of murderers. In the former case a reward may stimulate vigilance and prove justified by results. In the latter it usually operates, or at any rate would almost certainly on this occasion operate in impelling persons of an impecunious and inventive turn of mind to draw on their imaginations and really embarrass the police by the multiplication of their suggestions and clues. The deep feeling aroused throughout

London, and indeed, the country at large by the horrible series of atrocities, is believed to be ample assurance of the full co-operation of the public in helping in the discovery of the murderer.

That the London police themselves felt the seriousness of the situation and the slur on their characters that the continued non-detection of the killer produced is certain. Within a few days of the murders Dr. Robert Anderson had been recalled from his sick leave at the orders of Sir Charles Warren and personally took over the reigns of leading the investigation from Chief Inspector Donald Swanson. Towards this end he appears to have enlisted the help of James Monro, an action which did not go down well with Sir Charles but which, considering the latter gentleman's long experience of detective work, was probably a smart move. The actions of the City Police are, unfortunately, less certain as their records of the investigation were destroyed by fire during the blitz in World War II and only a report made to the Home Office by Inspector McWilliam survives.

However, the Irish Republican press were by now having a field day, and were often hard pressed to disguise their glee at the continued embarrassment of the English authorities. The time was a turbulent one for Irish politics, so that whatever could be latched upon would be made to show to the detriment of their English counterparts. Throughout the first half of October the Ripper crimes competed for space in the Irish press with tales of evictions, moonlighting outrages, arrests of Irish members, riots, coercion trials, and Star Chamber inquiries. By the second half the events of Whitechapel took a decided back seat to probably the largest single story in the history of Irish reporting up to that point.

CHAPTER EIGHT ENDNOTES

1   In a letter to Sims in 1913, Chief Inspector John George Littlechild would later put forward the name of Tom Bulling of the Central News Agency as the author.

2   No report of this escape has been traced to date. James Kelly, who had murdered his wife by stabbing her in the neck in 1883, escaped from Broadmoor in January 1888 and was still on the loose at the time of the murders. His name has been mentioned as the possible perpetrator of the crimes frequently, and indeed the Home Office files contain a note inquiring if he had been located.

3   In all fairness to Mr Matthews, there is no record of him ever having made such a statement.

CHAPTER NINE

Another Irish Interlude

O N OCTOBER 2ND, the London Correspondent of the *Cork Examiner* told a brief anecdote which was instructive in terms of the fact that while the Whitechapel murders had, for a time, eclipsed the "Irish Question" in the eyes of press and public, there was no diminution in public policy:

> It is a curious fact that in spite of the disgraceful break down of the Metropolitan police as detectors of crime, Home Secretary Mathews still insists upon a large number of detectives shadowing the Irish members when they are in town. I walked along the Strand with an Irish member to-night and two detectives followed us all the way. The cost of the two or three hundred men who are employed upon [the] Irish detective force in England ought really to be added to the Irish estimates in order that the British public may have an accurate estimate of the cost of governing Ireland against the will of her people.

The late 1880s were not a good time for Irish Republicanism. Things had seemed much better in the earlier part of the decade when Charles Stewart Parnell, imprisoned for slandering the Prime Minister William Gladstone in print, had then come to an agreement with him through intermediaries which led to his release from Kilmainham Prison and the Irish Party acceptance of the 1881 Land Bill in return for Gladstone's promise to tackle the issue of rent arrears and to work towards Home Rule. Apart from a short setback during 1885, the Parnellite Irish Party and Gladstone's Liberals worked together relatively successfully for the following five years. However, 1886 saw the failure in Parliament of Gladstone's Home Rule Bill, a plan which had proposed the setting up of an independent Irish legislature within the United Kingdom. The defeat of the bill forced Gladstone to go to the country and in the ensuing election he was heavily defeated by the coalition of Conservatives and Liberal-Unionists.

By the autumn of 1888 the situation was effectively one of open war between the Nationalist policies of the Irish Party and Chief Secretary Balfour's open determination to smash the National League and put an end to the Plan of Campaign. And despite talking a good game, it was a war in which the Nationalists were incurring some heavy defeats. Wholesale evictions and imprisonment of rebel MPs were occurring across the country. The Ripper murders must have seemed almost a godsend for the Nationalist press, providing as they did an opportunity for criticism of the English Government which was irrefutable, and for the first time in a long time, the Tories and Unionists found themselves on the back foot on this issue at least.

The two main Republican periodicals both printed leader columns on the murders on the Saturday following the double event, October 6th. *The Nation* confined its comments to another suggestion of a double standard between the English and Irish criminal laws:

> London has again been the scene of two ghastly tragedies. Within the area of Whitechapel, where the four previous murders were committed, the bodies of two women were discovered early on Sunday morning, one of them mutilated with the same barbarity as characterised the preceding cases. Every circumstance points to the conclusion that both crimes were committed by one and the same person. Both were marked by the same reckless daring and brutality. The unfortunate women were murdered within a few feet of crowded haunts, one woman almost in sight of a policeman. Yet the murderer has so far escaped. The police are utterly powerless. Were such a thing to happen in any part of Ireland, every Tory paper would denounce the people of the neighbourhood as in league with crime, and attribute the escape of the assassin to their sympathy. The moral would be drawn from this inability of the authorities to discharge their duties, that the country was wholly unfitted for self-government. Yet no one makes such a suggestion on the case of London; coercion and the suspension of the Habeas Corpus have not been asked for as the remedy. Six murders since Christmas is now the record for Whitechapel. That these have been committed in such rapid succession and with the same unvarying circumstances of atrocity, is, perhaps, due to the furore made over the first tragedy by the English press. The gruesome story of its sickening horrors was dilated on with a morbid regard to details. The taste for sensation was deliberately pandered to by even the most respectable papers. The murderer became a sort of hero of the hour, and the importance thus bestowed upon him has fired him to new efforts; or has, perhaps, inspired some imitator to continue his revolting work. The publication of these horrors in elaborate grossness of detail is a terrible abuse of the powers of the press.

The *United Ireland* editorialised at much greater length, taking as the basis of their column a letter which had been printed in one of the London dailies during the week:

> The unparalleled series of murders with mutilation – all undetected – which have taken place in London within the past few weeks suggest one thought pertinent to the Irish controversy. Suppose they had occurred in Ireland, and suppose, as in the case of London, the murderer or murderers had all remained undetected! The first consequence would be an immediate reassembling of Parliament to pass a new and fiercer Coercion Act, and the general effect would in all probability be to postpone the settlement of the Irish difficulty for another half-dozen years. But the Whitehapel atrocities are, after all, an exceptional outbreak of British crime. If we take up the ordinary calendar – from which these crimes differ only in the peculiar circumstances of horror and mystery surrounding them – we might, if we chose to judge our neighbour from the same data as they do us, read quite as terrible a story of the depravity of the superior race. The very day on which the latest Whitechapel murders were reported in our papers, there was reported in an obscure corner the murder of a wife by almost cutting her head off in Westminster.[1] Every other day a similar crime is reported. Nor are the crimes themselves the worst evidence of the state of public morality. Worse still is the comparatively slight degree of enormity with which some of the most horrible of them are viewed by the judges and juries before whom the culprits are tried. An English lady (Mrs. FENWICK MILLER) writes a striking letter on this subject in Tuesday's *Daily News*.
>
> "Is it not worse," she asks, "to hack and mutilate a living woman's sentient body than to kill and cut at the insensible corpse. Is it not a more terrible fate to be slowly beaten to death in instalments than to be sent from the earth by one swift stroke? Yet week by week, month by month women are kicked, beaten, jumped on till they are crushed, crippled, stabbed, seamed with vitriol, bitten, eviscerated with red-hot pokers, and deliberately set on fire – and this sort of outrage, if the woman dies, is called 'manslaughter;' if she lives, it is a 'common assault.'"
>
> Mrs. MILLER gives a few samples out of many of these cases. Let the offences and the sentences be compared with the offences and the sentences to be read of every day in the administration of Mr. BALFOUR'S Coercion Act:
>
> "Here is Mr Edlin, the Assistant Judge of the Middlesex sessions, dealing with a case of burglary, cutting a watchdog's throat, and stabbing the

woman of the house to the throat when she resisted an attempted rape, cutting seriously both her throat and the hands put up to protect it – six months imprisonment!" (The same sentence which Mr Balfour's Removables and County Court Judge Kisbey thought proper for John Dillon.)

Mr EDLIN, who has inflicted other such sentences, has just received the honour of a knighthood.

"Mr Justice Charles a fortnight ago had a miscreant who had inflicted months of acute agony and disfigured a poor girl for life by pouring vitriol over her face because she refused to live with him – sentence, eighteen months. The same judge had a man who chopped a woman's head open with an axe – sentence, nine months. Mr Edlin again had a case of a savage brute biting an old woman's cheek through to her teeth, and 'worrying it like a dog' – eighteen months. Here, a fortnight ago, is Mr de Ruizen; a man biting a woman's arm, when her baby was a month old – six months. Mr Chance: for beating a woman with a ginger-beer bottle, and turning her out of doors in her night-gown – three months. The country magistrates are even worse. The Barnsley magistrates, for a brutal assault with a brick, kicking, and attempted rape, last week gave four months imprisonment. The Whitehaven magistrates, for breaking a woman's jaw in two places and knocking out six teeth, six months. Here is Edward Doyle, who, not content with breaking a woman's ribs and scalding her with hot water, next thrust a red-hot poker up into her abdomen, and let her lie dying for two days: manslaughter, fifteen years prison. He will be let out to go on again while still quite in the prime of life; he is no murderer. John Freshfield, tearing off his wife's ear, breaking her breast-bone and also eight of her ribs on one side and nine on the other: manslaughter (Mr Justice Hawkins), eighteen months prison. John Finnemore, stabbing his wife in the abdomen with a knife because his dinner, ordered for three, was not nice when he returned at midnight; manslaughter, twenty years. T. Leyland, setting a woman on fire, with express intention to kill her, by holding a lighted paper to her clothes and then shutting her out in a high walled yard away from rescue; manslaughter, 'recommended to mercy because he looked a soft sort of man!' James Kelly, Edinburgh, fifty wounds on the head and elsewhere, the end of a long course of brutal usage; culpable homicide, ten years. John Jones, a murder described by the judge as one 'for which we might search in vain amongst the records of barbarians to find a case so bad'; manslaughter (Mr Justice Grantham) twelve months imprisonment."

If we were to judge of the English people from such a record of judges' sentences, juries' findings, and crimes, frightful indeed should the state of public morality amongst such a people be pronounced. But of course it would be highly unfair to judge the English people by such a standard. Yet that is the standard by which the dominant party in England, headed by the *Times* and Mr. BALFOUR, apply to Ireland every day of the week.

The Unionist press naturally responded in kind, supporting the Government in the face of the onslaught it was receiving both in Ireland and from the radical press in England. The *Kerry Evening Post* printed this article on October 13th:

Now that the panic which accompanied the discovery of the latest crime has somewhat abated, and the popular excitement to which they gave rise has calmed down, we can look back on the occurrences with composure, and can judge whether there was sufficient cause for such an outburst of unreasoning terror, as whether the obloquy to which the authorities, from the Home Secretary downwards, have been assailed was deserved. We have no intention of describing afresh the incidents of the tragedies. That the murders were carried out with the same secrecy, with identical absence of motive, and that discovery of the criminal has not yet been effected, need not be further dwelt upon. But that they have been made the vehicle for bitter and undeserved attacks upon public servants, disheartening their energy and damaging their efficiency, is one of the most regrettable facts in connection with a public calamity. There was absolutely no justification for it. The outrages were limited to one particular quarter, and to a class of women whose habits render it extremely difficult for the police to afford them ordinary protection. The persons and dwellings of decent citizens have been as safe as at any other time. The police of the metropolis have been increased in numbers and efficiency during the last two years, and London, as regards ordinary crime, compares most favourably with any foreign capital. Yet, because a single murderer, acting with peculiar cunning, and with extraordinary advantages, has not been instantly captured, an outcry has been raised for the dismissal of the Home Secretary, the resignation of Sir Charles Warren, and a change in the whole system of police management. The followers of Mr. Gladstone in the press have not hesitated to denounce the failure to secure the criminal as the natural result of the inaptitude of a Tory Government, and the reader is left in doubt as to whether they or the unknown murderer deserve the greatest punishment. All this is, perhaps, the outcome of the new method in politics which has been introduced by Mr. Gladstone at the bidding of his Parnellite allies. To hamper and attack the constabulary in Ireland in the discharge of their duties has become one of the recognised weapons of the Gladstonian armoury. It had a certain amount of success for a time, but has latterly become somewhat rusty and ineffective. If we are now to have it brought into use in England, whenever a social calamity like the Whitechapel murders occur, political warfare will, indeed, have reached its lowest level.

An attempt to explain the land situation in Ireland here would be futile. Whole books have been written on the subject and still only manage to scratch the surface. But to boil things down to the most basic component, everything revolved around a concept known as the three Fs, these being Fair rent, Fixity of tenure and Free sale. These were effectively provided for in the 1881 Land Act which recognised the right of yearly tenants who had occupied land continuously for a considerable period of time to a statutory tenure defeasible only on decree from a Land Court, and for that Land Court also to have the power to fix rents independently of both tenant and landlord. The tenant would thus have fixity of tenure so long as the rent was paid up to date, and the legal right to sell on the tenancy, which had been loosely provided for by the previous act of 1870, was now legally granted.

Unfortunately, although the bill granted the rights for which the tenants had been fighting for most of the century, it had come too late. Great damage had been done in landlord-tenant relations by the 1860 Landlord and Tenant Law (Amendment) Act, popularly known as the Deasy Act, which had unequivocally placed absolute ownership of the land in the hands of the landlord. Although the 1870 act had given some legal status back to the tenant, it had not gone far enough, and by now the idea had become fixed in the minds of the Irish that what was really needed was an end to landlordism in its entirety. The question became: had one sovereign nation a right to govern the leasing back of the land of another territory to its indigenous population? The Parnellites in Parliament may have been reasonably content with their lot, but the same could not be said of the more extreme elements of the Republican movement, and the result was increased land agitation and dynamite plots in London organised from America by the hardline Clan-na-Gael and the Fenian Brotherhood.

The 1885 Land Act, known as the Ashbourne Act, was a further concession, providing for £5 million to be made available as 100% loans to allow tenants to purchase their holdings from their landlords at a cost of 17 years' rent. The problem with the act was that no provision was made for tenants in arrears, albeit the 1882 Settled Land Act had empowered the Land Commission to write off arrears not in excess of £30. The concept behind this lack of provision was understandable enough, i.e. how could a tenant who had fallen into arrears on their rent then be trusted to keep up payments on a loan for purchase?

However, the counter-argument ran that much of the arrears was the result of too-high rents set by absentee landlords during years when poor crops and falling agricultural prices had resulted in the tenants making scant profit on their yield. It was exactly this situation that the Plan of Campaign was designed to combat.

The Plan was not universally accepted among the Nationalist movement, most notably by Parnell and Michael Davitt, the co-founder of the Land League, both of whom refused to support it publicly, albeit for very different reasons. It was seen by certain elements in the party that its aims had their basis more in separationist politics than in securing actual aid for the tenant farmers. Davitt wrote to John Dillon in 1887 expressing his strong opinion that money raised in America for the aid of evicted tenants should not be given to those whose evictions had come about as a result of participation in the plan. He saw the plan as a political statement of tenant strength and a form of blackmail, providing the landlords with the choice of either accepting rents lower than those judicially set by the land courts, or receiving none at all and risking financial ruin.

However, it was not the plan itself which brought about the precarious state in which the country found itself it that autumn of 1888. Rather it was Arthur Balfour's heavy-handed efforts to defeat it. His sacrifice of the subtle politics and negotiation of his predecessor Michael Hicks-Beach in favour of a strict adherence to the application of "rule of law" in its narrowest sense through the Perpetual Coercion Act met with great approval within his own party, but in Ireland it served as a rallying cry for the Nationalist movement. Even though politically the times were not good for them, the positive epidemic of evictions and imprisonments resulting from Balfour's policies made it a boom time in terms of membership recruitment.

The activity of the Nationalist land agitators was intense throughout the period. The release of John Dillon from prison shortly before a judicial order was due to be issued for the same from the Parnell Commission was trumpeted from the rooftops as a great victory against "Balfourian oppression." Wherever they went in the land Dillon and William O'Brien were greeted as heroes, and despite the proscription of the National League they used various subterfuge methods to organise Nationalist rallies in secret on estates all across the country where the Plan of Campaign was in operation. In the week of the double event a mass Nationalist rally was held at Carrick-on-Suir, near Waterford, ostensibly to honour O'Brien and grant him the freedom of the city. The reporting of the event in the *Waterford News* of October 5th left little doubt as to the true purpose of the meeting, as the newspaper gave over almost its entire issue to detailed transcripts of the lengthy speeches made. The article, headed "The Call to Action" began as follows:

It is impossible to over estimate the importance of the proceedings at Carrick-on-Suir which marked the opening days of this week. Mr. O'Brien and his brother campaigners called into fresh life a spirit of dogged determination to continue the fight for home and freedom, which nothing can withstand. In our columns this evening we publish in full the programme which those who profess to be actuated with sentiments of nationality are fully expected to follow. This is not the time for snivelling patriotism; the Convention pointed to the path which each man is called on to tread, and he who does not adopt the decision, in its minutest detail, should be drummed out of the ranks of those who are deemed worthy to carry on the fight against the present Tory despotism practised in this country. It is a self evident fact that if the people do not stand with an impregnable front this winter, they cannot hope to contend against the tyrannical rent collectors, backed up by the despots in Dublin Castle, who have almost pledged themselves to make the Irish contented, whilst oppression, discontent and misery stalks the land. The call to action is simply an appeal to defy the law, as administered in this country, and to carry on the campaign for the preservation of the tenants of Ireland from the decimating influence which landlordism, even in a minor degree, still exercises over our people. Resistance to the law as it is at present framed is in the abstract a duty. Prudence must determine the exact amount of resistance necessary in particular instances. We would direct special attention to the fiery denunciation of the crime of land grabbing, and the punishment that should be meted out to those who offend in this particular. What is the use of William O'Brien and John Dillon risking their liberty and their lives, if in the very heart of the farming community a reptile is allowed to live and thrive that is undermining all the work which the brave campaigners are doing in Ireland? Dealing with the land grabbers' specific offence a very effective resolution was passed at the Convention, on the motion of Mr. Laurence Power, Carrigeen, seconded by Mr. Cusack, of Drangan, and strongly supported by Mr. John O'Connor, M.P., who said he would be very happy to defend its adoption from any platform even in England. The resolution, which is of paramount importance, runs as follows:– "That the names of land grabbers, grass grabbers, emergency men, and their supporters, as well as those that deal with them, be sent to each branch attending this Convention from the branches in which they are, as well as to all cattle dealers, and pig buyers; and that a vigilance committee of six be appointed in each branch to carry out this resolution." If this resolution is rigidly adhered to the landlords of this county will think very often before they set out on a crusade of eviction, which can bring them no relief.

Already there are signs that the determination of the people to carry out judicious boycotting has made the landlords chary about calling the forces of eviction to their aid. This should encourage the people to appoint the vigilance committees suggested in the above resolution, in order to make it impossible for the arch enemy of the Irish people – the land grabber – to exist in the country. The other resolutions adopted must be adhered to to the letter, now that the fight of right against might is to be waged to the bitter end.

The Boycott was one of the most powerful weapons in the arsenal of the National League. Named after Captain Charles Boycott on whose estate near Ballinrobe, County Mayo, it was first put into action after the eviction of three of his tenants in August 1879. The scheme called for what Charles Stewart Parnell called "a moral Coventry" of landlords, emergency men and new tenants on evicted properties, such that there would be no possibility of the tenancy being operated at a profit as they could neither purchase seed nor sell the produce of their land. Not only would local merchants refuse the trade of those being subjected to the boycott, but vigilante supporters of the National League would watch the roads leading to the property to prevent relief in the form of supplies from further off. On the Boycott estate the Government attempted to smash this new scheme at its inception by ensuring that the crops on the estate were harvested by a work force of fifty volunteers from the Orange Order, but the campaign, known as the "Boycott Relief Expedition" cost the Government an estimated £10,000, or as Parnell put it, "one shilling for every turnip dug from Boycott's land," and was obviously an unrepeatable exercise.

By 1888 the rights of tenant farmers were well defined, eviction only being permitted by order obtained from the Land Court, and the landlord being responsible to compensate the evictee for any improvements for which he was responsible. In this sense the Plan of Campaign could be said to have played into the hands of the more ruthless landlords, providing as it did legal grounds for obtaining such orders on the more unruly of their tenants. Whatever one might think of the rights and wrongs of eviction orders, it cannot be denied that the actual eviction scenes were often ones of almost heart wrenching tragedy, involving families being turfed out of properties they had often held for generations. On October 17th, the *Belfast Morning News* printed a letter from Handel Cossham, an English Member of Parliament for Bristol East, who had attended a number of evictions on the estate of Captain Singleton at Belpatrick, near Drogheda. He described several scenes in heartbreaking detail, including this one:

> Marching orders were issued, and away went the hundred representatives of the law, attended by the land agents, sheriff's officers, &c, for about a

mile to the hut of James Dunne. I was told on the road that this was a very bad case, and that eviction must positively take place here. Father Taff opened the door of the hut, and I followed in with the land agents, head police officers, &c, and oh! what a sight met the eye here. In the chimney corner sat the tenant who was to be evicted – an old man over eighty years of age – bent and tottering. A bit of peat was burning on the hearth, most of the smoke from which came into the room, where I could dimly see several young men, whom I understood to be the sons of the old man, and one or two women, who I presume were daughters or daughters in law. I had never looked upon such a sight and such a home before. £130 was the amount demanded, and I could well believe the declarations of the old man and his sons that they were really destitute, but they said there was about £65 worth of crops on the land, and they could and would sell all they had and pay not less than £65 by Dec 1, and more if the crops yielded more. But the agent explained that his orders were definite, and he could take no less than the £130. So the evictions began. The emergency men brought out the few bits of furniture, which certainly were not worth more than £2 or £3. "I have lived here," cried the old man, "all my life; I have lived here under four generations of Singletons, and this is how I am served at last. I have always paid the rent in the past, when I could," he passionately added, "and they know it, but they are going to turn me out to die." The loud cry of the women mingled with the wail of the old man, was more than I could stand, and I had to leave before the occupants were actually turned out. But all this is done in the presence of nearly 100 policemen and legal officials, most of whom are paid out of the taxes of the United Kingdom, and the whole thing done in the name of the Queen and the people of the United Kingdom.

This is no random eviction report, for as chance would have it this particular case would become something of a cause celebre in the Nationalist press. As the same newspaper had reported four days earlier on October 13th, under the headline "KILLED BY EVICTION – A REAL SENTENCE OF DEATH", matters had taken a worse turn after Mr Cossham's departure:

Last night James Dunne, the old man of eighty years of age, who was evicted on Captain Singleton's estate in the early part of the day, breathed his last. The circumstances of the old man's fate are most melancholy. When the sheriff came to evict him yesterday, with Messrs Dudgeon and Emerson, and the host of emergency men and police, he declared that he had paid rent for sixty years, but was now utterly unable to meet the landlord's claims. He was suffering from bronchitis, and presented a miser-

able spectacle as he crouched before his kitchen fire. He warned the evic-
tioners that if the process of the law was carried out it would result in his
death. Despite his entreaties he was put out upon the road side, and left
sitting on a stool in the midst of his broken furniture. When the evictors
left a passer-by heard the old man exclaim:– "Emerson, Emerson, get me
the poorhouse van for God's sake. I have not a half hour to live." He was
removed to a barn at hand by some friends, and at about nine o'clock last
night expired. The occurrence has given rise to a very strong feeling in
this district.

The leader column of the newspaper commented further:

Eviction was once declared by Mr Gladstone to be the equivalent to a
sentence of death. The truth of this sentence has, alas! only too often
proved to be literally correct. Such a case is that which has just occurred
at Belpatrick, near Drogheda. An old man named James Dunne, aged 80,
who had been turned out of his humble home for the non-payment of an
impossible rent, died the next night after the landlord had obtained his
"rights." Such is the law. Such is the Christianity of the Government,
administered by the gentleman who talks so sweetly of the beauties of
the doctrines of the Christian religion! We will be told of course that it
is the dishonesty of the Irish peasantry that leads to such occurrences. Or
perhaps it will be said that it is the anxiety for stage effect. What a curious country Ireland must be, where men submit to eviction and die on
the roadside merely for the sake of stage effect.

The holding in question was a large one, some one hundred and five acres in
extent, and the man's family had occupied the land for almost three hundred
years. Rent on the land was in the region of thirty shillings per acre, and the
landlord had offered a reduction of four shillings in the pound, but the tenant,
unable to pay that much, had gone to the Land Court to have the rent judicially reviewed and had been turned away on account of arrears. An inquest was
arranged on the body, and a host of witnesses paraded before it to express the
opinion that the evictors had been aware of the precarious state of Dunne's
health and had ignored the warning signs. The result of the inquest caused a
sensation when a verdict of manslaughter was returned against the land agents
Dudgeon and Emerson. The case would never come to trial, however, the verdict being overturned on appeal. The names of the two accused men would
appear again in the *Freeman's Journal* of November 27th in which an advertise-
ment spotted in the *Down Recorder* was reprinted as an example of what they
considered to be the actual central motives of the land agents.

VACANT FARMS
IMPORTANT TO PROTESTANT TENANT-FARMERS AND THEIR SONS
THERE ARE SEVERAL VACANT FARMS TO LET in the Counties of
Louth and Meath, in close proximity to the important Seaport and
Market Town of Drogheda.
None but Protestants need apply.
Special advantages offered to suitable Tenants.
For further particulars apply to
Messrs DUDGEON & EMERSON
Land Agents and Solicitors, 14 Upper Sackville street, Dublin[2]

Another event which caused a scandal in the first week in November was commented on by the *United Ireland* on November 10th:

> Another murder, for which in all probability no one will ever be brought
> to justice, has been perpetrated by the Irish police. It is in many respects
> one of the worst ever laid to the charge of that callous body, for the victim
> was done to death without the smallest shred of an excuse. A perfectly
> inoffensive man, named Patrick Ahearne, was walking home
> through the streets of Midleton on Thursday night, when he was set
> upon by a policeman armed with a rifle and bayonet, who, without a
> word, ran his steel right through him. Ahearne lived long enough barely
> to allow of his dispositions being taken and to have himself spiritually
> prepared for that world where Balfourism and police blood-guiltiness will
> meet their just deserts. The only reason apparent for the slaughter of
> poor Ahearne is that a row was going on between some other policemen
> and a group of men whom they were trying to arrest, and a party of
> armed constables under the command of District-Inspector Creagh, had
> set out from the barracks to go to their comrades assistance. Despite the
> remonstration of Father O'Donoghue, the inspector ordered his men to
> charge the people in the street, instead of doing what they were first
> about to do – dispersing them with powder and ball. They did charge
> most ferociously, striking everyone they met, without respect for age or
> sex. Poor Ahearne, it appears, was not one of the crowd; he was merely
> just coming out from a place of refreshment when he was set upon and
> done to death. It is difficult to write or speak calmly about a system under
> which such savage deeds are not only tolerated but absolutely encouraged.
> Whatever the findings of the coroner's jury in the case, there is but
> faint hope of anyone being held to account for this fresh deed of blood.

In spite of the hyperbole of this account, it is actually quite accurate as to the events in question, except that the victim was not "run through" but died from the effect of a sword bayonet puncturing the right groin and severing the femoral artery. The inquest again led to a verdict against the authorities, this time one of murder, and on this occasion the trial did indeed go ahead, albeit the result was much as the *United Ireland* had suspected. On December 13th, Constable Edward Swindell was charged at the Munster Assizes with the murder of Patrick Ahern but the Attorney General indicated that he was unwilling to go ahead with the case until a judicial inquiry had been heard. This inquiry began on January 10th, and, after several days deliberations, found that Mr Ahern would undoubtedly still be alive if there had not been a riot going on in the streets, and that if he had been stabbed by a policeman, then the fault lay with the rioting mob and not with the policeman himself.

As well as Balfour going on the offensive in Ireland itself, the British Government were equally vigorous in their fight against the Irish Party in Parliament, and it was seen that the best way to attack that organisation was through its figurehead, Charles Stewart Parnell. Much of the Unionist press criticism of the Home Rule movement focussed its energy in this direction, as shown in this leader column from the *Belfast News-Letter* of September 14th, dealing with a pamphlet published by a Barrister named Thomas Harrison which sought to demonstrate that support for Home Rule was not widespread in Ireland:[3]

> It seems to us that too great emphasis cannot be laid upon the fact that the *personnel,* not merely of the Parliamentary representatives whom Mr. Parnell is supposed to control, but of the general rank and file of Nationalists in Ireland, is far from respectable, to say the least that could be said about it. It is time that the English people were made aware of the fact that the Home Rule conspiracy might with every appropriateness be compared to a movement on the part of the inhabitants of Whitechapel to obtain the control of the government of London. Mr. Harrison does not make this comparison, but he might have done so without its having any other effect than to make the readers of his pamphlet more fully acquainted with the relative position of the Unionists and the Nationalists in Ireland. If the same strong light which is at present being thrown upon the inhabitants of the most undesirable quarter of the East of London were to be cast upon the great body of the Nationalists of Ireland we are convinced that the result would be less prejudicial to Whitechapel than to Nationalist Ireland. If the suggestion were made that it would be desirable to place the control of the government of London in the hands of delegates from Whitechapel, it would not be more ridiculous than the serious proposal to hand Ireland over to the representatives of Parnellism. The people of England should know this. In Ireland it is pretty well known

already. If the Parliamentary representatives of Irish Nationalism were to endeavour to raise a loan of £10,000 on the joint security of their own names they would simply be laughed at in Ireland. It is said that the people of England will subscribe to any loan that is floated; but we fancy they would show considerable shyness in offering their money to the Parnellite members on personal security. Mr. Harrison deals exhaustively with this point in his pamphlet. He shows how even the leading Roman Catholics of Ireland are as bitterly opposed to Parnellism as the leading Protestants. Dublin, for example, cannot furnish from its Catholic Nationalists one member of Parliament able to defray his own Parliamentary expenses. Nothing better illustrates the hostile attitude of the leading Roman Catholics to the Nationalist movement than this extreme scarcity of self-supporting members of Parliament.[4] Newspaper editors and reporters, briefless barristers, retired schoolmasters, bankrupt farmers, broken merchants, travelling clock-menders, are a drug in the market; but those Roman Catholics unwilling to trade in the misfortunes of their country, who have succeeded in business, who have nothing to gain, but everything to lose, by social disorder, are conspicuous by their absence. The majority of Mr. Parnell's members, as he is fond of calling them, are not free representatives, but hired delegates, most of whom, in a healthy state of society, would be earning an honest living in some respectable employment. The fact, indeed, that such a large number of the "Irish Parliamentary Party" are salaried, voting ciphers, is proof sufficient that the Roman Catholics cannot be obtained from a self-supporting stratum of society. These have, in their most deliberate manner, joined forces with their Protestant brethren against an enemy which they distrust, and an issue which they dread.

As far as the Conservative Government of Lord Salisbury went, the most effective medium for attacking Parnell was the *Times* newspaper and the series of articles on *Parnellism and Crime* whose effects were felt throughout much of 1887. In May and June of that year it published a number of articles in the series written by Dr Robert Anderson and based on information passed him by his personal spy Thomas Billis Beach (alias Henri le Caron), under the title *Behind the Scenes in America*. The June 1st article named one of the more obscure Irish members, Frank Hugh O'Donnell, as a supporter of the Parnellite party, although incidentally he had never supported Parnell's leadership. As the article of March 7th had stated that the Land League and the National League were organisations founded on brutal intimidation and the sanction of murder, O'Donnell stated that his name was thus connected with these crimes, declared himself personally libelled and set out to sue the newspaper.

The case came to court on July 2nd, 1888, and quickly turned into a farce. O'Donnell refused to call Parnell as a witness, or to take the stand himself, and the judge ruled that only direct references to the plaintiff were admissible as evidence, of which there were actually none in the March 7th article in question. Much of the Nationalist press suggested that O'Donnell was in fact in league with the *Times* newspaper, and had brought the action solely to provide the Attorney-General, chief counsel for that newspaper, the opportunity of speaking out against the Parnellites and specifying the charges against them. This he did in a speech which lasted three days, and during which he produced six more letters implicating Parnell and his followers in seditious activity.

On July 5th the jury found in favour of the defendant without even retiring to discuss the matter. However, during the trial Parnell secured evidence that the signature on the letter published on April 18th, and various other incriminatory letters produced by the *Times* since, had been forged by Richard Pigott, the former owner of the *Flag of Ireland* newspaper which he had sold to Parnell in 1881, obtaining the documents from which he had copied the signature in the process.

Parnell was persuaded by former Dublin and Home Office "spymaster-general" Sir Edward Jenkinson, the man whom James Monro had replaced as head of the secret Irish department in January 1887, to press home in Parliament his case against the *Times*. Jenkinson's tenure at the Home Office had come to an end over his support for the Home Rule issue, and he had since become one of Parnell's strongest allies. In a letter to former Liberal Home Secretary Sir William Harcourt he offered "every assistance in my power" to Parnell and the Irish Party. So began what was to become a game of political cat and mouse between Parnell, the Government, and the *Times*.

Parnell demanded that the House of Commons appoint a Parliamentary committee to investigate the fraudulent letters. It was a reasonable request, but one the Government could not allow to be fulfilled, considering the danger that certain high-profile Tory members might be implicated in the fraud. They couldn't just ignore the problem, however, and so they chose a course of action designed to bury the letters as deeply as possible in a much larger context. They passed an act of Parliament on August 13th setting up a Special Commission whose brief was "to inquire into the charges and allegations made against certain members of Parliament and other persons by the defendants in the recent trial of an action, entitled O'Donnell v Walter and another."

The Government having countered his opening move, Parnell showed what an astute political manoeuvrer he could be. He had not dared take the *Times* to task for slander in the English courts, for fear of being subject to a Star Chamber inquiry of his own. Scotland, however, was a very different matter, and a legal tactic unique to that country gave him his opening. In Scotland he was entitled to use a practice known as "arrestment for founding jurisdiction", which allowed for a person beyond the jurisdiction of the Scottish court to be sued in the Scottish tribunals if they owned any property in that country. The *Times* were accordingly served with papers announcing that they would be liable to a law suit in Edinburgh for the defamation of Parnell's character. *The Nation* positively crowed on August 18th regarding this master-stroke:

> The unmasked plotters of Printinghouse-square have been making very ugly grimaces within the past few days. The slanderous gang were up to Saturday last very fond of baiting Mr. Parnell on his apparent unwilling-ness to meet them before any jury in the British islands. The Irish leader, quoth the *Times*, does not dare to deny our allegations, for we defy him to bring any case against us in the law courts. Now, however, Mr. Parnell has appealed to Scottish justice to defend him against the wanton attacks of the "leading journal," and that very consistent publication complains that there is no necessity for such a move, inasmuch as a Commission has been constituted. Mr. Parnell's latest move has in fact created a veritable tempest in the offices of the *Times*. Mr. Walter and his confederates were cock-sure of having a quiet time of it throughout the long and vague inquiry which was to have taken place. The question of the forged letters, they thought, could be slyly shelved while the judicial dignitaries were plunged up to their eyes in discussing the French, American, and Australian ramifications of the League, or were trotting all over the world in quest of fee-faw-fum romances connecting Mr. Harrington with the Moonlighters. They fancied that they could get out of the scrape by enlarging the scope of the inquiry to these fantastic limits. Mr. Parnell, however, determined not to allow the oracles of Printinghouse-square to run off with his character in such a spanking style. Lord John Russell, after having on one occasion chalked up "No Popery" on his political signboard, bolted immediately from the arena where he was to play the *role* of doughty knight. The *Times* followed the example of the little lord. It impudently forged several letters attributed to Mr. Parnell, and lo and behold! when Mr. Parnell appears on the scene, the arch-forger disap-pears like a spectre. Unlike a spectre, however, it will have, nilly-willy, to come back and atone for its abominations in a court of justice.

On September 17th the first preliminary hearing of the Commission sat. The result was a resounding victory for the Parnellites. The Attorney-General, who was scheduled to appear for the *Times,* did not show up, and it was left to a jun-ior counsel, a Mr Graham, to argue the case for the newspaper, against the legal wit of Sir Charles Russell, Parnell's chief counsel and one of the leading bar-risters of the day. What resulted was something akin to a lamb being led to slaughter. *Freeman's Journal* told the story the following day.

> The result of the proceedings at the Forgeries Commission yesterday will not be regarded, we venture to anticipate, as favourable to those who have originated the charges against Mr. Parnell and his colleagues. The sitting was brief, but it went in a remarkably searching way to the point. This was suggested in the first two or three words of the short business-like statement with which the President of the Commission, Sir James Hannen, opened the inquiry. He said that the issues are to be restricted both as to the persons and the charges and allegations made in the late action of O'Donnell against the *Times*. Whatever the result of the Commission may be, the public will learn with great satisfaction that the Judges, so far as yesterday's proceedings indicate, are determined to be the head of no roving or fishing Commission. They are likewise resolved, as it would seem, to clear the air of the vagueness that has distinguished the charges so far. It is an unexpected development of "Parnellism and Crime" to find the authors of that precious production cultivating an unyielding reticence just as the opportunities for proving the truth of their charges and the validity and genuineness of their documentary evidence present themselves. We expect our Unionist friends will read with some apprehension the backing down performance of the counsel for the *Times*. If there was one thing which the *Times* vaunted, it was the specific character of the charges it made, and the convincing clearness with which they could be brought home to certain individual leaders of the Irish movement. This position is now vacated by the *Times*. It not only refuses to repeat its charges, but it declines to make any "charges and allegations" at all. But it does not end there. Mr. Graham, the *Times*' counsel, substantially averred in Court yesterday that any charges and allegations that he had made were preferred, not by the *Times*, but by the Attorney-General! We cannot refrain from quoting this portion of the sitting. It is altogether so unlike anything the public can have anticipated that we prefer to repeat here the *ipsissima verba* of the conversation between Sir James Hannen and Mr. Graham:–
>
> SIR J HANNEN – But the act deals with "charges and allegations." Do you propose to substantiate any charges and allegations?
>
> MR. GRAHAM – I do not know, my lord. I propose to lay before you all the information that we have in regard to the charges and allegations.
>
> SIR J HANNEN – Which charges and allegations?
>
> MR. GRAHAM – I cannot tell, I am not in a position to say. We will lay before your lordship such evidence as we can.
>
> SIR J HANNEN – The question is what you do know at present, and who

are the particular persons against whom the charges and allegations are made.

MR. GRAHAM – We don't charge particular persons; we make charges against organisations.

SIR J HANNEN – Who are implicated in the "things charged and alleged?"

MR. GRAHAM – I respectfully submit that that is what your lordships are to find out.

SIR J HANNEN – Then you decline to say against what persons you make the allegations, and what the allegations are?

MR. GRAHAM – Yes.

SIR J HANNEN – Who, then, did make these charges and allegations? Did anybody make them?

Mr Graham said the Attorney-General had made certain charges and allegations against Mr. Parnell and others in the recent action. The charges and allegations, however, were principally against an organisation.

SIR J HANNEN – No, no; the charges are against particular persons, "members of Parliament and others."

The President then directed counsel for the *Times* to draw up a list of the charges made, a suggestion to which the counsel strongly demurred. For the present we must leave this striking incident of yesterday's sitting to the opinion of the public. We withhold our comment both as to the effect which such an attitude on the part of the *Times'* counsel must have upon the entire case from the outset, and as to the extremely peculiar position in which it places the Attorney-General and the Government in relation to the charges.

The decision of the preliminary hearing was that the Commission would operate as any court of law, with the *Times* acting as prosecutors, the Parnellites as the defence. The *Times* were ordered to cite specific charges and allegations, and to list specifically the persons against whom those charges and allegations would be brought. They would then be charged with proving their case. During the hearing Mr Graham set forth his understanding of the purport of the "Parnellism and Crime" articles, and thus the basis of what those charges would be. This quote is from *Freeman's Journal*, September 18th:

Broadly speaking the allegations in these articles are this: that what is known as the Parnellite party formed an association in Ireland which was known as the Land League in 1879; that the association was formed for the purpose of dealing with the agrarian difficulty and with the question of Home Rule; that the party who formed the association have enforced the decrees of that association by means of a system of boycotting and outrages of various descriptions and also by murder, that the members of the League, while posing as a constitutional party, went about Ireland making inflammatory speeches in which persons who had made themselves offensive to the party were named; that those speeches were followed by crimes of violence of various descriptions, and that the parties committing those crimes were supported and recognised by this association; that eventually the Phoenix Park murders were committed; that those who mainly formed the executive of the League then fled to America; that while they have been in America they have boasted of their connection with those murders; that they have boasted of their connection with extreme parties who were known as the Invincibles; and that they have collected large sums both for the benefit of the families of those who were convicted of murder and for the purpose of defending the persons who were alleged to have committed those various crimes; that the members of the Parnellite Party have continued, notwithstanding what they knew of the avowed conduct of these men, to act with them, to receive money from them from America, and that very large sums of money amounting to some millions of dollars were from time to time applied as to part of them, for the very purpose of paying people who were committing crimes.

Enumerating the "charges and allegations" was the last thing that the *Times* or the Government, both of whom had hoped for as wide a remit as possible from the inquiry, wanted. Even the staunchest of Unionist newspapers were unable to make any kind of political capital. The *Dublin Evening Mail* could do nothing but admit that they had lost the first battle, and point out that the war was yet to be decided:

> Yesterday's preliminary proceedings have been followed by the public with much interest, and it is satisfactory to note that our Parnellite contemporaries are quite delighted with the way in which the Judges have, so far, comported themselves. This, of course, will not save them from being most emphatically cursed by the same journals, should it happen, any day, that the scales turn in favour of the *Times*. Yesterday, the opening day, Mr. PARNELL's star was, according to the *Freeman*, in the ascendent, and on that account the Judges are fine fellows, without even the exception of Mr. Justice DAY…. But we fear that before the inquiry is over the *Freeman* may be tempted to modify if not reverse this satisfactory opinion, when the results of the investigation are not such as the *Freeman* and its friends would like.

As referred to earlier in the chapter, another result of the preliminary hearing was the issuing of an order by Mr Justice Hannen that John Dillon should be released from prison to hear the charges against him and respond to them. The ruling was that he would be released on a £1,000 surety that he would take part in no other proceedings than the Commission. However, the very day after this order was given, events took a different turn, as explained by the *Freeman's Journal* on September 19th:

> The release of Mr. John Dillon from Dundalk Jail yesterday morning will come with a pleasant surprise upon the country. He has been liberated unconditionally upon the warrant of the Lord Lieutenant. This, it is scarcely necessary to say, has nothing to do with that order for Mr Dillon's release which the President of the Forgeries Commission intimated his intention of granting a month hence. Mr. Dillon is now at liberty to go where and do what he likes, unfettered by the restrictions which Sir James Hannen intended to make conditional to the order for his liberation. We wish we could add that Mr Dillon comes out of prison with the strength to avail himself to the full of his freedom. But it requires no words of ours to make it clear why he has been released three months before his time. As Mr. O'Brien said a short time ago, Dundalk Jail presented the pleasing spectacle, illustrative of the Coercion Act, of Mr. Balfour's doctors keeping their fingers on Mr. Dillon's pulse to see "how much more he could stand." We assume the Executive has exercised its "merciful discretion" only when it felt it no longer safe to withhold it. We deeply regret to learn that his appearance only too vividly betrays how severely his three months' imprisonment has told upon his nearly shattered frame. While his presence and voice are invaluable to the public life of Ireland, we are sure it is the wish of his countrymen that he should husband his great resources, and that he should benefit by some recruiting rest before resuming his place in political affairs. One thing must afford Mr. Dillon no small satisfaction. As Mr. Parnell's message of congratulation says, his "triumph over the brutalities of his imprisonment is a great victory for Ireland, and a signal discomfiture to Balfour's Coercion." No single act of Mr. Balfour's system produced so powerful an effect upon the minds of the people of the Three Kingdoms as Mr. Dillon's sentence. Its very savagery was its strongest condemnation. He was sentenced to six months imprisonment for recommending to tenants on the Massareene estate in Louth not to pay exorbitant rents. This is no offence. It is not an offence in England, and, as was pointed out at the time, even under the Coercion Act it was declared by the Exchequer in the Killeagh case not to be an offence. So that Mr. Dillon was not only the victim of a brutal exercise of power by a brace of Removables and a partisan Judge of the County Court, but he was the victim of an illegal sentence. It

was so felt at the time. The public will not forget that on the very threshold of the prison Mr. Dillon was presented with an address of sympathy from a hundred and fifty English, Welsh, and Scotch members of Parliament; and leaders and people alike have made the welkin ring across the Channel ever since Mr. County Court Judge Kisbey confirmed the sentence of the Removables. It was an effort to break the spirit of Mr. Dillon. How far Mr. Balfour has succeeded in that we may leave to the public to gather from the few stirring words which Mr. Dillon addressed to the people who gathered at his residence last night to give him a ringing welcome home. Mr. Dillon may be injured in health. Mr. Balfour and the Executive are entitled to the full benefit of their gain there. But can they count another scalp upon their girdle? How far has the movement for which Mr. Dillon was imprisoned been got under during the three months he was in Dundalk Jail? May we not refer to Lord Massareene for an answer? He will tell how much rent he has got, or rather how much he has not got, from his tenants. And has not the spirit of the people of Louth been inflamed and their organisation strengthened and consolidated by the attempt to bring Mr. Dillon to earth? So far, therefore, it is easy to understand who has benefited from Mr. Dillon's imprisonment. It is as he said himself last night. Every prisoner under the Coercion Act marks an advance of one step forward for the National cause.

The *Times* eventually produced their specific charges on October 15th, a week before the Commission was due to open and at the very last hour before which they been ordered to do so, in which they charged a total of sixty-four members of Parliament.[5] The charges enumerated eight very generalised charges and six further more specific ones, the last of which were with respect to the forged letters which they still stood behind.

That the Nationalist press of Ireland stood solidly behind Parnell need hardly be said, and is nowhere better demonstrated than in this short item which appeared in the *Eagle and County Cork Advertiser* of October 27th under the title "May God Defend the Right."

Comment on the PARNELL COMMISSION while the Judges are sitting and the investigation is proceeding would be not only unseemly but highly reprehensible, in fact almost criminal in the eye of the law. We are, however, not travelling outside the rights of journalism in saying that history does not furnish a parallel to the case now being tried before three English legal functionaries, whose abilities and high sense of justice cannot for a moment be questioned; nor, indeed, are they, even by those who stand charged by the *Times* with being the aiders and abetters to the foulest crimes that could possibly stain a criminal calendar. We can only here express our firm conviction that the Irish Party will come scatheless out of this fearful battle, this terrible ordeal; will, like burnished gold, come forth clearer, brighter, and certainly more endeared than ever to their fellow-countrymen, even those who may differ with them in politics. This week we devote the greater portion of our space to the proceedings taking place in London, and in order that our readers may be kept well posted on this important trial, we have decided on letting loose the MONSTER "EAGLE" next week, and during the sitting of the Commission. This huge bird will be able to carry on its expanded wings a full, almost verbatim report each week of a trial that will be watched not only with great interest, but intense anxiety, by Irishmen of every class; by Irishmen of every creed; nay, eagerly watched, it may be said, by the civilised world; in a word, the report will be anxiously read wherever the million-tongued Press can reach to tell the tale; for on the result of this important enquiry depends the future of our brave people, the fate of our unfortunate country, once the seat of learning, once the envy, and once the pride of other nations. Alas! it is a trying time for dear old Erin. Oft and earnestly, then, in this sad hour of trouble, will go forth from the lips of her devoted sons and daughters, wherever scattered, the fervent and heart-felt prayer –

GOD SAVE IRELAND!

CHAPTER NINE ENDNOTES

1   On the night of the Double Event a man named John Brown murdered his wife Sarah by cutting her throat in Regent Gardens, Westminster. Having committed the deed Brown proceeded immediately to the Rochester Row Police Station and gave himself up.

2   My italics.

3   Having read the pamphlet it has to be said that it signally failed in its purpose, its somewhat weak conclusion being that as a little less than twice as many of the population of Ireland supported Home Rule as supported Unionism, this wasn't the "overwhelming majority" that Parnell claimed.

4   This is something of a specious argument. It ignores the fact that most of the independent wealth in Ireland, and particularly in Dublin, was in the hands of the Protestant population. It also suggests that only Roman Catholic members of the population supported Home Rule. In fact the National League had a sizeable Protestant representation. Parnell was, himself, a Protestant.

5   Full details of the charges are specified in Appendix Five.

CHAPTER TEN

Bloodhounds, Policemen and Politicians

THE DETAILS OF THE RIPPER investigation during September, while not entirely known due to the incompleteness of the files, are at least fairly well defined through the regular and detailed reports issued by Chief Inspector Donald Swanson to Sir Charles Warren. After the night of the double event Dr Robert Anderson was urgently recalled from his sick leave and took personal control of the investigation, and possibly as a result of this change in the chain of command the files from this time on are less comprehensive.

Although the Home Secretary may have continued to resist the public pressure to offer a reward for the capture of the killer, not all public suggestions met with such disapproval, and one of the most high-profile ideas taken up was the proposal for the use of bloodhounds.

Suggestions that these dogs should be used for the tracking of the criminal had appeared on a regular basis since the beginning of September, and it was not long after the double event that these resurfaced. The *Longford Journal* of October 6th stated:

> The suggestion that a bloodhound should be employed to track out the Whitechapel murderer is, of course, rather revolting to those who consider the immense reliance that we should thus be placing upon the mere instinct of a dog. But the same method was tried with success at Blackburn twelve years ago; and it is probable that the scent of a bloodhound is, at any rate, as keen and as discriminating as that of an average English detective.[1]

The same day's *Kilkenny Moderator* considered the idea at some length:

> We have seen a suggestion in the newspapers that bloodhounds should

be set on the traces of the Whitechapel Thug. Well, but have we got the bloodhounds ready; or are we to import them from Cuba, or from wherever in the Southern States of America the breed still lingers? The trail, we fancy, will be weak when they arrive. Moreover, a bloodhound which has been wont to follow fugitives through swamp and jungle may well be "at fault" in a city, and when the trail has been crossed and re-crossed at a hundred points. If we mistake not some such wild move in the matter of bloodhounds as the newspapers suggest was made in England some time since, with the result that the bloodhound dragged down and nearly killed an old gentleman returning from a club of the first rank – which was awkward. Without attaching very much importance to the suggestion, it would seem to us that the services of dogs, not necessarily bloodhounds – the very name of which is alarming and disagreeable – might be utilised for the detection of crime. The dog has what the policeman has not – viz., a nose. A dog can find out his lost master by the smell, which shows that the smell of his master is as peculiar to the master as his own personality, and therefore that every man emits an odour, imperceptible to most animals but very perceptible to a dog. That being so, there seems to be no *a priori* reason why a trained dog should not be able to follow the track of an individual through streets, and no matter how it may be crossed and re-crossed by other tracks. The dog, in his own miraculous nose, possesses that strange faculty, and a man having leisure and a taste that way ought to be able to develop it and turn it to account. So far as one can judge, it is all a matter of time and patience, and perhaps of breeding. With short excursions and exercises, growing each day more difficult, with rewards and punishments and the other methods known to dog-trainers, we see no reason why a well-selected and patiently trained dog ought not to be able to follow the tracks of a certain man's feet when put fresh upon the scent. Of course we only throw out this as a suggestion, not affecting any unusual knowledge upon the subject, but at the same time surprised that no serious attempt seems to have been made by detectives to train dogs for this purpose. So, by degrees, a certain breed of animals would be specialized, marked in high degree with the necessary qualifications. The root of the whole matter, of course, lies in the before-mentioned fact – that "the friend of man" has what man has not; that the dog has got a nose, and the policeman has none. Save his smell, a clever criminal will take very good care not to leave behind him any clue or trace; and we fancy the resources of civilization have not yet discovered anything which will enable a criminal to do away with his peculiar odour, save by the employment of something whose smell is still more unique and powerful.

Not all the newspapers commented so positively on the theory. The *Dublin Evening Mail* of October 8th was rather less complimentary in its opinion:

> The statement that Sir Charles Warren has decided upon the employment of bloodhounds with a view to track the murderer, has been published far and wide without calling forth any official contradiction. Yet it is almost incredible that the report is authentic. Sir Charles Warren must surely know that bloodhounds are of practically no use except when they are well trained – and where can well-trained animals be obtained now? And Sir Charles must also be aware that the most perfectly trained bloodhound is almost invariably a failure if he be not set on an "unfoiled scent." In the streets of London, no matter what hour of the night, the scent would of necessity be lost in less than five minutes after a murder was committed. Such, at all events, is the deliberately expressed opinion of all whose knowledge of bloodhounds and their capabilities entitles them to be regarded as experts. The bloodhound theory is consequently now voted absurd.

The Irish Times comment of the same day speaks for itself:

> As for Sir Charles Warren's notion of employing bloodhounds in case of another murder, while we challenge the judgement and sagacity of the Chief Commissioner, we refuse to believe him actually possessed by so preposterous an idea. Fancy the possibility of preserving the trail in London. The mere suggestion reduces the alleged intention to the dimensions of rank absurdity.

Sir Charles had indeed been in contact with an expert bloodhound breeder by the name of Edwin Brough, and had arranged from him the loan of two of his champion dogs, Barnaby and Burgho, for use by the Metropolitan Police. The dogs were stabled with a veterinary surgeon named Alfred Joseph Sewell of Eaton Square, and instructions were sent out to the police that in the event of any further discoveries Mr Sewell was to be telegraphed at once to bring the dogs with all urgency. It was a situation on which the press both in England and Ireland showed a great deal of fascination, and not a little criticism, and kept close tabs. The *Cork Examiner* of October 10th had this comment to make:

> The theory of using bloodhounds to track the Whitechapel murderer has called forth many letters to the papers of considerable interest. We are all accustomed to hear since childhood of the terrible accuracy with which these brutes hunt down their prey, but the circumstances are all different,

and we fear they will prove no better than the detectives. Where they were used to track men up to this was in dense wildernesses, but they are expected to follow their victims through the heart of London now, and that without previous training. One might as well go shooting with an unbroken setter or try to rescue a person lost in the snow with one of the St Bernard dogs that were exhibited at the last dog show. The suggestion, however, will have, we believe, an important effect. It will do more to prevent a recurrence of these outrages than would an addition of a thousand men to the police force, and probably we have heard of the last murder in Whitechapel, for the coward, even though a maniac, knows how to take care of his skin, and will be slow to tempt this new and wholly unexpected danger. So the "friend of man" has still his use.

In truth, this was one of the more complimentary comments on the idea. Reaction from most sections of the press was not good, and kept coming back to that same fact, that by the time the hounds could be laid on a trail in Whitechapel it would have been crossed so many times that the dogs would have almost no chance of following it. Trials were held in Hyde Park with Warren himself acting as the fugitive in at least one run, and although they were reported relatively successful, the point was mentioned several times that an empty park in the early morning, and the busy streets of one of the most overcrowded areas of the metropolis were two very different propositions.

On October 19th a report was circulated widely and carried by all the Irish dailies that the dogs had bolted while being exercised on Tooting Common and were now lost. The story was not true, in fact Burgho was in training in Hemel Hemstead at the time while Barnaby had been withdrawn by Mr Brough in order to be shown in Brighton, but the report was never retracted and the general opinion was that the experiment had ended in farce. This was not far from the truth, as shortly afterwards they were withdrawn after Brough objected to their being used to try to track a burglar, fearing that the dogs might be set upon by the East End criminal fraternity and badly injured or killed.

On October 10th, *The People* published an article under the headline of "BLOODHOUNDS" which used the experiment as a metaphor for the English attitudes to Ireland:

> What a contrast between bloodhound-hunting in England and Ireland! In London, as a last resort, bloodhounds are employed for detective purposes against the wanton, ruthless, diabolical murderer who rips up his victims for gratification of a morbid craving for blood and horror. In Ireland the detective is employed as a bloodhound to hunt down the honour, the honesty, the virtue of our country – the pure souled peasant and his noble pro-

tector, the *Soggarth* – every man who strives for right, justice, or humanity is certain to have the bloodhounds upon his trail. What is the meaning of the grand ceremony in the graveyard of Kilninor – the unveiling of the monument to poor, murdered Kinsella, of Coolgreany, on Sunday, where priests and people, members of Parliament, and the *elite* of the patriotism of Wexford and Wicklow assembled to honour the memory of a murdered man? How do you read the meaning of the scene? The bloodhound! The bloodhound let loose against, not the murderer, but against the poor victims of landlord plunder and tyranny! What agency was resorted to in order to hunt down, and hunt out of the county, ten honest virtuous families in Coolroe? Bloodhounds!! What means have been adopted to hunt out thousands of equally honest and virtuous families from every part of this county? Bloodhounds! – ay of deadlier, more dogged, more fierce determination than the poor brutes employed against the perpetrators of the most ghastly and bloodcurdling crimes in London!! And this represents the perfect similarity of law and its administration which we experience in England and Ireland, and the perfect equality with which her Majesty's subjects are treated in the sister countries!!! What a mockery, what a scandal to every human feeling – to every Divine precept! What a blind, devilish confounding of morality, Christianity, and foulest barbarity and heathenism!!! There is just another contrast between the manner in which public opinion is exercised upon crimes committed in Ireland and in England. If a murder happens to be committed in Ireland, the ready assumption of the English Press is, that the whole population are in sympathy with the perpetrator of the crime, otherwise they say he would be delivered up to justice. Not infrequently has the horrid and inhuman threat been made of clearing a whole countryside because some unknown murderer has escaped detection. But what happens in London – "the heart of civilization and the centre of Christianity"? The gory-handed murderer stalks abroad, undetected by all the most refined and systematic agencies of police surveillance of which the world can boast, and no threat is held out of clearing out the filthy depravity of the most debased city slums, the thieves' homes, the murderers' dens, well known to police and public. And here lies the admission, and reward of sympathy with crime. A bribe is offered to overcome the reluctant scruples of the wretches who decline otherwise to peach upon their pals, and thus induce them to assert the high-toned civilization and exalted Christianity of the Capital of Christian England. It might seem ludicrous to institute one other contrast between the test which is applied to the sense of humanity of public men in the two countries. If an old cow's tail is cut off in Kerry, a pious howl is raised because the leaders of the people do not come forward and dissociate themselves from the odious barbarity, but murder follows murder in England, like horrors in a dream, and no public man is expected to stand on a platform and declare himself free from sympathy with or participation in the crime. Well, who but a drivelling dotard would expect it? And yet we find the cream of English journalism enforcing this ridiculous test upon our public men here. What a hollow mockery. What a hideous farce!!

Barnaby and Burgho were not the only dogs to make news that month, and it was no commendation to the police when this subsequent canine made the headlines. This report from the *Ballina Journal* of October 22nd will elucidate:

There is a strange want of keenness on the part of the London police in searching out the murderer, or murderers, concerned in the recent atrocities. Eight or nine feet from the spot where the headless and limbless body of a woman was found a fortnight ago, in one of the vaults of the new police buildings, there has been lying one of the legs also, and they did not make the least exertion to find it as they might have done by an examination of the place. It occurred to a Mr Jasper Waring that a search ought to be made, and he got permission from them to employ a dog to examine the vault. The dog very quickly found the leg in a little mound of earth in the vault, which mound of earth was caused by the excavation of a drain or trench eight or ten weeks ago. The leg must have been lying there at least as long as the body, for it could not have been deposited since that was discovered without the knowledge of the police, who have been in continuous watch of the place ever since.

The discovery was made on October 17th, and the following day the London Correspondent of the *Dublin Evening Mail* pulled off a scoop. An interview with the dog himself!

Later in the day I had an opportunity of seeing the dog and questioning its owner. The animal is nine or ten years old and is as sharp as a needle. He will sit up, beg, and perform a number of tricks at the word of command, and what is more, he is essentially a loyal and patriotic dog. At the mention of the words "the Queen" he perches himself on his hind legs, sets his ears up quite waggishly, and gives three sharp, ringing barks. On the other hand, the mention of the word "Gladstone" excites his wrath to such an extent that he flies at the individual who has had the temerity to utter it. This is a fact. I witnessed the powers of the sagacious animal this afternoon. The first experiment amused me vastly; the second was far less diverting.

Throughout October the parade of individuals arrested "on suspicion" and released a few hours later continued unabated, leaving the public with little hope of an actual apprehension and less and less confidence in the detective abilities of the London police. In the Irish Nationalist press not only the police but the whole of English society was held up for condemnation. The *Munster News* of October 3rd commented:

> One thing that strikes the readers of the details of those fiendish brutalities most forcibly is that when the descriptions of the districts or structures where the crimes were perpetrated are read over, they are found to be filthy and squalid near noble edifices, but badly inhabited by foreign races, no more observant of Sunday worship than Mahomadens or Hindoos. They carry on a sort of small miscellaneous traffic, fight dogs, and violate Sunday in every possible form. They contribute some of the revenue paid to the revenue by the Corporation, and would have a right to improvements by which light and air and health and sanitation could be introduced to the kennels near the palatial piles that belong to London. It is through a dark and gloomy lane and dirty square that a clubhouse of foreigners is approached in the city, and one of the mangled bodies was lying regurgitating its life stream before it was perceived. If in place of guzzling and swilling the London Corporation had laid out the funds drawn from the poorest of the population, and opened up the vile courts and closes, it would not be possible that the maniac could waylay the victims in the reckless and daring manner in which the wretches had slaughtered the six. Of course there is no telling whether the lunatic, if he be one, may not consider he is doing the British metropolis a series of important services, inasmuch as he is ridding it of the instrumentality of vice in which it abounds, but this is apparent, that if the fiend had not found his opportunity in obscure and narrow passages, no terrible crime would have been enacted under the banner of Whitechapel. As it is, a most lamentable lack of sagacity is wanting on the part of the police. The body comprehends about 12,000, about as many as the force for all Ireland, and out of that host, despite its familiarity with the retreats of the weasels, sneaks and serpents of society, not an officer has been able to capture one of the venomous and poisonous set, covered in the holes hollowed and concealed by crime. Jobbery and corruption are common practices of the London Corporation. They bestow "freedoms" in gold boxes, and vote statues and such like to heroes who are shot in the back, because they are pious. They are misspending heavy sums, by which they could make sunshine gleam where gloom reigns day and night, and cruel murder is paramount. When BONAPARTE straightened the Boulevards, revolution was

arrested. When mail roads were made, the Queen's write would run, and civilisation hold its own in the kingdom of Kerry. If the Tories did in the modern Babylon what the BONAPARTISTS did in Paris, and British ministers did a little of what the Board of Works did in Kerry, caitiffes and cutthroats could not work their will amid crowded thoroughfares, nor assassins work their dreadful wickedness upon wretched womankind.

Comparison with crime in Ireland continued to be a common theme, used to good effect again and again in editorials which sought to propound Nationalist principles, or simply to drive another sharp rebuke home to the "mother nation." The *Ballina Journal* of October 8th carried this leader column:

"The cry is, 'still they come'." London is in a state of panic. Murder succeeds murder, and if there are degrees of horror which this fearful and unnatural crime excite, the murders at the East End have reached the highest pitch. In comparison with them the crimes of a homicidal character in the present age are trifling; such murderers as Mr. Palmer of Rugby, the turf speculator, Wainright, Peace, Muller and fiends of that ilk pale into insignificance when gauged by the standard of "Jack the Ripper;" and although Whitechapel and other parts of London are nightly patrolled by an augmented force of police and amateur detectives, their efforts so far have been fruitless. The murderer is still at large. We say murderer; perhaps we should have pluralised the noun; but, the popular theory is that there is but one hand engaged in this diabolical work. When the "murder is out," as it surely must finally come to light, and we trust speedily, we shall then, and only then know, whether there was one or more engaged in this amateur work of the devil. Not in the annals of crime in these realms have London murders been surpassed either in their atrocity and barbarity, or in the awfully mysterious manner in which they have up to the present been effected. Our country has of recent years incurred the odium of all peace-abiding men on account of its agrarian crimes, moonlighting and the rest. The shooting of an odd landlord who has demanded impossible rents, however, does not strike the people with much horror. When a family in the depth of misery and want – a family of father & mother with their helpless starving children are thrown out on the roadside like rubbish from the dust bin, to live or die as they may, it is not very unnatural that feelings of rancour and vengeance against their cruel oppressor should uprise in their breasts. When the hearts of the myrmidons of the law are so moved in compassion for those whom they have been deputed to persecute, as to subscribe a sum for their immediate relief, no one will deny that there is oppression stalking abroad. A charitable and humane D.I., who, in charge of a number of constabulary deputed to carry out the eviction of a feeble old man of 80 years, drove off to the nearest union to have him conveyed away in an ambulance before he expired did a noble act. The *lex talions* is provoked by scenes of this nature; but the Whitechapel and East End tragedies appear to be attributable to no such cause – they are simply an unfathomable mystery, and baffle all the ingenuity of Sir C. Warren, C.B.

The Irish Times continued to be at the forefront of those most critical of the London police force. On October 5th they printed yet another rebuke in their editorial:

Those who of late have given attention to the reports of proceedings in the police courts of London and its outlying districts must have noticed that there has been a remarkable recrudescence of crime. To mention but one instance, it appears that Clapham and its neighbourhood have been made the happy hunting ground of the burglar. When in any form crime is successful the result is surely that its enterprises are extended, and we now find that cases of robbery with violence are more frequent than at any previous period known in criminal records. All this represents a serious warning. If once it is supposed that the police are incapable, it follows as certainly as the night the day that the criminal classes, organised as now most perfectly they are, will take advantage of that ineptitude. There is, taking all circumstances into consideration, only too good reason to believe that the London Police Force, though highly experienced and trained, is insufficiently controlled and directed. It is provided for sufficiently in the national expenditure, and it is not the fault of the men that their duty is incapably rendered. No blame attaches to them as a body. They are brave and well instructed, skilled in their duty and sufficiently acquainted with their responsibilities. But it is very clear that the heads of the Department have failed to use the materials at their command to the best account in the interests of the public service. Their rank and file cannot be held to account while the leaders exhibit a lapse in their responsibility. There is under the command of the HOME SECRETARY and of the Commissioners of Police in London a vast and ably instructed force, most highly trained and experienced. If there occurs a failure to trace the designs of criminal impulse – as recently manifested – to their ultimate sources, the reproach will be perilous and permanent. We believe that sooner or later the criminals now being sought will be tracked to their lair, but in the meantime the public cannot cease to condemn the failure to seize them, nor can they avoid the conclusion that had the knowledge of the detective department been properly applied – with acuteness, with precision, and with timely prevision – some of the terrible tragedies that have shocked the sense of humanity might have been avoided. An awful lesson has been taught, and it remains to be seen whether its dismal teaching will be appreciated.

Meanwhile the *Belfast Morning News* of October 9th printed a lengthy letter from one of their readers on the subject:

SIR, – Not perhaps during the past century has anything taken place which has so horrified the people of England and Scotland, and I might say of the entire world, as the diabolical and cold blooded murders which have been committed in the east end of London during the past couple of months. Many reasons have been assigned for them, and many suggestions offered as to the way in which the murderer might be caught – female detectives, clairvoyance, gutta percha shoes, bloodhounds, and many other things have been suggested; but although the lives of seven unfortunate victims have been sacrificed yet up to the present time no active steps have been taken in the matter. No doubt numerous arrests have been made on suspicion, but in each and every instance the accused man was discharged. I observe that now at the eleventh hour Sir Charles Warren has decided to employ bloodhounds. This is a step which should have been taken after the second or third murder was committed, and I say that it is a shame and a scandal to think that it is only when seven human beings have been murdered and seven unfortunate victims hurried unprepared and without a moment's warning to face their Creator, that Sir Charles thinks of doing anything in earnest. It has often been remarked in the papers that the police have obtained certain information, but they are very reticent as to the nature of it. Now, sir, in my humble opinion, had they been a little more reticent than they have been, in all probability the murderer would have been caught before he had carried his bloody and inhuman butcheries so far. The fact of publishing in the newspapers the various suggestions offered as to how he could be captured, has, in my opinion, only tended to enable him to avoid detection, and to laugh at the success and impunity with which he can carry on his work and evade capture. Persons desirous of offering suggestions to the authorities should have done so privately by letter, and these suggestions should not have been made public. The letters and post cards received from "Jack the Ripper" in a great measure confirm my opinion. He reads the various suggestions offered as to the mode of capture, and of course can then guard against each and every one of them. Had Sir Charles only

been half as energetic as he was to suppress the meeting in Trafalgar square some time back, I think his efforts would have been crowned with success long ago. If only one of these brutal murders had been committed in the South or West of Ireland the criminal would have been caught before twenty-four hours. It is, therefore, high time I think for Sir Charles to do something in the matter. I am afraid the adoption of bloodhounds is rather late now to trace the assassin, as another murder must be committed before they could be of any use, and then as likely as not some innocent person would be laid hold of. Sir Charles says though not in words, "at present I can do nothing. I am powerless and wholly unable to trace the murderer, but if another life is taken I will try what the bloodhounds can do." This is the only means can be taken from his resolve to employ bloodhounds now when they are no use. Now, sir, what I would respectfully say is that any person who can offer a feasible suggestion for the detection of the murderer should communicate same to the authorities, and that such suggestion should be kept strictly private and not circulated through the columns of the Press, and further, that the authorities should try every possible means that they can, but that they let it not be known what they intend doing, what they have done, or the result of any action they may have taken. In this way the inhuman monster would not know what to guard against, and consequently would be more readily captured. Trusting you will kindly pardon me for thus trespassing, and excuse my lengthy letter and also that "Jack the Ripper" or whoever the murderer may be will be caught before he has the satisfaction (to him) of taking another life. – I remain, yours, &c,
FRANCIS P HUGHES
8 Garnet street,
Belfast, 6th Oct, '88.

The London Correspondent of the *Dublin Evening Mail* on October 19th obtained the opinion of another policeman working on the case:

I was speaking this evening with a member of the police force who is in anything but a subordinate position, and this is what he said – "We are somewhat nonplussed, we confess. Still, we believe we shall catch the murderer ere long. There is far more to contend with than the great bulk of the outside public think of, or at all appreciate. It should be remembered that there was no apparent motive for the crime, and that – what is all important – the victims, besides being apparently strangers to their assassin, deliberately led him into their own trap. As to any further murders being committed, that is a matter of opinion; but for my own part, I think another will at least be attempted. With what success can only be conjectured. One thing is very certain – the police authorities in the East End will not relax their exceptional precautions for a very long time to come."

Criticism of the police was hitting home, however, and as this item from the *Belfast News-Letter* of October 20th indicates, Sir Charles Warren was preparing to hit back at his critics. It would be an action which would have far-reaching consequences:

Very seldom, indeed, has the London Press made such a combined attack upon any public man as it has recently directed against Sir Charles Warren, the Chief Commissioner of the Metropolitan Police. Sir Charles considers that he is a badly-used individual. He has had, it is true, an extraordinary series of startling crimes to deal with of late, and up to the present he has not shown that he possesses any of the instinctive genius of a Fouché. The force over which he presides is not remarkable for the affection in which it regards him. For this and other reasons Sir Charles Warren has written a vindication, which is to appear in the forthcoming number of *Murray's Magazine.*

On Monday, October 8th the *Freeman's Journal* reported on a thankfully murder-free weekend, and also noted another curious occurrence:

Saturday the 6th October, will be marked with a red letter in these times of grace, as it has providentially passed over without a diabolical murder or two having been committed in East London. That is as much as can be hoped for nowadays, when we have to be thankful for the smallest of small mercies. In our wildest moments we never now entertain the hope that the police will find the man or men responsible for the horrors of the last two months. If by due precautions their recurrence can be obviated then there will be ground for congratulation. But here again it is to be feared that the people of Whitechapel are depending on a broken road. A vigilance committee of local residents has been formed for the protection of life in the district on which the deeds of the Whitechapel monster has riveted the eyes of the world. But it would appear from the story of the president of this committee that a man who from his general description and manner might well have been the author of all the atrocities was in his house, and in conversation with him for a quarter of an hour, after which he was permitted to depart in peace. Indeed, if the story as recorded means anything, it means that Mr. Lusk's visitor was animated by the ambition to add the President of the Vigilance Association to the list of his victims. This would have been a daring stroke of humour, and, if carried out, it would have shown that the murderer has no object in view beyond that of creating a sensation.

Whether he had sought to become one or not, it was a fact that George Lusk was now a well-known character in the drama being played out on the streets of Whitechapel. The mysterious stranger with whom he had conversed had in fact come to his house but, not finding him there, had been redirected to a tavern owned by Lusk's son, where the pair had a conversation while the man acted in what Lusk considered to be a suspicious manner and tried to induce him into a private room. Lusk became convinced during the month that he was being tailed by a sinister bearded man who was watching his house, and he asked for police protection. On October 16th he became more involved in the case than he could ever have wished, on the arrival through his door of a small parcel. On opening the parcel he found it to contain a fleshy substance, and accompanying it was a letter:

> *From hell*
> *Mr Lusk*
> *Sor I send you half the kidne I took from one woman prasarved it for you tother piece I fried and ate it was very nise. I may send you the bloody knif that took it out if you only wate a whil longer.*
> *Signed Catch Me when you Can*
> *Mishter Lusk*

Lusk asked the opinion of the Vigilance Committee who suggested it should be seen by a medical expert. So saying they took it to Dr Thomas Openshaw, the pathological curator of the London Hospital Museum, who examined it and pronounced it to be a left kidney and human, preserved in spirits of wine. He was reported to have further stated the opinion that it was taken from a woman of about forty-five years of age who had drunk heavily, and that it had been taken from the body within the previous three weeks.[2] The letter and kidney were handed over to the police who had it independently examined. The *Dublin Evening Mail* commented on October 20th:

> The mysterious parcel sent to Mr. Lusk, the Chairman of the Whitechapel Vigilance Committee, is not regarded seriously either by the police or by the bulk of the medical men who have been asked to express an opinion regarding it. The general impression is that it is the work either of a butcher or a stupidly "larkish" medical student. There is a conflict of opinion as to whether the kidney is even a human one, some

of the medical men believing that it may have belonged to a pig.

Whatever the true explanation of the sending of the extraordinary package, the receipt of it has quite unnerved Mr. Lusk. He has altered altogether in manner since the parcel came into his hands, and apparently his firm conviction is that the organ sent to him is that of the woman so foully mutilated in Mitre Square. Arguments have been used to try to persuade him differently, but apparently with no effect. He has quite made up his mind that the half kidney sent to him through the post, is portion of the left missing organ of the woman Eddowes.

In fact the first part of this statement is not true. A report from Chief Inspector Swanson in the police files show that their own experts confirmed the kidney to be human, and the matter was certainly taken seriously, but the indistinctness of the post mark on the parcel made it impossible to trace. Most Ripper experts today agree that if any of the supposed communications from the killer is genuine, it is this one.

The publication of the original "Jack the Ripper" letter had by now led to a positive epidemic of letter writing, and a flood of letters were delivered to police, public servants, and newspapers every day, most of them beginning with the by now familiar "Dear Boss" and signed "Jack the Ripper."[3] The *Dublin Evening Mail* commented on November 23rd:

> The extent to which threatening letters are being written, under the influence of the present atrocities scare, can scarcely be appreciated by the general public. I hear on very good authority, that some scores of "Jack the Ripper" letters are being received almost daily by coroners, magistrates and officials connected with the higher branches of the police force. These missives are all very carefully scrutinised and filed, but, of course, no importance is attached to them except as illustrating the extraordinary effect produced on morbid minds by a sensation like that recently associated with the East End. It is, I am told, in a large measure owing to the letter-writing epidemic, that the authorities decided to prohibit the exposure in shop windows of anatomical models and drawings.

Of course nobody with a modicum of sense could possibly have ever believed all of the letters to have been sent by the killer himself, and the police quickly relegated their importance to one of minor annoyance, but they were variously reported as making good copy for the newspapers. Albeit there is some fun to be had in studying their ever more ludicrous contents[4] there was a darker side as expressed by the *Belfast News-Letter* on October 25th:

The person who considered it an excellent joke of a practical character to write and distribute letters under a name which he pretended was assumed by the Whitechapel assassin has suggested to several other equally silly individuals a system of jocularity which has already resulted in the actual death of one person. Up to the present, indeed, it would appear that the horrible name adopted by the original "humorist" had brought about two fatalities. Yesterday a coroner's inquest was held at Sheffield on the body of a woman who committed suicide out of sheer terror, which was the result of allowing her mind to dwell upon the revolting *sobriquet*;[5] and we learn now that a young lady in County Down, when out walking some time ago with a few friends, was accosted on the road by a ruffian who brandished a knife, proclaiming himself to be the assassin under the same hideous designation. So overcome was the young lady at the mention of the words that on returning to her home she was found to be in a state of high fever, to which she has just succumbed. It is to be hoped that the search by the police for the perpetrator of this last outrage will be successful and that the scoundrel will be made to answer to a proper tribunal for his crime. The impulse that causes persons presumably sane to impersonate "as a joke" the most unusual monster of the century is an extraordinary one.

Another annoying phenomenon for the police was the positive rash of drunken men confessing to the murders. When John Fitzgerald had confessed on September 26th he had been taken seriously by both police and press. By mid-October, however, so many confessions had been made that one can imagine each new confessee on application at the police station being met with little other than a roll of the eyes and a heavy sigh. A correspondent to *The Irish Times* commented on the subject on October 12th:

> SIR, – From time to time I have read in your journal of the manner in which the police authorities have and are being troubled and deceived by persons coming forward and making voluntary confessions that they are the persons guilty of these horrible butcheries.
>
> On investigation these self-accusations turn out either to be the ravings of a drunken person or a deliberate attempt to hoax the authorities, ending in the discharge of the self-incriminated.
>
> Is there no law, sir, to grapple with such persons and under which they could be committed to prison until their heads would cool, and thus give them ample time for recovering their judgement? A few lashes of the cat would be very effective in teaching such troublesomeness a lesson.
>
> The authorities, in my opinion, are liable to enough public odium in

their tracing of crime without having to undergo the perplexity and annoy-
ance entailed by the idle and groundless accusations which, especially in
connection with the above murders, they have been troubled with.
A READER
Cookstown, County Tyrone,
Oct. 10th, 1888.

In fact that newspaper had already commented on the phenomenon itself the
previous week in the October 6th edition, after the story had appeared of a man
named William Bull, claiming to be a student at the London Hospital who confessed themselves entirely ignorant of him, being sentenced to a period of
imprisonment for claiming to be the perpetrator of the Mitre Square murder:

> It is hoped that the four days' confinement undergone by the young man
> Bull, who, in a drunken freak, describing himself as a medical student, sur-
> rendered as the Whitechapel murderer, will have a deterrent effect on the
> notoriety-mongers who appear to think they are perpetrating a good joke
> by hoaxing the police. During the last day or two there have been several
> of these bogus confessions, consequently the police have been occupied in
> examining the truth of these reports, verifying the accounts given by the
> self-accused man of his identity, and ascertaining his whereabouts at the
> time of the murders, therefore considering a sharp punishment should be
> inflicted upon fellows who thus needlessly occupy the time of magistrates
> and add to the work of the police. At a time like the present it is absolute-
> ly necessary that every one of these confessions should be carefully exam-
> ined into, because there is no real clue as to the age, appearance, or posi-
> tion in life of the murderer. Indeed, scarcely a murder takes place in which
> the criminal's identity is not clearly defined without men coming forward
> to denounce themselves. Sometimes the self-denunciation is made by a
> drunken man, but it must none the less be inquired into, for although it
> may be only a tipsy freak it may also be a case in which liquor has unsealed
> the lips. In other cases it appears to be a craving for notoriety, while in a
> third it is the outcome of the feeling prevalent among a section of the
> lower class of satisfaction at bamboozling the police. For whatever the
> object, the offence should be a punishable one, and a good flogging would
> be the most suitable penalty and the best deterrent.

By late October the story had virtually dropped out of the papers, partly
because the attention of the entire country had now been diverted to the
Parnell Commission, but also I suspect because the public were tired of daily
reports which essentially said the same thing: "The murderer has not been

caught." The London Correspondents were mainly assigned to spend their days at Probate Court Number One in the Royal Courts of Justice where Sir Charles Russell, Parnell's chief counsel, was busily fighting for the honour of Ireland.

The London Correspondent of the *Dublin Evening Mail* continued to be the one Irish pressman whose fascination with the case led him to return to the subject again and again, and by following his columns we can get some idea of the mood in Whitechapel over the period. On Monday, October 15th he reported as follows:

> The scandal of the streets is assuming a new phase. The miserable class of depraved beings against whom the Whitechapel murderer has recently directed his murderous schemes have, under the influence of a great fear, flitted in a body from the East to the West End. In the streets along which roll the carriages of the great, and where vice when it struts abroad is ordinarily clothed in purple and fine linen, one now sees hundreds of ragged and wretched females, seemingly dazed by their strange surroundings, and unutterably miserable, lonely and bereft of hope. Around the doors of theatres and restaurants they hang in little groups, begging from the well-dressed crowds, whenever the policeman's eye is not upon them, and then in the small hours of the morning, shuffling off to the bridges and the Embankment to try and snatch a few hours sleep on the stone seats, and in exposed places where the wind whistles shrilly all night long.
>
> Some good at least has resulted from the changed conditions brought about by the East End scare. The wretched women to whom I have referred have been absolutely compelled to abandon their former miserable calling. They may suffer more privations for a time, but their sin is less. Moreover, the shopkeepers and others in the West End have taken up their cause in quite a hearty way. A number of meetings are being organised, and it is intended to hire thee or four unoccupied houses for the temporary shelter of the lonely wanderers. In the meantime, an appeal will be issued to the wealthy and philanthropic, and it is hoped that subscriptions will flow in at a rate that will admit of great good being done.
>
> During the whole of last night and this morning the police and amateur detectives paced the streets of Whitechapel with a feeling of apprehension not a whit less keen than that manifested a week ago. Every stranger met with in the by-ways and alleys was regarded half in the light of the supposed murderer, and as on some former occasions, some of the mistakes made in the way of policemen dogging the steps of other policemen, were extremely ludicrous. When the morning broke, and inquiries proved that no fresh tragedy had been brought to light, there was a great feeling of relief, for undoubtedly the feeling of terror with

which the recent murders have inspired the residents has scarcely, if at all, subsided. The weekly newspaper offices were, of course, equal to the occasion. Staffs of compositors were kept on duty the whole night through, and quite a small army of reporters were perambulating the East End streets and making inquiries at the various police stations until long after sunrise. Everyone agrees that there has never been a series of tragedies perpetrated in London that has for so long a time held possession of the nervous apprehensions of the great bulk of the population.

His column two weeks later on October 29th shows that, notwithstanding the lack of press interest, in the locality of the murders themselves there was still a considerable level of vigilance:

I strolled through Whitechapel again on Saturday night just to note the effect which the lapse of a few weeks' time might have had upon the recently terrorised population in that locality. There were not wanting signs that the panic which prevailed a month ago has to a large extent subsided, but, at the same time, it is remarkable how many individuals still voluntarily pace the streets at night on the look out for the much-dreaded murderer. The possibility of claiming either the whole or a portion of the reward offered for his arrest has acted as a wonderful stimulus to energy. Several men have walked the streets every night up to daybreak since the tragedies in Mitre-square and Berner-street were committed. Not a few have suffered in health in consequence, and many have neglected their work to such an extent as to bring down upon their heads a sharp reprimand from their employers. The wildest rumours have been afloat since Saturday night, respecting an alleged important clue obtained by the police, and the possibility of the immediate arrest of the murderer. The police, however, will say nothing on the subject. They are known to be watching night and day one or two suspected individuals, but the extent and importance of their knowledge can only be conjectured.

That Saturday, November 3rd, he reported again on preparations for the weekend:

The effect of the latest sensational reports from Whitechapel and South Kensington will, it is said, be forcibly manifested to-morrow night, for the supposition that another atrocious crime will be committed again on a Saturday night has taken such a firm hold of the people that now that fresh rumours of a suspected man and the discovery of blood-stained knives are abroad the popular imagination is excited to quite a painful

extent. The end of the week is looked forward to with feelings of undis-
guised dread. To-morrow night the "Vigilance Committee" intend to
turn out in full force, and the East End will bristle with the official police
presence. The discovery of knives at Kensington is not considered by the
authorities to have any connection with the East End horrors. The residents of the fashionable West End suburb are, however, greatly concerned about the matter, and, in obedience to their demands, a large
extra force of police has been drafted into the locality.

The prime event of interest at the end of the month was the promised magazine article from Sir Charles Warren, on which the *Belfast News-Letter* published
an exclusive on October 26th:

> Sir Charles Warren's defence of his administration of the metropolitan
> police has leaked out before its publication in magazine form. He shows
> that for years past the streets of London have been stirred up into spas-
> modic action by certain demagogues who affect and lead the mob. By
> their operation they had exercised undue influence on the Government
> of the day, and, consequently, the capital had become more prone to dan-
> gerous panics, which, if permitted to increase in intensity, must certainly
> lead to disastrous consequences. These are some of the kingly words
> which, we hear to-night, Sir Charles Warren uses in defence of his action.
> He is probably right in his estimate of the "let-it-slide" policy of past
> Governments; but the question most people will ask – was it the duty of
> Sir Charles to set all Governments right? I am afraid many people will
> come to the conclusion that he takes too high an estimate of his position.
> The leaders of the Opposition will be furious at this statement of fact. "It
> is still more to be regretted that ex-Ministers, while in Opposition, have
> not hesitated to embarrass those in power by smiling on the insurgent
> mob." Unlike the "Continental Press, the English Press ventures to dis-
> cuss the operations of detectives, and thereby hampers inquiries. He
> denies that he has "militarised" the force, and makes light of all the crit-
> icisms that have been passed upon his rule at Scotland Yard. He has put
> his back against the wall, and invites all his assailants to "come on." As a
> strategic move it is not without merit.

Meanwhile as October slipped into November, the population of London had
other things on their minds. The Whitechapel murders infiltrated the usual
November 5th celebrations in something of an unusual way, as described in the
Dublin Evening Mail the following day:

Guy Fawkes, could he revisit the English metropolis in the present year of grace, would probably be very disgusted by the evidences of his decline in popularity which are everywhere observable. What was only a few years ago a great annual *fete* among the juvenile population has sunk almost into the limbo of forgotten events. The Fifth of November this year has been the quietest that I ever remember to have seen. There have, of course, been a few effigies of the wicked Guy hawked about certain of the suburbs, and the playful youths of the East-end have done their best to impress the populace by christening their dummies "Jack the Ripper." The production of one of these effigies in a street near to the scene of the Berner-street outrage had such an effect upon the feelings of the residents that a bevy of muscular females fell upon it with great energy and tore the stuffed conspirator into shreds and patches. The nocturnal displays resulted in some accidents, but these were less numerous than in many previous years.

The main event of the week, however, would come on the Friday, with the Lord Mayor's Show, an annual procession through the streets of the city. The day traditionally held a festival or party atmosphere, although it was also seized upon by militants and Socialists, and this year was no different. Coming just one year after the Bloody Sunday riot, Sir Charles Warren was determined not to see a repetition of such public displays and took precautions. The *Belfast Morning News* reported on November 1st:

> I hear that Sir C Warren is much troubled about the suggested Socialistic-Radical march through Trafalgar square on Lord Mayor's Day. Preparations are being made to occupy good positions all through London with the military, who are to be ready in all suspicious and all possible places to "assist the police." The Socialists have been spying lately, and have observed military men taking careful notes in various parts of London, and those note takers have been particularly busy among the houses of the working classes.

The Socialists showed themselves to have a sense of humour, however, as the same newspaper noted on November 7th:

> A good deal of amusement has been caused in London by the appearance on several street hoardings of a proclamation announcing that "I, Charles Warren, would allow no other procession but that of Socialists on November 9th." A contingent of Socialists, armed with gummed slips, has followed close upon the official bill poster and inserted the name of their

own society over that of London's chief magistrate. The original read "no other procession but that of the Lord Mayor." After this practical joke, says a London contemporary, Sir Charles will be more convinced than ever of the dangerous and desperate character of the London "mob."

That Saturday, November 10th, the London Correspondent of the *Meath Herald* provided readers of that journal with an idea of the mood in London on the previous weekend:

> The publication of letters signed "Jack the Ripper" is to be much deplored, but they do answer the purpose of keeping the alarm alive. The panic was so great at the time that a reaction was setting in unusually soon, and the East-end Vigilance Committee is about to be dissolved. The general impression is that the murderer has got clear away. The fogs of the last week have revived the fears of the poor East-end people who have so long been living in terror. On Saturday forenoon I was compelled to walk abroad in a darkness as complete as midnight, and through streets in which the public lamps were not lighted. There was no fog in them, but it spread high overhead like a dense pall of funeral drape. If I heard the name of "Jack the Ripper" mentioned by passers-by once, I heard it fifty times, and I noticed that everybody regarded everybody else with suspicion. At the sound of approaching footsteps we seemed involuntarily to step aside, every man avoiding his fellow.

The words came too late. The previous day London had celebrated with their new Lord Mayor. In the middle of the festivities came the news they had been dreading to hear for the past five weeks.

CHAPTER TEN ENDNOTES

1   See Appendix One for a full account of the use of bloodhounds at Blackburn.

2   In truth these further details appear to have been the invention of an enterprising journalist, Openshaw having merely pronounced the kidney to be human and from the left side. The details were later repeated by Sir Henry Smith, the Acting Commissioner of the City Police during the crimes, in his autobiography *From Constable to Commissioner*. Probably for this reason these details have tended to be widely accepted over the years, although there is no actual provenance.

3   A cross-section of reporting on these letters appears in Appendix Four.

4   For anyone with an interest, *Jack the Ripper: Letters From Hell* by Stewart Evans and Keith Skinner is an excellent study of the letter writing phenomenon (see Bibliography for details).

5   A report of this incident appears in Appendix Two.

CHAPTER ELEVEN

In Mary's Room

I N THE NOVEMBER 14TH EDITION, the London Correspondent of the *Kerry Evening Post* opened his column with an account of the previous Friday's festivities at the Lord Mayor's Show. It was a subdued affair, the new holder of the office being a devout quaker, and thus opposed to showy spectacle, had requested a more restrained performance than usual:

It was a typical Lord Mayor's Day – muddy and sloppy, but not actually raining. The curtailed glories of the show caused, as far as I could see, little or no diminution of the popular interest. The Strand and Fleet Street were thronged as usual with a very vulgar and noisy, but perfectly good tempered crowd. A Mayor's Day crowd has a character of its own. It is overpoweringly jolly about nothing. It elbows and crushes and is elbowed and crushed with boisterous delight. Half the fun of the fair is this throng in the streets, of which many thousands of 'Arries in league and concert with a still greater number of 'Arriets, take advantage for purposes of horseplay and flirtation, which indeed appear to be very much the same thing. There was really hardly anything worth walking across the street to see; there were the gold coach and the banners of the different companies, and that was all. But it must be remembered that the denizens of Poplar and Bermondsey, of Battersea and Hammersmith, are almost strangers to the great thoroughfares of the City and Westminster. The streets have to them very much the same attraction as they have to country cousins; the 9th of November is the day upon which from "immemorial user," as the lawyers say, they come to see the twin cities.

There is an inclination on the part of the Socialists to get up some more Unemployed demonstrations. Lord Mayor's Day was proposed as a good opportunity for trying on the old game at Trafalgar Square. Sir Charles Warren, however, was not caught napping. From early morning the Square was occupied by the police, and notwithstanding the many demands made upon the force during the day, there was always a large reserve in readiness to crush any attempt at disorder. It is not thought that there is likely to be much trouble this year with the "Unemployed." The bubble was pretty well pinched last year. Now trade is tolerably flourishing, and work comparatively easy to obtain.

Whilst the constabulary – horse, foot, and I was going to say artillery – were mustering in battalions in the Square, there was evil abroad in Whitechapel, and by twelve o'clock the electric news ran through the holiday crowd that the Whitechapel murderer had added another victim to his dread list. The sensation was quite indescribable. At first, people believed a joke was being played upon them, but the repeated editions of the evening newspapers only confirmed the rumour; every sheet sold like wildfire, and public attention was immediately diverted from gay to grave. The last murder is even more revolting than its predecessors. Further comment is absolutely useless.

At a quarter to eleven that morning, John McCarthy, a young man who ran a chandlers shop in Dorset Street and rented out rooms in a lodging house and some tenements in a narrow court to the rear, sent his man to see if he could obtain some overdue rent from one of his tenants. Mary Jane Kelly lived in No. 13 Millers Court, a small room, approximately twelve feet square which was actually the back parlour of No. 26 Dorset Street, but was partitioned off from the rest of the house. She had lived there for eight or nine months, co-habiting initially with a man named Joseph Barnett, but he had left after an argument nine days earlier in which a window had been smashed. Now Mary was several weeks behind in her rent and owing twenty-nine shillings, and McCarthy's patience must have been running thin. In the *Irish Times* of November 10th he told what happened next:

> I sent my man to ask her if she could pay the money. He knocked at the door, but received no answer. Thinking this very strange, he looked in at the window, and, to his horror, he saw the body of Kelly lying on the bed covered with blood. He immediately came back to me and told me what he had seen. I was, of course, as horrified as he was, and I went with him to the house and looked in at the window. The sight I saw was more ghastly even than I had prepared myself for. On the bed lay the body as my man had told me, while the table was covered with what seemed to me to be lumps of flesh. I said to my man "Harry go at once to the police station and fetch some one here."

Thomas Bowyer, known to his acquaintances as "Indian Harry", rushed to the Commercial Street Police Station where he found Inspector Walter Beck on duty. McCarthy followed him there and together they explained to Beck what they had seen, and McCarthy requested Inspector Edmund Reid, with whom he was acquainted, but he was unavailable and Beck accompanied the two men back to Miller's Court.

As soon as he saw the horrible sight through the window Beck called for assistance, and by a quarter past eleven Inspector Abberline and Dr George Bagster Phillips were both on the scene. One look through the window was enough to tell Phillips that life was extinct, and Abberline ordered that the room remain sealed while he called headquarters for the bloodhounds to be brought. He was unaware of two important facts, the first of them being that the dogs were no longer in London, the second that the man by whose orders this course of action had been decreed, had resigned as his superior officer. It wasn't until half past one that Superintendent Arnold arrived and, announcing that the dogs would not be coming, ordered that the door be forced. McCarthy continues his story.

> I at once forced the door with a pickaxe, and we entered the room. The sight we saw I cannot drive away from my mind. It looked more like the work of a devil than of a man. The poor woman's body was lying on the bed undressed. She had been completely disembowelled, and her entrails had been taken out and placed on the table. It was those that I had seen when I looked through the window. The woman's nose had been cut off and her face gashed and mutilated, so that she was quite beyond recognition. Both her breasts too had been cut clean away and placed by the side of the intestines on the table. The body was, of course, covered with blood, and so was the bed. The whole scene is more than I can describe.

Once again the *Dublin Evening Mail* was the first Irish newspaper to carry the news, printing a brief and somewhat confused report on the evening of the murder itself. The following day most of the dailies carried full details of the discovery, and the *Limerick Chronicle* had something special to say:

> A rumour prevailed in Limerick to-day that the murdered woman was in some way connected with the city, where it is said her parents at one time resided; but this may be found to be one of those vague reports which are so freely circulated on occasions such as this. However, we are informed that the police in this city have been communicated with, and that inquiries are now being instigated to ascertain the truth or otherwise of the rumour in question.

The truth of that rumour has not to this day been ascertained, but it is generally accepted to be the case. Mary had told several people, Joe Barnett included, that she had been born in Limerick, but had moved to Wales as a child when her father, whose name she gave as John Kelly, took a job as a foreman at an iron works. In researching this book I made an attempt to trace a record of her birth. There was no central registration of births at that time, and the census records for the period no longer exist. Searching the baptism records for the various diocese for the County of Limerick for the period I was able to find only one Mary Kelly born in the right period with the father's name of John. She was baptised on March 31st, 1863 in the parish of St John in the city of Limerick, and her mother's name was Catherine Jordan. Whether this is the same Mary Kelly or not, it is impossible to confirm.

According to her own story she was married at a young age to a miner named Davies who was killed in a pit explosion within two years of their wedding. After this she had moved to Cardiff where she had drifted into a life of vice. From there she travelled to London's West End where she had apparently worked as a high-class call girl, and one of her paramours had taken her to France for a time, although she had not liked it there and had returned after a few weeks.

How she had fallen from there to a dingy room in Whitechapel in the course of just a few years is not really known. There are confused tales of her movements in between, but none can be confirmed. All that is really known is that she was the youngest of the Ripper victims, at just twenty five years of age, was described as a well formed woman and was said to be both prettier and more intelligent than most of her class. She was, however, like the other four murdered women, almost certainly an inveterate alcoholic, and it was likely this addiction which had led to her condition of life.

As well as being the youngest of the Ripper's victims, she was also the only one to have been killed indoors. The additional time and privacy this had given him was something he appeared to have take full advantage of, for the mutilation he exacted on her body was not merely the worst of the series, but indeed the crime scene was one of the most hideous recorded in the history of any police force in the world. The full details were not reported in any newspaper, English or Irish, at the time, and indeed were lost to researchers until 1987 when the notes of Dr Thomas Bond, the senior police surgeon of the Metropolitan Police who was asked to attend the scene personally by Robert Anderson, were recovered by Scotland Yard in a packet of lost documents returned to them anonymously.[1] Bond described the scene in the following words:

> The body was lying naked in the middle of the bed, the shoulders flat, but the axis of the body inclined to the left side of the bed. The head was turned on the left cheek. The left arm was close to the body with the

forearm flexed at a right angle and lying across the abdomen. The right arm was slightly abducted from the body and rested on the mattress, the elbow bent and the forearm supine with the fingers clenched. The legs were wide apart, the left thigh at right angles to the trunk and the right forming an obtuse angle with the pubes.

The whole of the surface of the abdomen and thighs was removed and the abdominal cavity emptied of its viscera. The breasts were cut off, the arms mutilated by several jagged wounds and the face hacked beyond recognition of the features. The tissues of the neck were severed all round down to the bone.

The viscera were found in various parts, viz; the uterus and kidneys with one breast under the head, the other breast by the left foot, the liver between the feet, the intestines by the right side and the spleen by the left side of the body. The flaps removed from the abdomen and thighs were on a table.

The bed clothing at the right corner was saturated with blood, and on the floor beneath was a pool of blood covering about 2 feet square. The wall by the right side of the bed and in a line with the neck was marked by blood which had struck it in a number of separate splashes.

It is a description which almost beggars belief that one human being could do such things to another. Notwithstanding that all but the throat wound were performed post-mortem, it still displays such extreme vicious ferocity that even the words on the page make the stomach churn. It is hardly any wonder that John McCarthy could not drive the scene from his mind. On November 13th, the London Correspondent of the *Dublin Evening Mail* gave a personal account of a visit to the room:

I accompanied the jurymen this afternoon to the miserable apology for a dwelling where the woman Kelly met with her terrible death. It is the most squalid and depressing of dens – a small room, not more than twelve feet long, with a bed in one corner behind the door, two tables, one chair, and a small cupboard buried in the wall, containing a few broken crocks, two old knives and forks, and a battered spoon or two. In this miserable den was perpetrated the fiendish butchery of Friday morning, and on the table nearest to the bed were found the breasts and pieces of flesh that had been ruthlessly slashed from the victim's body.[2] These, of course, had been removed with the corpse, but the dirty bed linen and bed, stained with the woman's gore, bore ghastly evidence of the terrible tragedy that had been enacted. The sight was so gruesome that some of the jury turned faint, and all who were present were glad enough to be out in the open air again, though it was only to breath the thick and pestiferous atmosphere of the East End in November.

The *Irish Times* of November 10th provided its readers with a description of the general locality of the murder:

> Dorset street is a fairly wide thoroughfare, and at night, owing to the lamps in the windows and over the doors of the numerous lodging-houses, it may be described as well-lighted. Miller court is approached by an arched passage not more than three feet wide, which is unlighted, and from this passage open two doors leading into the houses on each side. The house on the left hand side is kept as a chandler's shop by a respectable man named M'Carthy, to whom also belongs the house in the court in which the crime was committed. The court is a very small one, about 30 feet long by 10 broad. On both sides are three or four small houses, cleanly whitewashed up to the first floor windows. The ground floor of the house to the right of this court is used as a store, with a gate entrance, and the upper floors are let off in tenements, as is the case also with M'Carthy's house. Opposite the court is a very large lodging-house, of a somewhat inferior character.[3] This house is well lighted and people hang about it nearly all night. There is another well frequented lodging-house next door to M'Carthy's, and within a yard or two to the entrance to the court is a wall lamp, the light from which is thrown nearly on to the passage. But perhaps the most curious item in the entire surrounding is a large placard posted on the wall of the next house but one from the right hand side, offering, in the name of an illustrated weekly paper, a reward of one hundred pounds for the discovery of the man who murdered the woman Nicholls in Hanbury street [*sic*].

The police quickly cordoned off the area and called in a photographer to photograph the body *in situ,* the first time in the case this had been done. Once again the order was handed down for complete non-cooperation with the press. Even the man from the *Dublin Evening Post* for once was unable to worm his way into "the know." His report on November 10th:

> So strong is the feeling now manifested at the inability of the police to lay hands on the assassin that it will not be surprising in the event of his non-arrest if something like a revolt takes place in the East End. The police are almost scared by their lack of success in obtaining a clue to the murderer's whereabouts. They take shelter in taciturnity, and refuse to impart the slightest vestige of information to the press. This afternoon,

immediately on learning of the latest tragedy, I repaired hurriedly to the spot with a view to ascertain the whole of the facts, and transmit them by wire for the benefit of your readers. Yet, to get the merest semblance of a story from any police officer was a matter of impossibility. The street in which the crime was committed was barred at each end by a thick band of police, who rigidly refused to allow anyone but detectives and the medical men to pass. Driving to the Commercial-street Police Station, my modest request for "a few facts" was met by a positive and almost rude refusal to say anything on the subject. "You do not deny that a murder has been committed?" I asked. "I cannot tell you even that much," was the reply. "We dare not tell; we are forbidden to say a word on the subject; it is of no use your questioning me. I can tell the representatives of the press nothing." Hurrying back to Dorset-street, I succeeded by a ruse in passing the cordon of police, but at the court in which the crime was committed I found another bar to my further progress, and here also even the slightest scrap of information was withheld.

Despite the paucity of information, the London evening papers grasped eagerly at whatever vague and often inaccurate accounts of the murder and the victim they could obtain from the inhabitants of the area, and had hastily thrown together early editions on the streets before the day's festivities in the City were completed. The *Bray Herald* described the scene on November 17th:

The almost fatalistic horror which is beginning to settle down over a large portion of the people of the metropolis, and particularly those dwelling in the East-end, because of the continuance of the atrocious crimes, generally known as "the Whitechapel Horrors," is not to be wondered at. After remaining in perfectly secure hiding for close upon five weeks, the miscreant to whom it is generally believed that the series is due once again made his malefic presence felt; and on the very morning when sight-seeing London was all agog with desire to witness the Lord Mayor's procession, he committed yet another of these appalling crimes. There was a grim contrast between the laughing, pushing crowds which thronged the streets, and the eager, noisy newsboys who ran up and down crying the details of the latest horror; and as the news coursed from lip to lip, popular indignation began to run high. No one could suggest what ought to be done, that ought to be left undone, but everybody had an idea of his own that there must be something very wrong in the state of society which witnessed the perpetration of such crimes. And in this inarticulate and utterly unpractical fashion the popular feeling found vent, only speedily to realise for itself that mere ejaculation of complaint could secure no remedy.

Although panic reigned through London on the day of the murder, and once again crowds descended on the area of the crime scene, several of the newspapers were commenting by the Monday on how quickly this seems to have dissipated. *The Irish Times* commented:

> It is amazing how comparatively slight the effect on the public of the latest Whitechapel murder has been. People have supped so full with this class of horror that it has palled upon their faculty for sensation, and no more interest is now shown in these familiar butcheries than in ordinary crime. It is an instructive fact that so far as the large force of police on detective and usual duty in the East End have observed the class to which the latest victim, like her six unfortunate sisters, belonged appear to have grown callous to peril, and are not terrified by the latest warning of their possible fate.

The *Dublin Evening Mail* reported on the same phenomenon:

> I spent the early hours of this morning in the Whitechapel district, and was very much struck with the fact that though a large number of degraded women have evidently been driven from the locality by panic, a very considerable number still remain to pursue their miserable life in the face of a terrible risk. The rapid recurrence of crime seems to have made them only the more indifferent to its horrors. They are warned by the police, but they persist in pursuing the only life which presumably they consider open to them.

The murder coming just a few weeks after the opening of the Parnell Commission, the radical *Freeman's Journal* on November 10th provided a political slant on the killing:

> The irony of appointing a Special Commission to inquire into Irish crime ten years old, most of which has been long ago expiated on the scaffold or in the prison, while London reeks with the fresh-spilt blood of the victims of the most horrible and wanton criminal of the century, will suggest itself to most minds. The resurrection of "Jack the Ripper" will possibly detract somewhat from the impression caused by the Times catalogue of Irish agrarian murders. Even the most sensational of the English papers recoil from the task of describing the aggravated abomination

with which the murderer has accompanied his latest atrocity. The police are more at fault than ever as to the criminal, and the bloodhounds have proved a lamentable fiasco. Last evening the report was current that the accumulated discredit and misfortunes which have come upon him will compel Sir C Warren's immediate resignation, and that Monday will find him no longer Chief Commissioner of Police.

In this last assertion, the *Freeman* was not correct. The murder of Mary Jane Kelly did not bring about the resignation of Sir Charles Warren. It was his magazine article which had already done so on the previous day, although this was a fact of which nobody was aware until the following week. The news was first presented to Parliament by the Home Secretary on the evening of Tuesday, November 12th and reported in the newspapers of the 13th, ironically the first anniversary of the Bloody Sunday riot. The *Belfast Morning News* gave full details of Mr Matthews' explanation on November 14th:

The HOME SECRETARY, in order to avoid any misunderstanding as to the ground of Sir Charles Warren's resignation asked leave of the House to make a short statement on the subject. On the 8th November, he said, he directed a letter to be sent from the Home Office to Sir Charles, calling attention to the fact that his recent article in *Murray's Magazine* was in violation of a Home Office minute directing that no officer in the force shall publish any work relating to the department unless the sanction of the Secretary of State had been previously obtained. The letter set forth that the minute applied to every officer of the force, from the commissioners downwards. On the same day he (Mr Matthews) received a reply from Sir Charles Warren stating that, had he known the minute applied he would not have accepted the post of Commissioner of Police. He disputed the power of the Home Secretary to issue any order to the force, and concluded – "I desire to say I decline to accept this instruction, and I have again to place my resignation in the hands of her Majesty's Government." The Home Secretary, replying to that said the position taken up by Sir Charles Warren was altogether inadmissible, and accordingly his resignation would be accepted. At the same time he had to acknowledge the services Sir Charles Warren had rendered to the Government during his administration of the force. The Home Secretary, continuing his statement to the House, said the resignation was accepted solely on the grounds set forth in the correspondence, and the failure of the police to discover the authors of the crime in the Metropolis, or the differences of opinion between Sir Charles Warren and Mr Munro had nothing to do with the action of the Government.

The resignation caused almost more furore with the Irish press than the Kelly murder had. Virtually every journal and periodical in the land editorialised at length on the matter, most of them relating his resignation back to either the failure of the Ripper investigation or the actions in Trafalgar Square the previous year. The *Kerry Evening Post* of November 17th had this to say:

> No one maintains for a moment that an official should be made a scapegoat to appease popular prejudice. But in the present case it must be admitted that people were right. The police have no cause to believe that the efforts made to discover the Whitechapel murderer reflect credit on the authorities. The extraordinary difficulty is generally admitted, but the means employed appear to have been too fussy and fitful, showing no ingenuity or originality in their conception at all in proportion to the intricacy of the terrible problem to be solved. They cannot persuade themselves that the detective skill of the police is adequate to the demand made upon it, and feel that their failure is a disgrace to the City; wont to believe its police organization the best in Europe. The prestige of the force has been lowered they think, under the administration of Sir Charles Warren, and when the repute of any body of men is lessened amongst the community they serve, whether it be by adverse circumstances beyond human control, or from the lack of certain requisite qualities in those to whom it looked for guidance, the individuals themselves become disheartened and mistrustful of their own capacity. The consequence is that their most difficult duties are discharged in a perfunctory manner and vigilance and alertness, which alone enable an organization to fulfil the manifold demands made upon them, slowly deteriorate. Entire confidence in the chief is necessary, and this can no longer be said to exist. For this reason alone Sir Charles Warren's resignation is a welcome event. The unfortunate loss of Mr. Munro at a moment of supreme need, the destruction of a clue by the erasure of the supposed murderer's hand writing on the wall, and the nonsense about the bloodhounds never destined to be tried when a chance of testing them occurred, killed whatever confidence in the Chief Commissioner his previous inefficiencies had permitted his subordinates to entertain.

The *United Ireland* of the same date, as might have been supposed, used the situation for an opportunity to attack the Home Secretary:

> The enforced resignation of Sir CHARLES WARREN is a nasty rock for a

Government none too steady. Mr. MATTHEWS might just as well not strive to blind the public to the real meaning of the incident, for no one is blinded. Sir CHARLES WARREN is not shunted because of a magazine article, nor yet because of the atrocities of "Jack the Ripper." Trafalgar Square is responsible for his downfall. The police attack on the public in Trafalgar Square was a very mild form indeed of the police outrages on peaceful public meetings which is of every-day occurrence in Ireland. But London has not been broken into the system as Ireland. The people grew restive and made their indignation felt. Sir CHARLES WARREN is the scapegoat of the cowardly cabinet, whose policy he too faithfully carried into effect. Mr. MATTHEWS' delight at his dismissal reminds one unpleasantly of the exultation of the informer in the witness-box, with the free pardon and the reward in his pocket, swearing against his accomplice in the dock.

Freeman's Journal did likewise on November 13th, and also suggested that Sir Charles had engineered the showdown with his superior:

The news will not be received by the public with any great surprise. Mr. Matthews' own resignation may not be far off. His administration at the Home Office has been one long series of dismal blunders and mistakes. Mr. Matthews has visited upon his subordinate all the consequences of his own unpopularity. He has wreaked upon Sir Charles Warren the chagrin of his own sense of failure. The public are aware that serious complaints have been lately made regarding the whole organisation of the London Metropolitan Police. Sir Charles Warren, as the head of that department, had, indeed, proved himself unequal to the task of conforming to Mr. Matthews's somewhat peculiar ideas on the subject of police regulation. For weeks past there have been clear indications, which Sir Charles Warren seems to have fully understood, that his room would be more highly valued than his presence. This being the case it would seem that Sir Charles Warren has ridden for a fall. In the November number of *Murray's Magazine* he published an extremely interesting and able article on the police organisation of London. Our idea is that when Sir Charles Warren wrote that article he knew that he committed a breach of the rule which forbids an official connected with the administration of the Home Office to publish information in any way relating to the department in which he serves. In other words, Sir Charles Warren knew that the inevitable result of his action was resignation. We were therefore not at all surprised at the public censure passed upon Sir Charles by Mr. Matthews in the House of Commons on Thursday night. It is the natural sequence that Sir Charles should have intimated to Mr. Matthews his inability to stand the severe reprimand administered, and that he should forthwith have tendered his resignation. The announcement is said to have been received with cheers upon both sides of the House. Now, it might have been expected that the Tory Party would have preserved at least a dignified silence over such an incident, and we think Sir Charles Warren has some right to complain of the manner in which his so-called friends have treated him.

In the November 20th issue the London Correspondent of the same newspaper also managed to draw a criticism of James Monro and his secret department into the issue:

> Your readers are aware that Mr. Munro recently resigned his place as head of the Criminal Investigation Department, and was immediately accommodated with an equally good post in the Home Office. It is now said that Sir Chas Warren objected to the action of Mr. Munro in utilising the detective force in working up the *Times* case both because he thought it was improper employment of their services and because it led to their neglect of other more important work. Mr. Munro's position would be quite untenable under such a charge. So that his withdrawal from the police department would have been imperative in order to avoid a scandal, while his appointment to another place would be the only and natural compensation the Government on whose behalf he came into conflict with his chief could offer him.[4]

The *Kilkenny Journal,* on November 17th, went further than any of the other newspapers, bringing Matthews' Irish Catholic beginnings into the equation and making a stinging accusation against him:

> Mr. Matthews let it be tacitly understood when announcing Sir Charles Warren's resignation that the gallant baronet's "resignation" was a polite form of dismissal, or was the result of a by no means gentle hint from the Home Secretary. It now appears that Sir Charles wanted to resign long since, but was implored by the Government to hold on, and that it was only characteristically mean conduct of the Home Secretary in attacking him outside and inside the House of Commons that brought matters to a crisis. We think the renegade Home Rule and ex-member for Dungarvan should return once more to the Divorce and Probate Court, and leave politics and everything above the narrow view which he seems only able to take to persons more suited to the work. How many a Judas

has buried his thirty talents in the potter's field, metaphorically at least, since Iscariot paid the price of his treachery 1,800 years ago?

While the political manoeuvrings went on around them, the police still had to contend with the not inconsiderable task of trying to catch the killer. As with the previous cases, witnesses were soon found, but their testimony was confused and contradictory. What was known was that the previous day Mary had spent some time with a friend, Maria Harvey, and later had a visit from another, Lizzie Albrook. At around seven or half past seven in the evening Joseph Barnett came to visit and Albrook left. Barnett had visited often since moving out, and usually gave Mary some money if he had any, but on this evening he was broke and apologised for not being able to give her anything before he left, sometime around eight.

What she was doing between then and midnight is not clear, although it seems likely that she spent at least part of the time in the Britannia Public House, the same one Annie Chapman had visited on the night of her murder. Just before midnight she was seen by Mary Ann Cox, who lived further up the court, returning to her room with a blotchy faced man with a carroty moustache who carried a beer can. Between then and one in the morning she was variously heard singing in her room. A man named George Hutchinson later saw and spoke to her in Commercial Street, and watched her return to her room with a well-dressed, wealthy looking man wearing a coat with an astrakhan collar. A highly detailed description he gave of the man was later widely circulated by the police.

Two women in the court, Elizabeth Prater, who lived in the room above Kelly's, and Sarah Lewis, who was visiting in a room opposite, both reported hearing a cry of "Murder!" some time around half past three or four in the morning coming from the direction of Mary's room, and as this tallied with the various police doctors estimates of the time of death, this seemed to suggest that this was the time that the murder took place.

Unfortunately this situation was confused by the story of one Caroline Maxwell, who insisted she had seen and spoken to Mary at half past eight on Friday morning. She appeared at the inquest to tell her story, and stuck to it unshakably despite the fact that few seem to have believed her. Another man, Maurice Lewis, who did not appear at the inquest, also claimed to have seen her that morning. The *Dublin Evening Mail* commented on November 12th:

> In the first place, the medical testimony indicates almost beyond doubt that the woman Kelly was murdered, not in broad daylight, between nine and ten o'clock, but during the early hours of the morning, some considerable time before sun rise. There are people who still declare that

they saw the deceased as late as eight and nine o'clock on Friday morning, but it is believed that those persons are mistaken as to the woman's identity. The fact of the murder having been committed during the quiet hours of the early morning certainly fits in best with the extraordinary disappearance of the assassin from the house and the court without being observed. It is more probable, at least, except in one particular, which is that from the terrible amount of mutilation effected it would seem improbable for the criminal to have performed his hideous work in the dark. If a light was burning in the room at the time, the reckless nature of the crime is all the more remarkable, for anyone might have witnessed its accomplishment by peeping in at the window through which the man looked who made the discovery. Of course, it is possible that the murderer did not observe the window, or, at least, that he did not know of the facilities that it afforded for inspecting the room from the outside. In this case the quietude of the night alone sheltered him from observation, and enabled him after the completion of his ghastly task to vanish like a spirit, observed by no one.

It is a curious fact that this most brutal of all the Ripper murders, either of the accepted five victims or of any of the others intimated as possibles, received the least press attention of any since Polly Nichols. It may have been as *The Irish Times* said that the people had "supped so full" of horrors that everything had been said already, or it may have been that by November with Parliament back in session, the Parnell Commission in full swing, and the US Presidential election having taken place the previous week, there was just too much other news for the papers to concentrate too much of their efforts on the case. Most likely it was a bit of both, but combined with a general public weariness of the subject, and a lack of belief that the result of investigations into this murder would prove any more fruitful than those of the previous four. The *Dublin Evening Mail* commented on November 12th:

> The police are now almost scared by their inability to secure a clue that holds out a reasonable hope of getting on the track of the assassin. They are thoroughly alive to the fact that a most indignant feeling prevails among the East End population, and that if they do not soon lay hands on the right man, they will provoke such a feeling of hostility that will jeopardise their personal safety as well as altogether destroy such reputation as they at present retain. Consequently, they are putting forward their best efforts, and the smartest of Scotland Yard men have been whipped up to do the most subtle part of the work. A great deal has really been done, though so far as can be ascertained, without any satisfac-

tory result. The room in which the murder was committed has been searched, every inch of it, by a score of the most astute London detectives. Yet not the shred of an article or a mark has been found that is considered likely to prove of the slightest use. Yesterday it was thought that the murderer had burnt something in the room before quitting it. Two or three hours were consequently employed in collecting every particle of dust from the fireplace, submitting it to the process of a sieve and then carefully examining and analysing the deposit. All, however, was to no purpose, and to-day the police seem as far off capturing the assassin as they ever were.

The same newspaper later noted:

That there will be more victims the authorities are quite convinced, unless, of course, the assassin be quickly run to earth. They are equally certain that the man will on one occasion make a slip of some kind in carrying out his fiendish programme and will find his career of bloodshed brought to an abrupt termination. Should such time happily arrive, there will take place one of the most sensational trials ever known in connection with the criminal history of this country.

The *Limerick Chronicle* of November 13th mused on who the murderer might be:

It is pretty clear that the murderer is in some unaccountable manner possessed by a religious mania, and that he considers himself divinely commissioned to do his utmost to extirpate a certain class of sin. He must also be a resident, if not exactly in the district where the crimes have been committed, yet within a short walk of the places rendered conspicuous by his diabolical savagery. It is clear also that he is one who, by previous occupation, has been accustomed to the shedding of blood. He need not necessarily have been a medical student, or acquainted with human anatomy. It is sufficient to say that he knows something of the position of the internal organs of the animal economy. Though the class to which his victims belong are anything but careful, yet in view of the last murder it must also be concluded that his appearance and manner are not such as to suggest his character, or likely to arouse a sense or even a suspicion of danger. That he is a resident in the neighbourhood is considered likely, and even highly probable, from the manner in which he has selected particular sites. The theory that he is a Malay who comes ashore occasionally, accomplishes his purpose, and then disappears, is, to say the least, untenable. It is more than probable that the perpetrator is well-dressed, and also well supplied with money, and that he first addresses the women as, perhaps, the agent of some charitable and philanthropic society, and persons of such a class could be found living in respectable streets within five minutes' walk of the points where the murders took place. These theories assume that the murderer is a man. Recently it has been broached that the perpetrator may be a woman. It is pointed out that "homicidal mania, religious fanaticism, or avenging mission can equally equate to both sexes; while the horrors of revolutionary epochs have proved that women when excited by revenge and drunk with blood are more cruel, relentless, and savage than men. The knowledge of surgery which has now been placed within female reach can account for the necessary proficiency in the use of the knife, and a study of anatomy could have been made to serve the fell purpose of a desperate resolve. An unbridled sectarian recklessness is not unfrequent among female reformers, resulting in insanity; the mutilation of the victims answering almost accurately the curses of the Bible on the class to which they belong (as set forth in certain chapters and verses especially in Ezekial) might seem to an unhinged mind but the meritorious execution of a divine command." Also, it is insisted that a woman has far greater opportunities of passing unnoticed in the streets and alleys or entering tenements unobserved. She does not excite the suspicion or alarm of other women, whose fears are directed in another quarter; and she possesses immense facilities, without carrying a bag or parcel, for disposing about her person the instruments of her crime. Her skirts, her wraps, are all safe hiding-places; by removing an apron, petticoat, or shawl, or covering her apparel with one before the deed, she can effectually avoid any vestige of blood to be apparent. Moreover it has been noticed that the one blood-stained garment found was an apron, and it is suggested that the ashes in the Dorset-street room were probably those of a lighter fabric than cloth. However unlikely the theory of a female murderer may appear, it evidently deserves attention.

The suggestion of a Malay had taken hold since a telegram from New York the previous month by a sailor named Dodge had suggested that a sailor of that nationality had told him he intended to rip up women in Whitechapel.[5] The *Freeman's Journal* of November 16th also mentions this story, while comparing the Ripper with a historical murderer:

> Since the days of 1812, when Williams struck terror into the heart of London by the complete annihilation of two whole families,[6] there has never been a series of crimes which so quickened the pulse of English

social feeling as the round of outrages that have lately taken place in Whitehapel. The notorious Williams is described as of a deadly and cadaverous aspect – a man through "whose veins there circulated, not red life blood such as could flush to the blush of wrath, of pity, or of shame, but a green sap that welled from no human heart." Whether the appearance of the Whitechapel assassin would furnish the text for an equally graphic description is a question which we are unable to answer for the present. But that in his heart there lurks the same diabolical fanaticism that prompted Williams to his deadly work, that there dwells in the brain of this fiend, be he Malay or not, a scheme of murder unaffected by taint of avarice – that lust of blood stands alone as the sole and awful motive of his crimes – of these things we are already too sure.

Another theory was mentioned by the *Dublin Evening Mail* of November 16th:

"Can it be true?" A considerable number of people are just now asking the connection with the theory that the Whitechapel atrocities are the work of one of the paid emissaries of the Irish faction. Probably by the majority of people the idea is scouted as absurd, but there is no denying that many – among them a few detectives – are strongly of the opinion that the suggestion rests upon a fair basis of probability. The number of men whose special duties are to watch the suspected dynamite and assassination party from America has been materially increased during the past few days, and the most elaborate inquiries are going on day after day. Messages in great number are also flying backwards and forwards between Scotland Yard and the police in New York.

This idea had first gone forth the previous month, and had met with little approval among the Nationalist press. The *Drogheda Argus* of October 13th had been particularly vehement in its condemnation of the suggestion:

Some English papers are now very bitter on the subject of Ireland, and as an example of how they write of the people of this country generally the following statement, taken from a London weekly, entitled *The Topical Times,* may be worth quoting. "I believe," says the writer, speaking of the Whitechapel murders in last Saturday's issue of his paper, "the cowardly assassinations to be the work of Irish American desperadoes, and that they are committed solely for the sake of showing that atrocities in England, or rather in London, are just as possible as they are in Ireland. Are not the gentlemen, who shoot from behind hedges, precisely those likely to select defenceless unfortunates as victims? The risk is small, the glory (?) is great, and so Jack the Ripper continues to ply his hellish trade with the same satisfaction that he used to feel when settling with land-lord, houghing cattle, or violating women in his native country." This statement is a most infamous one and ought in itself be sufficient to show how Ireland is libelled.

1   The returned documents were filed separately under the index reference MEPO 3/3153. They are available at the National Archive.
2   The fact that Mary Kelly's severed breasts were found on the table was variously report-ed at the time and was accepted as fact until the discovery of Dr Bond's report above. In truth it was the flesh from the thighs and abdomen which was found in this location and must have been mistaken for the breasts by the initial observers.
3   This was Crossingham's. It has been widely stated that this had been the home of Annie Chapman, however this was not the case. Crossingham owned several lodging-houses in Dorset Street. The one in which Chapman, and Pearly Poll, had both lived was at number 35 which was actually on the same side of the street as Miller's Court, further down the road next to the entrance to Paternoster Row.
4   In fact the opposite appears to have been the case. I mentioned in Chapter Two Monro's letter to his son in which he intimated that he resigned because he "refused to do what he considered to be wrong." In the summer of 1888 the *Times* and the Government were trying to inveigle the Fenian double agent General Frank Millen into testifying on behalf of the *Times* at the Parnell Commission. Millen was still a wanted man as the supposed organiser of the Jubilee plot on the life of Queen Victoria, and Monro by all accounts made it clear that should the man enter the country he would have him arrested immediately. It was this refusal to toe the Government line which most likely precipitated his resignation.
5   See Appendix Three for an account of this story from *Freeman's Journal*.
6   See Appendix One.

CHAPTER TWELVE

The End of the Terror

OVER A CENTURY has passed since the autumn of 1888 when Jack the Ripper stalked the streets of the East End of London, and for all the countless books, magazine articles, films, and television programmes devoted to the subject, we are frankly no nearer to knowing his identity today than the police were then. Everything is conjecture, including how many women he killed. Polly Nichols, Annie Chapman and Kate Eddowes we can say with a fair degree of certainty were victims of the same hand. Liz Stride, it has been suggested, may just have coincidentally been added to the list on account of the proximity of her murder to that of Kate. If she was not a Ripper victim then the prime suspect is her lover, Michael Kidney. Mary Kelly's murder also differed from the others in terms of location, age of victim, and degree of ferocity, but all things considered it seems fair to include her in the list.

Emma Smith was almost certainly not a Ripper victim. Martha Tabram may have been, and if so then another woman, Annie Millwood, who had been attacked in a very similar fashion the previous February may also be a good candidate. After the Kelly murder, three more Whitechapel prostitutes were found murdered and were linked at the time with the Ripper crimes. Rose Mylett was found strangled in a builders' yard in Poplar on December 20th and her killing most likely was not connected. Frances Coles was discovered in a foot tunnel beneath some railway tracks on February 13th, 1891 with her throat cut, and again the complete lack of any attempt to mutilate suggests that she was simply the victim of a disgruntled client. A man named Thomas James Sadler was arrested for her murder but was never brought to trial due to insufficient evidence.

Alice McKenzie is a different matter. Her body was found on the morning of July 17th, 1889, on a pavement in a narrow lane called Castle Alley. Her throat had been cut and her abdomen mutilated, albeit less brutally than those of the other victims. Her attacker, as with the other murders, had apparently struck silently and escaped without being noticed by a single person from an area that was swarming with police. However, Dr Phillips, who had personally examined three of the previous five victims and been present at the post mortem of a fourth, stated that he did not see the Ripper's hand at work in this case. It seems strange that after such an extreme experience as the slaying of Mary Kelly, that the killer should wait eight months and then carry out his work in such a comparatively mild manner. It is my personal belief that McKenzie was murdered by a different hand who, after the killing, decided to make it look like the Ripper's handiwork. For the purposes of this book I simply note here that she cannot be entirely discounted.

On November 16th, the *Dublin Evening Mail* noted the following:

> The pulse of the public quickens and becomes feeble again, as the different reported clues to the whereabouts of the Whitechapel murderer fasten upon their imagination, and are then shown to be altogether devoid of importance. The two very plausible stories, published during the past three days have put the police to a lot of trouble but are now declared to be of no account whatever. So far as I can ascertain, the police are absolutely no farther advanced along the road of discovery, than they were on the day that the last murder was committed.

This report sums up the remainder of 1888, as public interest in the case simply fizzled out in the absence of anything like actual news. For a short time in late November it was sparked into life again very briefly when a prostitute named Annie Farmer was attacked in a lodging house at 19 George Street, (coincidentally both Emma Smith and Rose Mylett lived nearby at number 18). Farmer was attacked in the mid morning of November 20th in an upstairs dormitory room. Her throat was cut, but not badly, and her attacker escaped through the kitchen and into the street where he was quickly lost to sight in the warren of alleys and courts.

Initially some of the newspapers reported the belief that her attacker was Jack the Ripper, but it was quickly apparent that the police thought otherwise, and the idea was soon dropped. Nonetheless, the incident was noteworthy in one respect, as commented on by the *Limerick Chronicle* of November 22nd:

> Of all the incidents connected with these murders the escape of this man is one of the most extraordinary. How he could possibly have been allowed to disappear in broad day light, with numbers in the streets ready to join in the pursuit, is not the least mysterious of these strange occurrences. The people should have searched every corner and crevice till they found the wretch, for he could not have been far off, and the area was limited. The populace seem utterly helpless either owing to their

dense stupidity or the panic which has seized them. They have let the murderer escape, as it were, out of their hands.

The slackening of interest in the case was commented on by the *Kerry Evening Post* on November 21st:

> The public are beginning to expect a periodical murder in Whitechapel, with the same regularity as they look for a new moon once a month, and unless the East End Fiend, as the newspapers have christened him in desperation after having used up most other epithets, be captured shortly, familiarity with horrors will produce comparative apathy in the public mind; and startling and bloodthirsty head-lines in the newspapers may cease to attract them. The last and most horrible crime did not excite panic in the neighbourhood where it was committed as the previous ones. As everyone has profounded [*sic*] his theory before the last ghastly outrage, we were spared a good deal of absurd discussion. The folly of some people lends a grotesque aspect even to the most shocking incident in modern criminal records.

On Monday, November 19th the *Dublin Evening Mail's* man in London provided another of his regular reports on the state of the streets at the weekend, and managed once again to obtain a comment from a local police officer on the situation:

> Whitechapel on last night and this morning again bristled with detectives, both professional and amateur, the number being always increased at the end of the week, in consequence of the murders having for the most part occurred on Fridays and Saturdays. While going the now familiar round at a late hour last night, I accidentally fell in with a Scotland Yard man, and succeeded in extracting from him a somewhat interesting account of his views of the situation. "It is all very well," he remarked, "to blame the police, but we have practically no clue to work upon. The very class – the unfortunate class – who could probably most help us, have given us the least assistance. As to the witnesses who have spoken to the description of a man seen in the company of the murdered woman, I regard the testimony as altogether worthless. Either it differs to an extent bewildering, or it is the product of an imaginative brain, created with the sole object of extracting money from the pockets of enterprising journalists and amateur detectives.[1] There has been more fiction hawked abroad in connection with the East End crimes than I ever remember in my experience. The statement that the woman Kelly was seen and spoken to a couple of hours before she was discovered mur-

dered, is entirely disproved by the medical evidence, which, if it were published at length, would show beyond doubt that the woman must have been murdered at two or three o'clock in the morning. As to who the murderer is, my theory is that he is a man who is accustomed to the sight of blood, who has some though perhaps rude anatomical knowledge, and that he is a monomaniac with a determination to exterminate, as far as possible, the class of woman at whose hands he has in some way suffered. I believe that he lives in the heart of the Whitechapel district. Not in a common lodginghouse, but in an apartment of his own to which he can obtain access at any time without disturbing others or exciting suspicion. I am also convinced in my own mind that he knows every inch of the locality well, and that in all probability, he meets and becomes familiar with his victims, and their habits, before he plans deliberately the commission of his deed."

A few days later he commented on a phenomenon which had been observable ever since the beginning of October. Following the night of the double event two people had reported incidents involving men carrying shiny black bags. Fanny Mortimer had seen such a man pass down Berner Street shortly before Liz Stride's body had been found, and Albert Bachert had had an encounter with a bag-carrying man behaving strangely and asking questions about the habits of street-walkers in the Three Tuns public house in Aldgate.[2] The idea of the black shiny bag had quickly got into the minds of the public, and indeed it has never gone away. Even today if you look at any artist's depiction of the murderer, the bag is nearly always present:

> Courageous indeed – or reckless – is the man who now ventures into the East End of London carrying a shiny black bag. The fact was strikingly illustrated at the funeral of the woman Kelly, the latest victim of the Whitechapel murderer. One of the spectators had the temerity to carry with him a bag such as is associated in the public mind with the criminal. Whereupon one of the crowd set up the cry of "Jack the Ripper." The words were taken up by some with terror, by others with coarse hilarity, until the poor, innocent, bag-encumbered gentleman found himself surrounded by a yelling mob who wanted but a hint to lynch him. Fortunately he had the good sense to at once seek police protection, and he was hurried, bag and all, into a neighbouring railway station from which he was speedily carried away from his tormentors. A similar incident is reported by police to have occurred on the average daily during the past fortnight.

The man from the *Meath Herald* had a similar story to tell on December 1st:

A friend of my own, an eminent chemical analyst, had to make some experiments in a Mile-end brewery, and to conduct these it was necessary to carry down a black bag of instruments. As it is a fixed idea with many men and women that Jack the Ripper always carries a black bag, my friend was soon followed by a menacing crowd, and had in self-defence to demand the protection of a constable to the nearest cab-stand. After witnessing the extraordinary panic in Whitechapel-road and Commercial-street last Monday, I am surprised that some innocent person has not been in one of the panics hanged to a lamp-post, or lynched in some fatal fashion.

Back with our man from the *Dublin Evening Mail,* another and much more detailed story on the same subject appeared in his column on November 23rd, which provides a flavour of the way public feeling still ran in the district:

Hogarth's "Enraged Musician" finds a novel counterpart in the experiences in the East End of London of an unoffending clarionet player at a West End theatre. This gentleman was walking briskly through the Whitechapel district last evening on his way to the Opera Comique. So to walk is a part of his daily occupation. Cheerily he trudged along, anticipating nothing to ruffle the even tenor of his way. In all probability nothing would have happened but for the fact that the musician with a commendable affection for his instrument is in the habit of carrying it to and from his home, and that the clarionet was comfortably ensconced within the padded lining of a black leather case. As he tripped merrily along it gradually dawned upon him that he was for some inexplicable reason an object of curiosity to a thin straggling crowd of miserably attired youths and women who eyed him with apparent fear, others will ill-concealed suspicion. Wondering, he stopped; the crowd stopped, too. He hurried forward, so did the crowd, every moment growing larger in bulk and more formidably threatening. The puzzled musician again stopped, and faced the enemy, demanding indignantly why they followed him. At this moment he had no suspicion of the fact, but he was soon enlightened. With eyes fixed glaringly upon the modest and inoffensive clarionet case, and fingers pointing towards it, some tremblingly, others defiantly, the miserable gathering of tag-rag and bob-tail sent up with piercing volume the cry of "Jack the Ripper." The musician stood aghast, turned pail, trembled at the danger of his position – as well he might – and gazed helplessly around for a uniformed Robert. "He wants to escape" shrieked the crowd as three boisterous females, with courage inspired by the bottle, rushed upon the embarrassed gentleman as if to lynch him on the spot. At this juncture the police happily put in an appearance, and forcing their way to the rescue, managed to keep off the mob, but not without considerable difficulty. By this time the road was completely blocked, and it was not until the distressed bandsman had withdrawn his clarionet from its case and held it aloft for inspection by the crowd that he was able to make a yard's progress, even though assisted by the officials in uniform. "Never," says the hero of the adventure, "will I carry my clarionet through Whitechapel again."

It wasn't only in Whitechapel that innocent suspects were being chased through the streets. The following story was printed in the *Irish Times* of November 28th and came from their Belfast Correspondent:

To-day, shortly after 12 o'clock, a man was pursued by a crowd through Royal avenue, and as many persons called "Jack the Ripper," the excitement became intense. The individual turned at the Free Library and ran up Little Donegall street. In addition to the increasing crowd, the police were now on his track as well. Scores of people from Union street, Charles street, Stephen street, and Birch street, joined in the pursuit. It was feared that the supposed "Jack" would bolt down Birch street and escape perchance through some familiar and mysterious haunt. These fears were but too well founded, though the fact that the visitor being called "Jack the Ripper" did not dispose the inhabitants to harbour him. "Jack" gained Carrick hill without being captured, and he rushed into the first door on turning the corner. Here it seems he frightened some children, and when the police arrived every facility was given them to enter. Constables Britten and M'Guirk went through the premises and ultimately found the so-called "Jack" secreted in a cellar between Carrick Hill and Birch street. The constables placed the man under arrest and conveyed him to the police office. As he was taken down Donegall street the crowd was still further augmented, and the cry of "Jack the Ripper" was kept up. When taken to the police office the crowd which were obliged to remain outside, gave vent to their feelings in frequent outbursts of cheering. It was discovered that the defendant was wearing two hats – a soft hat being inside a felt one – and carried two walking sticks. He gave his name as James Wilson, and appeared to be about 43 years of age. When asked his occupation he said "I am a comedian," which was interpreted by the sergeant in charge as meaning "a ballad singer." He stated that he had been on a tour through some of the provincial towns, and had called at Lisburn and several places in County Antrim. The charge entered against him was that of "indecent behaviour," but there can be no doubt that he was arrested more for his own safety than for any breach of the peace which he had committed.

One possible suspect was mentioned by name by the press at the time of the killings, the information being stated variously to have originated in Vienna, Lucerne or with Russian journal "Novosti", and the suspect being given the surname Vassili, Wassili or Vassilyoff in different newspapers. The *Munster News* told the story on December 1st:

> A fresh "theory" is under discussion as to whether the "Ripper" is not a Russian named NICOLAI VASSILYOFF, who sixteen years ago was committed to a Paris Asylum after he had shown a mania for murdering unfortunate women, and succeeded in terribly butchering a number of them. Shortly before the Whitechapel murders he was discharged from the French asylum "cured;" he has not since been heard of, and the "theory" is that he may be the assassin and that he is still possessed of the idea – that "unfortunates can only atone for their sins and obtain redemption by being put to death," which he had when in the Asylum, and circumstances seem to favour the idea.

The story which emerged from various newspaper accounts around the world was that this individual had been a member of a fanatical Russian religious sect which forbade sexual relations, and that he had stabbed five women to death in Paris in a five week period. Some of the newspapers claimed that after being released as cured from the Paris asylum on New Year's Day of 1888 he had expressed an intention to travel to London, and others claimed to have spoken to his countrymen in London who had known him and stated that he disappeared from view immediately the first murder occurred. In truth, however, considerable research since has failed to throw up any case which passed through the French legal system which matches either the details or the name.

The fact that so many of the newspapers latched on to this story demonstrates the paucity of other information available to them. The *Dublin Evening Mail* on November 20th complained again of the treatment the pressmen were receiving at the hands of the police:

> The metropolitan police are, as a matter of fact, a good deal too dogmatic in their treatment of the Press. No respectable newspaper would desire to publish clues that might have the effect of letting the uncaught criminal study the movements of his enemies, the police. Unfortunately, however, the police want to dictate to the Press precisely what it shall publish and what it shall ignore. Naturally, several of the newspapers

have firmly set up their backs against this ridiculous notion, and the police refusing any information whatever, reporters have to rely solely upon the evidence scraped up in the Whitechapel district, frequently under circumstances of extreme difficulty and inconvenience. At nine o'clock yesterday morning, I met one of the number returning home, who ruefully informed me that he had been patrolling the East End since four o'clock the previous afternoon – 17 hours at a stretch. Many of the London pressmen have had anything but an enviable time of it since the recent atrocities startled the town.

Another Ripper suspect reported in many newspapers, in lieu of any actual news on the capture of the villain, was identified by an altogether unusual source. In Cardiff a group of spiritualists had gathered to attempt to contact one of the victims and learn details of her killer. This account was published in the *Eagle and County Cork Advertiser* on October 13th:

"Who art thou?" queried the spokesman of the spiritualists in mechanical yet trembling tones.

Knock, knock, went the table, as it unerringly spelled out the words "Elizabeth Stride!"

"By whom wert thou murdered?" was the next question.

Again did the table oscillate, and rap out the necessary letters, "B-y a m-a-n n-a-m-e-d J-o-h-n-n-y D-o-n-n-e-l-l-y," and then warming vindictively to the congenial task of giving up to justice the foul slaughterer, "He lives at number thirteen, Commercial road" or "street" – which of the two thoroughfares it was the listeners in their excitement could not possibly determine.

"Did he commit all the Whitechapel murders?"

"No," replied the spirit, "He is one of a gang of twelve who have sworn to commit these crimes, and different members of the gang have done the various murders."

At this juncture the current of magnetism was suddenly broken.

The resignation of Sir Charles Warren continued to occupy many column inches, and a considerable amount of speculation was printed as to who his successor would be. For a time it was rumoured that Howard Vincent, a former head of the CID, had been offered the job. Vincent had resigned his post at the organisation in order to run for Parliament, but it was thought he might be willing to give up his seat in the House in order to take the top job in the police organisation. The two most frequently mentioned candidates were James Monro and Malcolm Wood, the Chief Constable of Manchester, although *Freeman's Journal* on November 13th made a more interesting suggestion as to who should be selected:

> The appointment of Sir Charles Warren's successor will be a ticklish affair for the Government. Jack the Ripper, who is undisputed master of the situation at present, would possibly be the ideal Chief Commissioner, but failing him the Government have to look around among the herd of commonplace and greedy hangers-on, from among whom the choice is sure to be made.

Little did the *Freeman* realise that their correspondent was shooting himself in the foot somewhat. The suggestion was seized on by the *Dublin Evening Mail* in a lengthy response that same day:

> Among the most attractive suggestions thrown out for the choice of a successor to Sir CHARLES is that which is made in this morning's *Freeman,* by the London Correspondent. The correspondent's favourite for the post is Jack the Ripper. The suggestion, however, is rather [more] brilliant than solid. The Ripper, after all, would not be, we think, a success. He has done his murders very cleverly, but he has been obliged to do them by his own hand. Now, if he could have contrived to get them done by other people while keeping himself in a position to defy a charge of conspiracy if he could have so managed those people as to instigate them or repress them, according as either course suited his own purposes, we would say he was a far fitter man for the post than the Whitechapel Reformer. About the latter, little is known, and it may turn out, when all is known, that luck had as much as skill to do in procuring for him the immunity he has hitherto enjoyed. We should say that, instead of Jack the Ripper, a more adroit detective would be found on application to "O'Connell"-street. In connection with that establishment are many persons who have operated on a larger scale than Jack the Ripper, and who have continued to do so without incurring the local unpopularity which is such a drawback on his success. He has not seen his way to make it anybody's interest to further his procedures. He has not enlisted the passion of greed on his side, nor yet the lust of domination, nor the instinct of envy. The consequence is that he is without visible supporters and professed admirers. From the point of view of the electoral meteorologist, he is absolutely worthless, and his wants and wishes of no account. For these reasons we decline to pin our

faith on Jack the Ripper, and would rather look for the necessary man in a circle with which we presume the *Freeman's* correspondent is more intimately acquainted. Some members of that circle, to be sure, have been obliged to make acquaintance with the inside of a jail, but then this was no penalty to themselves, nor was it the result of any awkwardness on their part. It was part of their policy, and has, in all cases, yielded them a handsome return.

Another suggestion of the possible replacement appeared in the *Belfast Morning News* of November 16th:

Some one has circulated the rumour that the place of Sir C Warren, officially killed by the Whitechapel murderer, is to be given to Mr. Harrell, Chief Commissioner of the Metropolitan Police. We have no doubt the Dublin Commissioner would be a capable enough man, but there is not the least likelihood of the transference taking place. Our Unionist friends, of course, proclaim perfect equality between Irishmen and Englishmen, and shout frantically "May the best man win," but in practice it is something very different. They would have no objection at all to sending over some Englishman to take a post of this kind in Dublin, but when it comes to reversing the process – oh, not likely. England does not exist for that sort of thing.

The position was finally filled on Saturday, November 24th. On the Monday, the *Dublin Evening Mail* had this to say:

No previous appointment of Chief Commissioner of the police in the metropolis has caused so much excitement as did the filling up on Saturday of the vacancy created by the resignation of Sir Charles Warren. The members of the Cabinet themselves took exceptional interest in the appointment, and the final discussion on the subject was, I hear, extremely piquant. The most popular man in London was unquestionably Mr Monro. The public have great faith in his ability, and among the police officers he seems to be perfectly adored. One of the chief detectives of the Criminal Investigation Department remarked to me on Saturday – "We would do anything to serve him. He is a man to whom all of us look up. When he says a thing we known that he means it, and we obey willingly, indeed cheerfully. On the other hand, he is as courteous and considerate as he is shrewd and exacting as a disciplinarian." Apart from the feeling in the force and among the outside public, it was said in official circles that the appointment of Mr Monro would greatly please the Queen. It was Mr

Monro who had sole control of the arrangements for her Majesty during the procession to Westminster Abbey and other celebrations associated with her Jubilee festivities of last year. Owing to his vigilance, a number of suspected gentlemen who travelled from America to London with the evident intention to commit outrages, were watched day and night for weeks at a stretch, and finally put to the rout and made to scatter – some going to the provinces, others to the Continent, and the remainder returning to the land of the Stars and Stripes. After the Jubilee celebrations the Queen expressed her warm approval of the admirable arrangements made for her safety and the compliment was echoed by the Prince of Wales, and many of the other notabilities who were assembled in the metropolis at the time. The appointment of Mr Monro may, therefore, be said to have given satisfaction to the bulk of Londoners, though in certain other quarters, no doubt, it has caused a feeling of disappointment.

Indeed, while the appointment was a popular one with the senior officers of the metropolitan police, it was anything but a satisfactory choice as far as the Nationalist press were concerned. The *Freeman's Journal* commented on November 29th:

Mr. Monro, as has been before stated, was removed from the directorship of the Criminal Investigation Department because of Sir Chas Warren's objection to his employment of the detective force in the attempt to get evidence for the *Times*. This was the cause of the correspondence between Mr. Matthews and Sir Chas Warren, which he has been publicly challenged to disclose by the latter. Mr. Matthews will now be pressed to produce this correspondence. The *Times* should be well off now if Scotland Yard can do anything to assist it. Mr. Munro is in chief command, and his sympathies are well known, while Mr. Anderson, the head of the detectives, is connected by every tie with the Castle and the gang of officials who are now hand in glove with the *Times*.[3] But, apart from Mr Monro's disabilities on this ground, there is a stronger reason for opposing his appointment, but which appeals exclusively to Londoners. During his tenure of office the Scotland yard staff was reduced to the condition of disorganisation and inefficiency which has been so powerfully exemplified in its helplessness to stop the Whitechapel murders, or, indeed, to do any of the commonest detective duties. The best men were employed by Mr. Monro in the idle and fruitless work of spying upon the movements of Irish members in the hope of manufacturing some political capital. The appointment is, therefore, anything but an improvement on that of Sir Charles Warren.

On December 8th, the *Meath Herald* printed a few words of warning for the incoming Chief Commissioner:

> If he fancies that it is a bed of roses which is spread for him, he will be mistaken. But he probably understands all about that. A gentleman in the front rank of superintendents assures me that Scotland-yard, from the Chief Commissioner down to the lowest grade of policeman, is fully aware that it will never satisfy the public. Of course, if the Whitechapel murderer should be captured between this and Christmas Mr. Monro will begin with flying colours. And it is unfortunate for him that the public expects this result. They argue that Sir Charles Warren's forte was military organisation, and that he devoted too much time to drilling his men and dragooning the public. Mr Monro's strong point, on the other hand, has been criminal investigation. He will, at any rate, have a fair trial, and the mere change may help to remove the undoubted soreness of feeling which has been gathering against the force generally.

As the year slipped away, so did the public interest in the Ripper case. With no further atrocities to report, and confidence in the police's ability to apprehend the killer running at precisely zero, there was really very little for the press to report. Even the ubiquitous man from the *Dublin Evening Mail* lost interest after a while. His last column of any note was on November 30th:

> The "Jack the Ripper" scare which has been so prominently developed during the past month or two has entered on quite a new phase within the past few days. It would have been strange indeed, if it had not been turned to account to furnish a silver lining to the pockets of the strange herds of rascals who prowl about the London streets with nothing to exist upon save what small wits they might happen to possess. The latest thing in roguery is, consequently, the personation of detective officers, and an arrest which has to be squared before the police station comes within the range of sight. Half a dozen cases of this nature have been reported to the police since Sunday last. Naturally a respectable individual is fixed upon for the victim. Two men walk up to him and tap him mysteriously on the shoulder. They ask him his name, and intimate that they would like three minutes private conversation with him. If the individual thus accosted at once acquiesce, the three adjourn to a quiet spot, and the men of mystery then unfold the startling information that they are connected with Scotland Yard and have reason to believe that the person they are addressing is connected with the recent tragedies perpetrated in the East End. The probability is that the inoffensive person so

accused almost collapses with fright, or, at all events, expresses a nervous anxiety to learn what reason there is for believing him to be associated with the murders. Then the artful rogues play their part with much ingenuity. There is, they are quite convinced, not the slightest justification for making so terrible an accusation. At the same time, they have their superior officers, who have given them orders, and though they are extremely sorry, and, in fact, seemed almost inclined not to proceed any further in the matter, to do so might be more than their place is worth. The bait, is so artistically dangled is swallowed voraciously in nine cases out of ten. Is there any way of getting out of so disagreeable and inconvenient an affair without going to the police station and appearing before the magistrate? Well, the artful ones reply, it might be done, though the game is such a risky one that it would have to be well paid for. What follows is not difficult to imagine. The dupe hands over a good round sum, and flatters himself that he is a lucky fellow to escape so easily. In a few cases reported to the police, the persons accused, having seen through the ruse, tackled the *pseudo* detectives with commendable vigour, and made an effort to give them in charge. In one case a city clerk set about his tormentors with an umbrella, and belaboured them to such an extent that they were glad to beat a hurried retreat down a convenient alley.

By the time of the Rose Mylett murder, interest had fallen to such a low extent that most of the Irish newspapers did not even carry the story, and those which did afforded it only a few brief lines. The Vigilance Committee patrols diminished and had all but stopped by January 1889. Inspector Abberline was re-assigned and his role continued by a local officer, Inspector Henry Moore. Letters continued to arrive from "Jack the Ripper" right up until 1896, but fewer and fewer every week and none were considered important enough for a second thought.

Henry Matthews kept his job for the remainder of the life of the Government, but proved as unable to work with his new Chief Commissioner as he had been with his old one. James Monro resigned the position after less than two years in office, as a result of interference from the Home Secretary attempting to appoint one of his political allies, Evelyn Ruggles-Brice, to an Assistant Commissionership.

A new land act was passed late in 1888 which effectively extended the terms of the 1885 Ashbourne Act. Gladstone had attempted to attach an amendment for the cancelling of tenant arrears but was defeated. During a debate on the issue an incident occurred in the House of Commons which permitted a great deal of indignation on behalf of Charles Stewart Parnell and his supporters and much discomfort to Arthur Balfour. This report from the *Freeman's Journal* of November 27th:

The debate in committee on the Land Purchase Bill had proceeded quietly for over an hour when it was suddenly interrupted by an incident which ultimately developed features of the very utmost moment. Mr. Sheehy, who had just returned to the house after an absence of a couple of minutes, interposed with a motion to report progress in order to call attention to a breach of privilege which had just been committed. The house filled instantly, and traces of excitement began to manifest themselves almost immediately on both sides. Mr. Sheehy in a few manly, straightforward sentences explained what had occurred. He had received a card from a visitor in the central lobby, and on going out he discovered an Irish policeman, who asked him to accept service of two summonses under the Coercion Act. Mr. Sheehy refused to take the summonses, and now asked the house whether it would allow its very precincts to be invaded in this manner by the emissaries of the Irish Government. The effect of this statement was electrical. Mr. Balfour, Mr. Goschen, Mr. Smith, and the Solicitor-General put their heads together in anxious converse, and were evidently at a loss to decide what should be done. Mr Bradlaugh rose, and in a few telling sentences supported Mr. Sheehy, and from the crowded benches of the Opposition there was immense cheering, while the Tories sat silent and irresolute, evidently beginning to realise that something ugly had happened. The doubts of a good many of them were set at rest when Mr. Hanbury rose from their midst and entered a powerful protest against the practice of dogging members of Parliament to the house in order to subject them and the house to the indignity of arrest, or, as in this case, to take a preliminary step towards that proceeding. The house rose to a fever heat of excitement during Mr Hanbury's speech, and the cheering from a good many members on the Tory side was quite as fierce as from the Opposition.

The Parnell Commission ran until November of the following year and cleared Charles Stewart Parnell of all the accusations against him, and his action against the *Times* in Edinburgh was settled out of court for a sum of £5,000. The Commission was not so good for Michael Davitt, who was declared "mainly instrumental" in brokering ties between the Irish Party and the American terrorist factions, and while the Irish Party was found not to have been seeking absolute independence for Ireland, some of its members were declared guilty of that action.

The tide of the Commission was turned by a surprise witness appearing on February 5th, 1889. In another example of how the Ripper murders and the Irish question intersected, the witness was Robert Anderson's personal double agent within the Fenian ranks, Thomas Billis Beach, alias Major Henri le Caron.[4] Up until this point proceedings had gone very much in favour of the

Nationalists, but le Caron breaking his cover and coming into the open proved a major blow against them. His evidence was damning, proving the link between the Home Rule party and the Fenian Brotherhood and Clan na Gael. Worst of all was his account of a meeting with Parnell in a corridor of the House of Commons in 1881 when he stated that the Irish Home Rule chief had told him, "I have long since ceased to believe that anything but force of arms will bring about the redemption of Ireland."

On February 20th the Nationalists recovered somewhat when Richard Pigott was called as a witness at the Commission, where he denied having forged the signatures on the Parnell letters. Sir Charles Russell then commenced a brutal cross-examination of the witness in which he all but proved Pigott to be the forger. The hearing was adjourned on Friday the 22nd until the following Tuesday. When Pigott was recalled to the stand at mid-day on the 26th he was nowhere to be found. He had left the country and travelled to Paris, from where he sent a letter to the commission which stated, "I grieve to have to confess that I myself fabricated them [the letters]." From Paris he travelled to Madrid. On Friday the 29th a Spanish police inspector arrived at his hotel with a warrant for an extradition hearing. Pigott asked if he could retrieve his hat from an adjoining room. He walked into the room, opened his bag, drew out a revolver, placed it in his mouth and ended his life.

Suggestions that the Ripper murders were a Fenian plot continued to surface from time to time for the next hundred years.

The deaths of Polly Nichols, Annie Chapman, Liz Stride, Kate Eddowes and Mary Kelly were never avenged.

On November 22nd, 1888, the Dublin Evening Mail published a poem sent in by one of its readers, Walter H.J. Beaurepaire:

THE MURDERED MAGDALEN
Oh! shattered outcast, 'midst thy midnight deep,
Sing on – and burst the trammels of thy gloom.
Sing on – and let "Sweet Violets" bring thee sleep,
And o'er thy spirit breathe their soft perfume;
Oh! broken heart 'midst thine anguish drear,
Let vi'lets breathe their sweet, mysterious balm;
For thee no friend with genial smile is near,
Thy restless heart with words of joy to calm.
Mayhap, tho' stricken 'midst that midnight's gloom,
"Recording angel" heard thy spirit's sigh,
"Recording angel" soars high o'er thy tomb,
And bears thy "contrite heart" to stainless homes on high.
Oh! vi'lets sweet, oh! flowers of rich perfume,

That song still breathed a transient summer joy –
An amber radiance o'er those hours of gloom;
Like golden fibre 'midst the base alloy;
That fain would mar the yearning spirit's love;
That struggling e'en amidst the waste of sin,
Would eager clasp one instinct from above;
That told of conscience still supreme within;
"One touch of nature" triumphed o'er the gloom;
"One touch of nature" with its thrill divine,
Finds echoes still that breathe their music o'er thy tomb.

CHAPTER TWELVE ENDNOTES

1   This is most likely a reference to an elderly fruit seller, Matthew Packer, whose shop adjoined Dutfield's Yard, the scene of the Liz Stride murder. Packer initially claimed to have seen nothing, but later told some private detectives that he had sold some grapes to the woman and a male companion shortly before the murder. Packer changed his description of both the incident and the man several times, and was quickly discounted by the police as a publicity or reward-seeker.

2   The name of the hotel was variously reported as The Three Tuns or The Three Nuns. In fact public houses of both names existed in the locality so it is impossible to be certain which is correct. The story is given in detail in Appendix Three.

3   This conjecture is slightly unfair to Monro. A man of strong personal morals, he resisted handing over the private files of the secret Irish department for use in the *Times'* case for a considerable time, finally succumbing to political pressure to do so only in May 1889.

4   Opinion is divided on whether Robert Anderson persuaded le Caron to testify. Christy Campbell in *Fenian Fire* states that Anderson's personal correspondence makes it clear that he did. However, in his autobiography, Anderson had this to say on the matter: "When Major Le Caron called on me in December, having been summoned to England by his father's death, he repeated the expression of his desire to give evidence before the Commission. He had written to me several times about this, and I had already tried to dissuade him from it." Le Caron himself, in his memoirs, agreed that Anderson had not initially been keen for him to testify, as he was unwilling to lose his information source. However he then states "On the eve of my departure for America I learned that my services might, after all, be utilised and my desire to drive the truth home given full play." He does not make it clear whether or not this information came from Anderson.

APPENDIX ONE

Referenced Crimes

A T SEVERAL POINTS in the book, various of the quoted news reports have referred to other crimes, the details of which would have been fresh in the memories of the readership in 1888 but about which we would have less knowledge today. This section contains reports from the Irish press of the time giving brief details of some of these cases.

We begin with a brief précis of undiscovered crime in London (which includes the Great Coram Street murder, referred to in more than one report), and then move on to articles on specific murder and attempted murder cases.

Derry Journal – September 14th
UNDISCOVERED LONDON CRIME
A TERRIBLE RECORD

A searcher into the annals of crime soon discovers that the list of undiscovered murders is very great. London, which surely has every means of tracking down its criminals, has a long record of this kind. Passing over the murder of Mrs. Squire and her daughter in their shop at Hoxton in broad daylight, the killing of Jane Maria Clousen in Kidbrook Lane, near Eltham the murder of the housekeeper to Bevingtons, of Cannon-street, we come to perhaps the best remembered and most sensational of the mysterious crimes of the past. On the morning of Christmas Day, 1872, Harriet Baswell was discovered with her throat cut. She was a ballet-girl employed at the Alhambra, and she had been accompanied to her home, 12, Great Coram Street, by a "gentleman" supposed to have been a German who was never found.

Mrs. Samuels was brutally done to death at her house in Burton Crescent, and a few doors further up Annie Yeats was murdered under precisely similar circumstances to those attending the death of Harriet Baswell.

Miss Hacker was found dead in a coal cellar in the house of one Sebastian Bashendorff, in Euston Square, and Hannah Dobbs was tried, but acquitted. An almost identical case happened in Harley-street. In this case the victim was unknown.

Another unknown woman was found lying in Burdett-row, Bow, murdered.

Mrs. Reville, a butcher's wife, of Slough, was found sitting in a chair with her throat cut, but no one was apprehended.

There was the murder of an unfortunate in her home near Pye-street, Westminster. A rough fellow was known to have gone home with her, and he left an old and dirty neckerchief behind, but he was never found.

Mrs. Samuels was killed with impunity in the Kentish Town Dairy.

The murderer of Miss Clark, who was found at the foot of the stairs in her house, George street, Marylebone, has gone unpunished.

Besides these, there are cases in which the victims have been men. A grocer's assistant was stabbed to death in the Walworth Road by a man who was stealing a pound of tea from a cart. The act was committed in the sight of a number of people, but the man got away, and to this day has not been captured. Mr. Tower, returning from midnight services on New Year's Eve, was found in the Stoke Newington Reservoir. The police, failing to get the faintest clue, adopted the theory of suicide, but could get nothing to substantiate it. On March 29, 1884, E. J. Perkins, a clerk in a city office at 2, Arthur-street West, was murdered, and from Saturday till Monday his body lay in a cellar in the basement of the building. Lieutenant Roper was shot at the top of the barrack stairs at Chatham, and though Percy Lefroy Mapleton, who was hanged for the murder of Mr. Gould on the Brighton Railway, accused himself of the murder, it was proved that he could have no connection with the lieutenant's death. Urban Napoleon Stanger, the baker of Whitechapel, who vanished so mysteriously, we pass over. The list, though incomplete, is ghastly enough.

Cork Examiner – September 15th

RATCLIFFE-HIGHWAY CRIME OF 1812.

The singular points of resemblance between the Whitechapel murders and those which fastened public attention upon Ratcliffe-highway in the beginning of the century are completed by this second crime. On a Saturday night in December, 1812, John Williams, the wretch whose story fascinated De Quincey, butchered a whole family in Ratcliffe highway. Master and mistress, a young apprentice, and a baby in a cradle, were all slaughtered with evidence of a certain fiendish joyousness that finds its parallel in the details of the killing of Annie Chapman. Williams first brained his victims with a mallet, then cut their throats. The discovery of the murder and the silent escape of the assassin filled the East-end with just such terror as now exists at Whitechapel. And, carrying out the parallel with curious detail, whilst the first murder was still being talked of, and the police were diligently in search of the murderer, there followed another crime of equal barbarity. Just twelve days later, Williams, entering another house close by the scene of the crime, murdered the inmates, watched from an upper landing by a terror-stricken youth, who, escaping out of the window, quickly brought together an angry crowd, the mustering of which, its rage and its roaring, were probably in the memory of Chas. Dickens when he described the capture of Bill Sikes.

Ballymena Advertiser – September 22nd
A FRENCH MURDERER

At a time when public attention is fixed upon the weird series of murders in Whitechapel, it might be of interest to recall the singular case of Phillippe, who was guillotined some 25 years ago in Paris, convicted of no less than 10 murders of women committed in Paris and other parts of France. This wretched being was a clerk in a well-known firm of chemists, and greatly respected. He was about 35 years of age, and fairly good looking. His manners were agreeable, and he was industrious and decidedly intelligent. He was frequently sent to different parts of Europe and the East as a commercial traveller. A series of mysterious murders in Paris and its neighbourhood having attracted a great deal of attention, it seems that on one occasion Phillippe dropped a razor enveloped in tissue paper at the feet of one of his mistresses. The woman picked it up, and, being suspicious, made a pretext to leave the room, and immediately summoned the police. Phillippe, on seeing the police enter the chamber, at once and without any hesitation gave himself up. "It is of no use," he said, "this horrible mania has caused me so much agony that my life is unbearable. Yes," he said, "I am guilty not only of the murder of which everybody is speaking, but of many others." In the course of his trial he was found guilty of ten different murders of women, all of them of the same unfortunate class, and he confessed himself guilty of seven others, which he had perpetrated in foreign countries. He was evidently the victim of a horrible mania, and it is said that so great was his cunning he was never suspected by his employer or by any of his most intimate friends of being otherwise than a most inoffensive person. He even on occasions disguised himself in the pursuit of his awful pleasure, if so it can be called, as an organ grinder, and it was by his extraordinary dexterity that he evaded the police for so long a time.

Limerick Chronicle – October 6th
THE WHITECHAPEL MURDERS

The Paris commentators on the crimes in Whitechapel expend much sarcasm on the inability of the London police to track the murderer or murderers. It would, however, be difficult for an assassin to commit six murders in quick succession in one particular part of Paris, and there is no locality in that

Metropolis which contains such a vast network of small streets, squares, and "slums" as that gigantic hive of humanity the East-end of London. Moreover, the *limiers* or "detectives of the Surete" have a better machinery at hand for the detection of crime than the experts at Scotland-yard. Nevertheless they too have frequently been baffled in their efforts to track out criminals. The only Parisian counterpart to the presumable murderer of Whitechapel – that is to say, of the person who wrote certain letters which have been published – was a cabman named Philippe, called "Le Tueur de Filles" who was "guillotined" at La-Roquette many years ago. This criminal, however, proceeded on different lines from the Whitechapel assassin. He first embraced his victims and then cut their throats. He boasted of his exploits in prison, and said that he liked women immensely – but after his own fashion. Of late years the murderers of "unfortunates" have been extremely common in Paris, the victims being of the wealthiest as well as of the poorest classes. One of the most sensational was that some years ago of a woman who lived in a notorious street of the Rue Saint Denis, which was called rather ironically "Rue des Filles-Dieu." Some workmen were one morning passing by a house in this "slum," when on looking up at a window they saw a woman, with blood streaming down the front of her white dress, who was endeavouring to gesticulate. After having made some signs to those in the street the woman fell back from the window, and the men rushing upstairs to her room found that her throat had been cut from ear to ear by some one whose motives were evidently dictated not by plunder but by personal revenge. The Rue des Filles-Dieu had for a long time the monopoly of crimes of this description, but it exists no longer, having quite lately been pulled down to make room for metropolitan improvements. The latest sensational murder of a "gay woman" in Paris was, of course, that of Marie Regnault, by Pranzini. In that instance, however, the woman was wealthy, and the object of her murderer was obviously plunder. In the case of the woman of the Rue des Filles-Dieu, as well as in those of many of her class, the cut throat was simply and solely actuated by revenge – a fact to which the police annals of Paris will bear ample testimony; but all these Paris crimes, although analogous in some details to those which are now stirring London to its depths, "pale their ineffectual fires" before the bloodthirstiness, the atrocity, and the magnitude of the "Whitechapel Murders."

Cork Examiner – October 9th

The acute and probably unerring instinct of those animals was most strikingly shown in the case of the Blackburn murder which was committed ten or twelve years ago where a barber named FISH killed a little girl and where guilt was brought home through the agency of a bloodhound. In FISH's case the police had previously searched his house several times without being able to find any traces of blood or any evidence to justify his arrest. The authorities were wholly at a loss when a man named TAYLOR volunteered the services of his two dogs, one a springer spaniel and the other a bloodhound and pointer dog, part bred. The police had made arrangements for visiting two barbers shops, one of them being that occupied by FISH. In the first house the blood-hound scented nothing. But when taken to FISH's shop the dog immediately began to scent all round the rooms, entering the closets, and smelling at all the corners and crevices of the place. The mystery was solved when one of the detectives opened the door leading to the upper rooms. The dog immediately rushed past the man upstairs, hunted round the back room, afterwards made its way into the front room, and came to a halt at last in front of the fireplace. There was no fire and the grate was empty, but TAYLOR, the owner of the dog, knew that the dog had reached the end of its search. The chimney was at once explored, and there was found concealed in it a human skull, that of the murdered girl. The canine detective had succeeded where the human detective had failed. FISH was forced to confess his crime, for which he was afterwards convicted and executed.

Ballinrobe Chronicle and Mayo Advertiser – October 13th
"THE MONSTER"

The recent series of enormities which have excited such horror in London and the country generally must in all probability be due to some distorted or monomaniacal appetite which has grown by what it fed on. That this theory is a probable explanation of these hideous incidents is supported by the fact that there are recorded instances of cases nearly analogous. Just ninety-eight years ago there was a general panic all over London, caused by the atrocious doings of a mysterious person, who came to be generally known as "the monster." This wretch pursued his work in the open streets, and seemed to defy detection. Women were always his victims. A lady would be walking unattended when she suddenly felt herself stabbed from behind. Often, if her dress happened to be thick, the stroke missed, though the depth of the cut showed how sharp was the instrument and how narrow the escape. More often, however, there was a serious stab or cut. The terror thus inspired could not be conceived; and nothing was talked of but "the monster."

A Miss Anne Porter and her sisters had often encountered a man in the streets who used to come up and, "leaning his head to their shoulder," utter some horrible words and then disappear. He was known to these ladies as "the wretch," and inspired them with a great deal of alarm. One night, when Miss Ann Porter was coming from a ball at St. James's walking home to her father's, the mysterious being stole up behind her as she was entering the house and struck her a blow on the hip; after which outrage he came up and stared into her face. It proved that she was terribly wounded, the cut being four or five inches deep. Yet strange to say, though his face was familiar to the sisters, no traces of him could be discovered. Six months passed away; and a Mr. Coleman chanced to be walking in St. James's-park, when Miss Porter called out that there was the man. Mr. Coleman followed him promptly and hunted him down. He was arrested, and proved to be a respectable tradesman named Renwick Williams. It was found at the trial that he was "the monster" from whom numbers had suffered in this extraordinary fashion. The shops were filled with portraits of the Monster, and the newspapers with extraordinary stories. Seventeen witnesses at the trial gave him the highest character for humanity, good-nature, and "kindness to the fair sex." He was found guilty; but a point of law being "saved" and determined in his favour, he appears to have got off. It will be noted what a similarity there is in this case and that of the Whitechapel assassin. The victims of "the monster" were women, and he seems by preference to have attempted something like the mutilations is described in the newspapers. The monster of our day is evidently a wretch with demoniac and homicidal propensities, which have been stimulated by notoriety and discussion; the other monster appears to have pursued his course for six months, and like his successor, to have used a sharp knife several inches long. Renwick Williams was undoubtedly a maniac; but a maniac who in ordinary life was mild, bland, and to all appearance quite inoffensive.

Sligo Champion – October 13th
A FRENCH MURDER MANIAC[1]

Last summer, while travelling in France (writes Michael Mack) I picked up and glanced over a French work resembling "Homes everyday book," which gave an account of a remarkable criminal who must have strongly resembled the fiend who has created such consternation in the East-End of London. For four months women of the lowest class of "unfortunates" were found murdered and mutilated in a shocking manner. The police seemed powerless. At last a girl one night was accosted in the street by a workman who asked her to take a walk with him. When by the light of the lamp,
SHE SAW HIS FACE,
it inspired her with a strange feeling of fear and aversion; and it instantly flashed upon her that he must be the murderer. She therefore gave him in charge to the police, who, on inquiry, found that her woman's instinct had accomplished what had baffled the skill and the exertions of all their detectives. The long-sought criminal had been at last found. It subsequently came to light that he had been impelled to commit these crimes by a brutal form of homicidal monomania. He had sense enough to know that from this class of woman being out late at night, and being friendless and unprotected, he could,

INDULGE HIS HORRIBLE CRAZE

on them with comparative safety and impunity, and he therefore avoided selecting his victims from a more respectable class. He was convicted and executed. The notorious case must be well known to the Parisien police and to thousands of persons in France, and if inquiry is made its history can easily be procured. No doubt a ruffian like him has turned up in East London, and will be also detected.

---

1   This could be a confused account of the murders of Philippe, already recounted above.

APPENDIX TWO

Related Incidents

THROUGHOUT THE PERIOD of the Ripper crimes the newspapers were full of stories which, while not directly related to the Whitechapel murders, referenced them in some way. Many of these involved incidents in which the name of "Leather Apron" or "Jack the Ripper" was invoked, or else they were crimes which were in some way reminiscent of or inspired by the East End atrocities. Some of these stories are reproduced here.

The Irish Times – October 6th
"LEATHER APRON" IN ARMAGH

This morning the tramp arrested last night who described himself as "Leather Apron," and in whose possession a blood-stained knife and a blood-stained letter addressed to the Roman Catholic Primate were found, was brought before Captain Preston, R. M., who remanded him for eight days. He opened the letter in the day room and read it for those present. It turned out to be a begging letter, and the signature was Mick M'Guire, from Co. Clare. It purported to give an account of what the M'Guires had done for the Church in days gone by. However he informed the police that his real name is William Robinson.

Derry Journal – October 8th
ANOTHER SUPPOSED MURDER

HAMBURG, FRIDAY NIGHT – An event which has come to the knowledge of the Hamburg police may be regarded as an addition to the list of London mysteries. Last August Altona Salenoyeman, an orphan, aged sixteen years, went from Hamburg to London, where she disappeared. No further trace was obtained of her until yesterday, when her former employer received a parcel containing wefts of her hair three feet long. The matter is being inquired into on the spot, and the London police have also been informed of the occurrence.

Morning News (Belfast) – October 9th

A woman named Anne Mulligan was charged by Constable Blakely with having assaulted her husband on Saturday evening. When arrested the prisoner admitted having struck her husband with the frying-pan, stating at the same time that she would do "Jack the Ripper with him too." Mulligan had to be conveyed to the Royal Hospital. The prisoner was discharged with a caution on condition that she would take the pledge.

Dublin Evening Mail – October 11th
"JACK THE RIPPER'S" SCARE

Considerable excitement was caused at Maryport on Tuesday by the report that a young woman had been savagely attacked by "Jack the Ripper." It appears that a young woman named Margaret Dixon, living in Eaglefield Terrace, Maryport, arrived at her work at Watergate Colliery, about five o'clock, in a most exhausted condition, with her hair dishevelled and garments torn. She was understood to say she had been chased and attacked by a man, but before she could give any details she fainted and lay semi-conscious for several hours. She was conveyed home, and on examination it was found that her corsets had been almost torn from her body. Dr Spurgin was soon in attendance, when it was found that the girl was unable to speak. In answer to questions put to her, however, she made signs that she had been attacked at a wood near the pit by a man, who endeavoured to take liberties with her. She succeeded in freeing herself, and ran to the colliery. The man wore a hard felt hat and had whiskers. It is also stated that another young woman was chased by a man near the same place. No arrests have yet been made.

The Irish Times – October 12th

The following curious story is vouched for as being strictly correct, at least so far as the young lady referred to is concerned:– On Wednesday evening the young lady in question was walking along Shiel road, Liverpool, not far from Shiel Park, when she was stopped by an elderly woman, aged about 60, who in an agitated and excited manner urged her most earnestly not to go into the Park. She explained that a few minutes previously she had been resting on one of the seats in the Park when she was accosted by a respectable-looking man dressed in a black coat, light trousers, and a soft felt hat, who inquired if she knew if there were any loose women about the neighbourhood, and immediately afterwards he produced a knife with a long thin blade, and sated that he intended to kill as many women in Liverpool as in London, adding that he would send the ears of the first victim to the Liverpool Daily Post. The old woman, who was trembling violently as she related this story, stated that she was so terribly frightened that she hardly knew how she got away from the man. She could not see anything of either a policeman or a park keeper, but in addition to warning the young lady she appears to have mentioned the matter to some workmen whom she met afterwards in Shiel road. The steamers leaving Liverpool for America and other ports are now being carefully watched by police, and the passengers are closely scrutinised by detectives, there being an idea that the perpetrator of the Whitechapel murders may endeavour to make his escape via Liverpool.

The Kerry Weekly Reporter and Commercial Advertiser – October 13th

"Leather Apron" in Tralee is the latest scare amongst the slaveys. Some nights ago a young man had occasion to go to the residence of a certain professional gentleman, who lives in one of the principal streets of the town. The door was opened by one of the servants, and the young fellow (who by the way was after a hard run), with much gasping tried to inform her that her master was required to attend immediately in his professional capacity at the house of a well-to-do being in another quarter of the town. But his message being wholly unintelligible to the girl, he again essayed to deliver it, and for this purpose moved into the hall, and familiarly placing his hand on the young woman's shoulder again tried, but failed miserably. The girl noticing that the young man was much excited, and probably the late London horrors occurring to her mind, she became terrified, and bounding up the stairs shrieked out, "Murder" and "Leather Apron." The owner of the house and one of his sons on hearing the girl screaming proceeded at once to the hall, but were only in time to catch a glance of the receding figure of the young man, who becoming as terrified as the servant, probably thought it best to beat a hasty retreat.

The Ballymena Advertiser – October 20th

AN EAST LONDON SUICIDE

The particulars of a case of suicide, which took place at No. 65, Hanbury-street, Spitalfields, a house a few doors away from the spot where the unfortunate woman Annie Chapman was murdered, reached Dr. Macdonald, the coroner for North-east Middlesex. It appears that the top floor of the address is occupied by a silk weaver named Sodeaux, his wife, and child aged eight years. For some time past Mrs. Sodeaux has been depressed, and since the perpetration of the horrible murders which have taken place in the district she has been greatly agitated. She was found to have a razor in her possession, and it was taken from her, as it was thought she meditated suicide. The following day she appeared to be more cheerful, and was left alone with her child. Subsequently, however, she left the room, saying she was going on an errand; but when some time had elapsed, and she did not return, her daughter went in search of her, and was horrified to find her hanging with a rope round her neck to the stair banisters. The child ran for assistance, but no one would go up to the body, and eventually the police were called in and the body cut down. Life was then extinct, but as the body was quite warm it is believed that, had assistance been rendered immediately on the discovery being made, the woman's life might have been saved.

Eagle and County Cork Advertiser – October 20th
THE MURDER MANIA

A man named Birchin, who lives at Portsmouth, has exhibited a most extraordinary ferocity since the occurrence of the Whitechapel murders. He has frequently rushed about the house with a knife in his hand, declaring that he would repeat the Whitechapel atrocities on his wife and three daughters. He was kneeling upon his wife on Sunday, and flourishing the knife over her head, when seized by the neighbours. On Monday at the Portsmouth Police-court, he was sentenced to three months hard labour.

Midland Tribune and King's County Vindicator – October 25th
"JACK THE RIPPER" IN BALLINASLOE
A STRANGE RUMOUR

On Monday evening a stranger with a florid complexion and black clothes was observed in Ballinasloe. Some evil disposed person put out a report that the stranger was "Jack the Ripper," and that two women had been killed in Athlone the previous night. He report spread quickly, and the streets were for a while deserted. Of course, the whole thing was a hoax, and the police, on inquiring into the matter, ascertained that the man was a harmless traveller, and in no way resembling the terrible Ripper. It was also ascertained that the story about Athlone was a gross fabrication.

Leitrim Advertiser – October 25th
STRANGE STORY OF MURDER BY LADS
CONFESSION WHEN UNDER THE INFLUENCE OF THE SALVATION ARMY

In all the history of crime, surely there exists no case which will quite match the record which comes from Tunbridge Wells. Two working lads determined upon the murder of a foreman who has offended one of them; then the poor man is lured into a quiet spot, and shot at close quarters by the youth whom the toss of a coin had designated as the person who was to do the actual killing. They afterwards calmly attended the funeral. When asked the other day, after his apprehension, "what grudge Dobell (the youth who fired the shot) could have against Lawrence (the foreman), seeing that he never worked under him?" Gower airily answered, "Oh, he's a friend of mine, and true as steel." The murderers not having been even suspected in the meanwhile, two months after the commission of the crime, Dobell, signing himself "Another Whitechapel Murderer," wrote to the local Advertiser, in which, having obtained "a small space in your valuable paper," he went on to recount, "a few facts concerning the death of the late Mr Lawrence." The letter contained a vivid description of the murder; but the local police, of course, treated it as a hoax, and the murderers remained undiscovered. About the beginning of this month, however, the two youths commenced to attend the services of the Salvation Army, for the purpose of obtaining a revenge upon some one who regularly went there, and, though really impenitent, they came to some extent under the influence of the "captain," and as a result one of them confessed to the murder. Their apprehension by the police following as a natural consequence, the lads proceeded to still further surprise the captain by confessing themselves guilty of a whole string of arsons that had startled the town, and declaring that they had repeatedly attempted to murder a "mate" who had cooled in his friendship.

Dublin Evening Mail – October 25th
DREAMING OF "JACK THE RIPPER"
SAD SUICIDE

A coroner's inquest was held at Sheffield on Wednesday on the body of Mrs Theresa Unwin, who had committed suicide by cutting her throat. She had recently been in low spirits, and was under medical treatment. On Monday last she told her husband that she had had a dream and thought that "Jack the Ripper" was after her. Soon afterwards she was found with her throat cut. A verdict of temporary insanity was returned.

Waterford News and General Advertiser – October 26th
THE "JACK THE RIPPER" SCARE
STRANGE INCIDENT IN THURLES WORKHOUSE

Great excitement was manifested in Thurles workhouse on Monday morning last under the following circumstances :– As early as about three o'clock that morning the inmates of the female wards were heard shrieking and shouting in a most extraordinary way, and they appeared to be in the greatest state of panic. When the officers of the house went to inquire the cause of all this disturbance and uproar they told them that a young man, respectably dressed, and who was a stranger to them, had entered the ward and approached the bed in which a young girl had been sleeping. Seeing the man she screamed aloud, and cried out that he was "Jack the Ripper"! All the inmates of the ward then joined in the uproar, and the intruder becoming alarmed as it is alleged, made his escape through the window. A search was made through the workhouse, but no person was found.

Kerry Weekly Reporter and Commercial Advertiser – October 27th
IMITATING WHITECHAPEL CRIME

At Pontadawe, near Swansea, on Saturday evening, the body of a boy named John Harper, aged five years, son of a tinplate annealer, was found in a wood with the throat cut and disembowelled. A butcher's boy named Thomas Lott, aged 18, was arrested, and he confessed he committed the deed with a butcher's knife. The motive is unknown. The crime was committed in a lonely wood. The prisoner is believed to be of weak intellect.

Dublin Evening Mail – November 15th
"JACK THE RIPPER" AND THE YOUNG LADY
SENSATIONAL STORY

A very sensational story is discussed in general society at the present moment. It is said to be undeniably true; if so, the East End horrors threaten to be repeated in the West End. A young lady of great personal attractions, residing in a fashionable square, has received many missives informing her that she is doomed to be the next victim of "Jack the Ripper." Her friends having communicated with the police, it was deemed advisable that she should be protected by a detective, and for a while the persecution ceased. Trusting that there was nothing more to fear, she accepted an invitation to a fashionable seaport ball, and naturally the detective did not accompany her. Wonderful to relate, when the dancing was over, and she sought her opera cloak, one of the paper placards, with a repetition of the same threats, was found pinned to it.

Morning News (Belfast) – November 16th
MADE MAD BY THE MURDERS

A painful scene occurred in Marylebone Court on the hearing of a charge against Philip Cornish, a schoolmaster, of Ratling Hope School, Pontesbury, near Shrewsbury. He was heard shouting and kicking violently at the door in the cells. Both his hands were pressed on the top of his head, and his eyes were glaring wildly. Constable 192F found the man in Praed street behaving like a mad man. There was a companion with Cornish. They had come to London to catch the Whitechapel murderer. The officer's evidence was frequently interrupted by the violent behaviour of Cornish, who shouted at the top of his voice, threw himself about, and stamped with his foot, and demanded that the witness who was, he said, the son of perdition, should be made to tell the truth. The young man who had accompanied the prisoner said he was a blacksmith. Cornish asked him to accompany him to London, as he had been appointed to come up and catch the author of the Whitechapel murders, for which he was to receive a large sum. The witness thought it was all right, so he left his work and accompanied Cornish to London. He thought Cornish was all right when they started, but he saw a change come over him while on the journey. Mr. de Rutzen directed that Cornish should be taken to the workhouse.

Drogheda Conservative – November 17th

At Clerkenwell Police Court John Brinkley was charged with being drunk and causing a crowd to assemble in Goswell Road by wearing a woman's skirt, shawl and hat over his ordinary clothes. He was drunk, and said he was going to find "Jack the Ripper." The magistrates sentenced him to fourteen days hard labour. John Avery was also charged with being drunk. He seized a hussar in York Road, and stating he was "Jack the Ripper," said he would show him how he committed the murders, and scratched his nose. The prisoner said he was respectably connected, but the magistrates inflicted a similar sentence.

Dublin Evening Mail – November 17th

A "Jack the Ripper" scare is reported to-day from Kilkenny. A tramp from Athlone, who describes himself as a painter, and a woman from Mullingar, both suspected of being "professional" pickpockets, arrived at Kilkenny on Tuesday evening, with the object, it is believed, of plying the active exercise of their "profession" upon the guileless and unwary at the fair on Wednesday. On Thursday night they were proceeding up Patrick-street, and when under the dark shadow of the Arch, the man attacked his female companion, and struck her some violent blows. The woman's cries rang out wildly, and the inhabitants were startled by a cry of "Jack the Ripper!" A number of people rushed out of their houses, and several started in pursuit of the man, who ran madly as if for his life, his pursuers flinging every missile they could find after him. The police, however, came quickly on the scene, in time, fortunately, to prevent the man from being very badly treated. He had to be escorted by police to the workhouse, where he was admitted for the night, and yesterday morning took his departure at the earliest hour permitted by the rules of that institution.

Drogheda Argus and *Leinster Journal* – December 1st
(From AMERICAN NOTES by William P. Garnett)

We have an imitator of the Whitechapel murderer here; he, however, was promptly arrested. Mrs Cooper, the victim, was found chopped to pieces by her servant. Her husband had been drinking and quarrelled with his wife, and as he had been reading an account of the Whitechapel murders and was excited he said, "he would fix her before Monday." He claims that his wife had been unfaithful to him, and that the killing was no more than any man would do under the circumstances.

Dublin Evening Mail – December 6th
A BOSTON "JACK THE RIPPER"

An American Correspondent writes:– "in Boston the Whitechapel fiend has been imitated by a man, who hides in dark corners and darts out at women brandishing a knife, and muttering threats. He is undoubtedly insane, and the police are arresting him numerously." Another outcome of the Whitechapel horror is a Chinese ghost with the face of a dragon, which appears in Pell-street, in the Chinese quarter, and frightens women. It is reported by cable from Europe that a certain person, whose name is known, sailed from Havre for New York, who is famous for his hatred of women, and who has repeatedly made threats against females of dissolute character. Whether this will throw light on the Whitechapel tragedies I must leave the London detectives to decide.

Munster News and Limerick and Clare Advocate – December 29th
ANOTHER TERRIBLE MURDER OF A BOY
HORRIBLE MUTILATION

A boy named John Gill, aged eight years, was found brutally murdered and mutilated in an outhouse in Thorncliffe Road, Bradford, this morning.

LATER – The murder of the little boy at Bradford is of a peculiarly atrocious character. He was last seen sliding with a number of boys on Thursday night. The body was found at seven o'clock this morning. Both legs were cut off close to the body; the abdomen was slit open and the intestines partially extracted; both ears were cut off; the legs were tied to the body. There were other shocking mutilations. Great excitement prevails. No arrests. The police refuse any information.

LATEST – Later details from Bradford show the body was even more shockingly mutilated than reported in previous messages. The lad's arms were hacked off and his heart torn out. The police believe the crime was committed by drunken lads desirous of emulating the Whitechapel murderer. The body was probably removed to an out-house after the murder had been committed elsewhere.

APPENDIX THREE

Arrests and Suspicions

ACONSIDERABLE NUMBER of arrests were made in respect of the Whitechapel murders and reported in the Irish newspapers. In most cases the apprehended persons were released almost immediately. Many more people came under suspicion, often for no other reason than that they resembled in some aspect one of the various vague reports of the appearance of the killer. I had neither the space nor inclination to include all of them in the main body of the text. Some of the reports, therefore, I reproduce here. If nothing else, they prove instructive as to how hopelessly confused the whole case was.

Dublin Evening Mail – October 1st
Shortly before midnight a man, whose name has not transpired, was arrested in the Borough on suspicion of being the perpetrator of the murders in the East End. This morning a tall, dark man, wearing an American hat, entered a lodginghouse in Union-street, known as Albert Chambers. He stayed there throughout the day, and his peculiar manner rivetted the attention of his fellow-lodgers. He displayed great willingness to converse with them and certain observations made regarding the topic of the day aroused suspicion. The mysterious individual attracted the notice of the deputy-keeper of the lodging-house, whose suspicions became so strong that he sent for a policeman. On the arrival of the officer the stranger was questioned as to his recent wanderings, but he could give no intelligible account of them, though he said he had spent the previous night on Blackfriars Bridge. He was conveyed to Stones End Police Station, Blackman-street, Borough.

Freeman's Journal – October 2nd
Albert Bachert says – "On Saturday night at about seven minutes to twelve, I entered the Three Tuns Hotel, Aldgate. While in there an elderly woman, shabbily dressed, came in and asked me to buy some matches. I refused, and she went out. A man who had been standing by me remarked that those persons

were a nuisance, to which I responded, 'Yes.' He then asked me to have a glass with him, but I refused as I had just called for one myself. He then asked me if I knew how old some of the women were who were in the habit of soliciting outside. I replied that I knew, or thought, that some of them who looked about twenty-five were over thirty-five, the reason they looked younger being on account of the powder and paint. He asked if I could tell him where they usually went with men, and I replied that I heard that some went to places in Oxford street, Whitechapel, others to some houses in Whitechapel road, and others to Bishopsgate street. He then asked whether I thought they would go with him down Northumberland alley, a dark and lonely court in Fenchurch street. I said I did not know, but supposed they would. He then went outside and spoke to the woman who was selling matches and gave her something, I believe. He returned to me and I bid him good night. At about ten minutes past twelve, I believe, the woman was waiting for him. I do not think I could identify the woman, as I did not take particular notice of her, but I should know the man again. He was a dark man, about thirty-eight years of age, height about five feet six or seven inches. He wore a black felt hat, dark clothes (morning coat), black tie and carried a black shiny bag.

The Irish Times – October 2nd

During last night and to-day no less than five men were arrested in the East End of London in connection with the murders. Three were at different times conveyed to Leman street Police Station, but one was immediately liberated. Another was detained until noon to-day, when he was set at liberty after giving a statement of his movements. He was found to have been in straitened circumstances and to have passed much of his time in common lodginghouses in Whitechapel, but there was nothing to show that he had anything to do with the murders. The third man was detained until the afternoon when he, after due inquiry, was also liberated. Of the two men detained at Commercial street, one was liberated soon after his arrest, but the other, named Frank Raper, was kept in custody. It appears he was arrested late on Saturday night at a publichouse known as "Dirty Dick's" near Liverpool street. He was standing in the bars while under the influence of liquor, and made a number of extravagant statements about the murder of Mrs Chapman and Mrs Nicholls. The bystanders sent out and obtained a constable, and when the policeman entered he was openly boasting of being the murderer, and complimenting himself on the means he had adopted to destroy all trace of his identity. He was removed to the police station, followed by a large and excited crowd. On being charged, Raper said he had no settled address, and inquiries have satisfied the police that he is not the man wanted, so he was set free later in the day.

The Irish Times – October 4th

At the Guildhall, London, this morning, William Bull, describing himself as a medical student in the London Hospital, and living at Stannard road, Dalston, was charged on his own confession with having committed the murder at Mitre square. Inspector Izzard said that at 10.40 last night the accused came to his room at Bishopsgate street Station, and made the following statement:–"My name is William Bull, and I live at Dalston. I am a medical student at the London Hospital. I wish to give myself up for murder in Aldgate, on Saturday night or Sunday morning about 2 o'clock. I think I met the woman in Aldgate. I went with her up a narrow street not far from the main road, for an immoral purpose. I promised to give her half-a-crown, which I did. While walking along together there was a second man, who came up and took the half-crown from her. I cannot endure this any longer. My poor head. (Here he put his hand to his head and cried, or pretended to cry) I shall go mad. I have done it, and I must put up with it." The inspector asked what had become of the clothing he had on when the murder was committed. Accused said, "If you wish to know, they are in the Lea, and the knife I threw away." At this point the prisoner declined to say any more. He was drunk. Part of the statement was made in the presence of Major Smith. The prisoner gave his correct address, but is not known at the London Hospital. His parents were respectable. The inspector asked for a remand to make inquiries, and this was granted. The prisoner now said he was drunk when he made the statement. He was remanded.

Carlow Sentinel – October 6th

Late last Thursday evening a man dressed in a black suit and white melton overcoat was observed waiting about the entrance to Mission Hall court, Shoreditch, where a tea was being given to a number of dissolute women who are in distress owing to the present agitation. On the police coming up a bayonet in sheath was found concealed under his overcoat. He said he was looking for the murderer, and would run him through. He was detained at the Commercial-street Police Station. He gave the name of John Kesel Joseph.

Freeman's Journal – October 6th
A STRANGE STORY FROM NEW YORK
SPECIAL TELEGRAM
New York, Friday

The atrocious crimes committed in Whitechapel have aroused intense interest here. The following statement has been made by an English sailor named Dodge. He says he arrived in London from China on August 18th, by the steamship Glenonrlie. He met at the Queen's Music Hall, Poplar, a Malay cook named Alaska. The Malay said he had been robbed by a woman of bad character in Whitechapel of two years savings, and he swore that unless he found the woman and recovered the money he would murder and mutilate every Whitechapel woman he met. He showed Dodge a double-edged knife which he always carried with him. He was about five feet seven inches in height, one hundred and twenty pounds in weight, and apparently thirty-five years of age. He was very dark.

The Irish Times – October 10th

Shortly before closing time this morning three men in the Black Swan public-house, Hanbury street – George Lucas, James Miller, and Thomas Pearman – being struck by the demeanour of a stranger who was present, submitted him to interrogation, and finally to a search. The three men assert that they took from him a large clasp knife, and that with the assistance of a constable they conveyed him to Commercial street Police Station, where two more knives were found upon him. After inquiries had been made, however, the man was liberated.

Drogheda Argus and *Leinster Journal* – October 13th

A suspicious affair is at present engaging the attention of the police authorities. On Saturday night a man, stated to have been intoxicated, entered the Bull Head publichouse, Oxford street, and gave the lady behind the bar a parcel to be left with the manager. On moving the parcel it fell, disclosing three large new knives, one 20 inches, one 14 inches, and one 10 inches in length, with sheath and belt to be wore around the waist. The knives were very sharp. On Sunday information was given to the police, and when the man called for the knives he was told to call again. Detectives watched the house with the intention of detaining the man until he accounted for the possession of the weapons, and the purpose to which they would be put, but he did not put in an appearance.

Freeman's Journal – October 16th

Superintendent Farmer, of the River Tyne police, has received information which it is thought may be a clue to the Whitechapel murderer. An Austrian seaman signed articles on board the Faversham vessel in Tyne on Saturday and sailed for a French port. It was found the signature corresponded with the fac-simile letters signed "Jack the Ripper," and that the man's description corresponded with that circulated by the metropolitan police, who have been informed of the result of Superintendent Farmer's inquiries.

Freeman's Journal – October 16th

A man wearing a slouched hat, carrying a black leather bag, speaking with a slightly American accent, and presenting a travel-stained appearance, was arrested at Limavaddy, near Londonderry, this morning by Constable Walsh, on suspicion of being the man who committed the recent murders in the East End of London. The arrest was made as a result of the police description of the man wanted. The prisoner refused to give his name or any information whatever about himself. A woman and child who were with him were also taken into custody.

APPENDIX FOUR

Letters and Communications

FOLLOWING THE RECEIPT of the "Dear Boss" letter and "Saucy Jacky" postcard, the police, newspapers, news agencies, important officials and private individuals were inundated with letters and communications, most of it signed "Jack the Ripper," "Leather Apron," or some other derivation of the kind. Here are a number of news reports from the Irish newspapers relating to these communications.

King's County Chronicle – 4th October 4th
A STRANGE CONFESSION

As usual in the case of mysterious murders there has been no lack of bogus confessions. One of the strangest is the following which was sent to the Birmingham *Daily Post* :–

Septr 28th 1888.
GENTLEMEN

I wish to give myself up as the White Chaple murderer. I am now in a desperate State of Mind and can console my feelings no longer. I was in a Hospital Corps in India, for ten years. The Climate affected My Brain so, that, At times I was Completely Mad and unconsous At My Doings. I was paid for My Crimes and Eagerly to Grasp the Gold I Slaughtered the Innocent defenceless creatures. I am now looking forward for nothing but death & hope God will forgive me for my desperate Crimes.

I Come to Birmingham with the intention of throwing the Police off my Scent. I can rest neither Day nor Night without some Gastley figure appears before my eyes. I startle in my dreams and fancy I am in the prison cell fettered down with iron chains. I can restrain my Conscious no longer, So I shall leave myself to the penalty of Crime.

I shall be at the Police Station Moorstreet On Saturday at Mid Day were I can make a full confession of my Crime.
Unfortunately
R. SMITH

Eagle and County Cork Advertiser – October 6th
ANOTHER LETTER FROM THE WHITECHAPEL MURDERER
A SHOCKING PRODUCTION

The Central Press has received the following letter bearing the "E.C." post-mark, written in red ink in roundhand, apparently by a person indifferent-ly educated. At foot is a rude drawing of a sharp pointed knife-blade measuring three inches and the handle one:–
"3 October,
"DEAR BOSS – Since last splendid success; two more, and never a squeal of I am master of the are. I am going to be heavy on the guilded w--s [insert 'sic'?]. Now we are. Some duchess will cut up nicely, and the lace will show nicely. You won-der how of we are masters. No education like a butcher's. No animal like a nice woman. The fat are best. Go to Brighton for a holiday; but we shan't idle. Splendid high-class women there. My mouth waters. Good luck there. If not, you will hear from me in West End. My pal will keep on at the East a while yet. When I get a nobility womb I will send it on to C. Warren, or perhaps to you, for a keepsake of. It is jolly.
"GEORGE OF THE HIGH RIP GANG.
"Red ink still, but a drop of the real in it."

Clare Journal and Ennis Advertiser – October 8th
AN EXTRAORDINARY TELEGRAM AND LETTER FROM "JACK THE RIPPER"

The following telegram was received by the Metropolitan police five minutes before midnight on Saturday having been handed in at 8 o'clock at an office in an Eastern district. "Charles Warren, head of the 'Police News,' Central Office. – Dear Boss, – If you are willing enough to catch me, I am now in the City-road, lodging, but number you will have to find out, and I mean to do another murder to-night in White chapel – Yours, Jack the Ripper."

A letter was also received at the Commercial-street Police station that morning, written in black lead pencil, couched in ridiculously extravagant lan-guage, hinting at committing another murder tonight in Goswell-road, and signed "Jack the Ripper." This has been handed to the G Division, in whose divi-sion Goswell-road is. The name of the office where the telegram was handled is not divulged, but the acceptance of such message is inexplicable.

A letter was received by a Manchester newspaper, and a postcard by a Brighton paper, signed "Jack the Ripper." Both are practical jokes.

At the Birmingham police court on Saturday, Alfred Nabier Blanchard, a canvasser from London, was remanded, because he had boasted in a public house that he was the Whitechapel murderer. He now retracted the statement, pleading excitement.

Freeman's Journal – October 10th

A letter was received by the police authorities at the Castle yesterday afternoon, purporting to have been forwarded by "Jack the Ripper," and stating that he intends visiting Dublin this week for the purpose of committing a murder. The letter, which was signed "Leather Apron" and "Jack the Ripper" is believed to have been written by some silly person who has been reading communications recently published in connection with the Whitechapel murders. The letter stated that a murder of a woman would be committed either in the east or west of Dublin; that the writer was determined to do away with unfortunates, and his reason for doing so was because his sister had joined them. He defied Mr. Malton and all his detectives to discover him.

Dublin Evening Mail – October 12th

Yesterday afternoon the following appeared in the third edition of the *Belfast Evening Telegraph*:– "Jack the Ripper" in Belfast. Extraordinary letter. A warning. Sensation in town. By this afternoon's post we have received the following extraordinary letter:– Dear Boss – I have arrived in your city as London was iss to warm for me just now, o the Belfast ---- had better look out, for I intend to commence operations on Saturday night, I have spotted some nice fat ones, who will cut up well. I am longing to begin, for I love my work – Yours, Jack the Ripper." The communication is written in red ink, like the letters received by the Central News in London, and there are several blotches evidently made in imitation of blood. The envelope was addressed – "The Editor, *Evening Telegraph*, Belfast," and bears the Belfast postmark.

Eagle and County Cork Advertiser – October 13th
THE LONDON MURDERS
"JIM THE RIPPER" NOW

The *Dublin Express* understands that the police authorities at Dublin Castle received a letter purporting to be from "Jim the Ripper," stating his intention to visit Dublin this week.

Dublin Evening Mail – October 13th
THE LONDON MURDERS
A PARISIAN "PARTNER"
A Paris Correspondent telegraphs – The Whitechapel murders have not only

been a newspaper sensation of the first magnitude here, but have got on weak brains and set madmen and lovers of practical jokes writing to the Prefect of Police. M. Goron, the Head of the Criminal Investigation Department, receives letters written from both. The following was received by him yesterday – "Sir – You must have heard of the Whitechapel murders. This is the explanation of their mysterious side. There are partners, I and another in this business. One is in England, and the other in France. I am at Brest, and am going to Paris to operate as does my London colleague in London. We are seeking in the human body that which the doctors have never found. You will try in vain to hunt us down. Our next victim will be a woman between twenty and thirty. We will cut her carotid artery, disembowel her, amputate four fingers of her left hand, leaving the thumb only. Meanwhile you will hear of me, and in three weeks at most. Look out, Signed – H. L. P. C."

Dublin Evening Mail – November 1st

By the last post on Tuesday night, a letter purporting to come from the Whitechapel assassin, was received at the Poplar Police Station, London, in which the writer said he was gong to commit three more crimes. The following is said to be the wording:– "October 30th, 1888 – Dear Boss – I am going to commit three more murders, two women and a child, and I shall take their hearts this time – Yours truly, (signed), JACK THE RIPPER." The letter was enclosed in an envelope which, in addition to the Poplar post-mark, also bore the Ealing post-mark, and was directed to the sergeant.

Clare Journal and Ennis Advertiser – November 8th
LORD SHEFFIELD'S LETTER-BOX

The following letter, bearing the Uskfield postmark of 27 Oct, has been received by the Earl of Sheffield. He has produced it in facsimile, and offered a reward of £250 for the writer:– "England, Oct 27, '88. – Dear Loard Sheffield, – I am sorry but feeling it my duty to let you know as I don't think you do, or you would not have the Heart to turn an old Tennent like poor old Mrs Grover out of her Home after such an hard struggle to maintain and bring up her family, not only that, but not allowing anyone to get an honest living there in the butchering line, as they have done for a great number of years, but it seems to me as though you and your faithul steward want it all, und if you had my wish you would get more than you wanted. Remember, this is a warning to you, and at the same time, I should be much obliged to you if you could arrange it for your steward to sleep under the same room as yourself on Monday night, Oct 29, or else I shall have to bring an assistant. My knife is nice and sharp. Oh for a gentleman this time instead of a lady. I am sorry for troubling you, but don't forget the 29th. – I remain yours truly, JACK THE RIPPER."

The Irish Times – November 12th

Last night there was found in the pillar-box at the corner of Northumberland street and Marylebone a letter directed to the police, and its contents were as follows:– "Dear Boss, – I shall be busy to-morrow night in Marylebone. I have two booked for blood – Yours Jack the Ripper – Look out about ten o'clock, Marylebone road."

The Irish Times – November 20th

A blank wall of a house in Newham street, Whitechapel, in which Albert Bachert, who gave a description of the supposed Whitechapel murderer lives, was found yesterday to have the following words chalked up:–
"DEAR BOSS – I am still about. Look out – Yours, 'JACK THE RIPPER.'"
The words were afterwards partly obliterated to avoid attracting a crowd.

Dublin Evening Mail – November 22nd
ANOTHER LETTER FROM "JACK THE RIPPER"

Mr Saunders, the sitting magistrate at the Thames Police Court, London, yesterday received a letter purporting to be from "Jack the Ripper." The envelope bore the Portsmouth post-mark and was directed "To the Head Magistrate, police Court, Whitechapel, London." It read as follows:–
No. 1 England 1888
DEAR BOSS, – It is no Good for You to look for me in London because I am not there dont trouble Yourself about me till I return which will not be Very Long. I like the work too well to leave it long. Oh it was such a jolly job the last one I had plenty of time to do it Properly ha ha. The next lot I mean to do with Vengeance cut off their heads and arms. You think it is the man with the black moustache ha ha ha. When I have done another you can catch me. So Good Bye Dear Boss till I return. Yours,
JACK THE RIPPER
The letter has been handed over by Mr. Sergent, chief clerk, to the police.

Drogheda Argus and *Leinster Journal* – November 24th
(From OUR DUBLIN LETTER)

A young lady residing in Clontarf a short time ago received a letter signed "Jack the Ripper," warning her that her end was near. She showed it to her father, who brought it to the police, by whom the affair was treated as of no consequence. The letter, which was couched in the most blood-curdling language was, no doubt, the work of a practical joker; but it caused the lady and her family a good deal of uneasiness, and as her relatives were foolish enough to speak about the matter, the affair was the subject of a good deal of gossip in the neighbourhood.

Dublin Evening Mail – November 26th

A Nottingham Correspondent telegraphs a remarkable letter signed "Jack the Ripper's Pal," which has been handed over to the police, and has been received by Mr Robert Porter, of Hucknall, Torkard, Notts. The writer says he is a Nottingham man, and feels as if he could blow up all the dens in Whitechapel with the filthy women in them. There were, he says, two concerned in the murders, and his pal taught him how to do it. He is now as bad as "Jack the Ripper," as he never feels frightened when cutting a woman up. When talking to a woman he can see the very devil, but he hopes the Lord will forgive him all his sins. His pal is a Bavarian, whom he met on a steamship as he was returning from Colorado. Through being mesmerised he found out the other man's hideous calling. They have become very intimate, and his pal casts a sort of spell over him. His pal said he had chucked two men overboard at sea. He is a wild wretch, but a great magician, and a clever man with plenty of money. The writer, in conclusion says he would be happier when he left England for good, but before then he and his pal will be heard of again.

Dublin Evening Mail – December 6th

Mr Saunders, the presiding magistrate at the Thames Police Court, London, has received a letter addressed to "Mr Saunders, chief magistrate, Police Court, Whitechapel." The letter read as follows:– "Dear Pal – I am still at liberty. The last job in Whitechapel was not bad, but I mean to surprise them with the next. Shall joint it. ha! ha! ha! After that shall try on the lazy louchers who live on unfortunates. We have just enrolled several for the job. I am in the country now for the benefit of my health. I met the super here (Wellinboro') the other day, and like him immense. He looks like a yard of pump water starched. Shall try a job here next, so look out for news from
"JACK THE RIPPER."

Charges and Allegations of the Parnell Commission

The specific list of charges and allegations issued by the *Times* to the Parnell Commission, as described in Chapter Nine, were reported in the *Freeman's Journal* of October 17th as follows:

SPECIAL COMMISSION ACT, 1888.

The following are the particulars of the charges or allegations made by the defendants in the action of O'Donnell v Walter (hereinafter referred to as the said defendants) delivered pursuant to the order of the Special Commission dated the 17th day of September, 1888.

The names of the members of Parliament against whom the charges and allegations are made are set out in the schedule hereto.

The members of Parliament mentioned in the schedule were members of the conspiracy and organisation hereinafter described, and took part in the work and operations thereof, with knowledge of its character, objects, and mode of action.

IRELAND A NATION.

From, and including, the year 1879 there have existed societies known as the Irish Land League and the Irish National Land League and Labour and Industrial Union, the Ladies' Land League, the Ladies' Irish Land League and Labour and Industrial Union, the National League, and the affiliated societies in Great Britain and America, all forming one connected and continuous organisation.

The ultimate object of that organisation was to establish the absolute independence of Ireland as a separate nation. With a view to effect this, one of the immediate objects of the said conspiracy or organisation was to promote an agrarian agitation against the payment of agricultural rents, thereby securing the co-operation of the tenant-farmers of Ireland, and at the same time the impoverishment and ultimate expulsion from the country of the Irish landlords, who were styled "the English garrison."

The mode of action was to organise a system of coercion and intimidation in Ireland, which was sustained and enforced by boycotting and the commission of crimes and outrages.

THE TIMES' "MATTERS."

The organisation was actively engaged in the following matters:–

1. The promotion of and inciting to the commission of crimes, outrages, boycotting, and intimidation.

2. The collection and providing of funds to be used, or which it was known were used, for the promotion of and the payment of persons engaged in the commission of crimes, outrages, boycotting and intimidation.

3. The payment of persons who assisted in, were effected by, or accidentally or otherwise injured in the commission of such crimes, outrages, and acts of boycotting, and intimidation.

4. Holding meetings and procuring to be made speeches inciting to the commission of crimes, outrages, boycotting and intimidation. Some of the meetings referred to, which were attended by members of Parliament, with the approximate dates and places of meeting are given in the schedule hereto.

5. The publication and dissemination of newspaper and other literature inciting to and approving of sedition and the commission of crimes, outrages, boycotting, and intimidation, particularly the *Irish World*, the *Chicago Citizen*, the *Boston Pilot*, the *Freeman's Journal*, *United Ireland*, the *Irishman*, the *Nation*, the *Weekly News*, the *Cork Daily Herald*, the *Kerry Sentinel*, the *Evening Telegraph*, and the *Sligo Champion*.

6. Advocating resistance to law and the constituted authorities, and impeding the detection and punishment of crime.

7. Making payments to or for persons who were guilty or supposed to be guilty of the commission of crimes, outrages, and acts of boycotting and intimidation for the defence or to enable them to escape from justice, and for the maintenance of such persons and their families.

8. It is charged and alleged that the members of Parliament mentioned in the schedule approved, and by their acts and conduct led people to believe that they approved, of resistance to the law and the commission of crimes, outrages, and acts of boycotting and intimidation when committed in furtherance of the objects and resolutions of the said societies, and that persons who engaged in the commission of such crimes, outrages, and acts would receive the support and protection of the said societies and their organisation and influence.

SPECIAL REFERENCES.

The acts and conduct specially referred to are as follow:–

9. They attended meetings of the said societies and other meetings at various places and made speeches, and caused and procured speeches to be made inciting to the commission of crimes, outrages, boycotting, and intimidation.

10. They were parties to and cognisant of the payment of moneys for the purposes of above mentioned, and as testimonials or rewards to persons who had been convicted or were notoriously guilty of crimes or outrages or to their families.

11. With knowledge that crimes, outrages, and acts of boycotting and intimidation had followed the delivery of speeches at the meetings they expressed no *bona fide* disapproval or public condemnation but, on the contrary, continued to be leading and active members of the said societies and to subscribe to their funds.

12. With such knowledge as aforesaid they continued to be intimately associated with the officers of the same societies (many of whom fled from justice) and with notorious criminals, and the agents and instruments of murder and conspiracies, and with the planners and paymasters of outrage, and with the advocates of sedition, violence, and the use of dynamite.

13. They and the said societies, with such knowledge as aforesaid, received

large sums of money, which were collected in America and elsewhere by criminals and persons who were known to advocate sedition, assassination, the use of dynamite, and the commission of crimes and outrages.

14. When on certain occasions they considered it politic to denounce, and did denounce certain crimes in public, they afterwards made communications to their associates and others with the intention of leading them to believe that such denunciation was not sincere. One instance of this, of which the said defendants propose to give evidence, is the following letters –

THE LETTERS

Letter from C S Parnell, dated 15th May, '82.
Letter from same, 16th June, '82.
Another letter from the same of the same date.

THE CRIME OF NOT BOYCOTTING

The following are the persons who are guilty of crime, or advocates of treason, sedition, assassination, and violence, with whom it is alleged the said members of Parliament continued to associate.

FRANK BYRNE, who admitted his connection with Phoenix Park murderers, and who was supplied with money by Mr. C S Parnell, which enabled him to escape to America.
PATRICK EGAN, the treasurer of the Land League, who, during the years '81 and '82, organised and procured the commission of crimes and outrages in various parts of Ireland.
PATRICK FORD, the editor of the *Irish World*, who remitted large sums of moneys to the said association, and for the purposes aforesaid.
JAMES CAREY, the Phoenix Park informer.
CAPT. M'CAFFERTY, implicated in the Phoenix Park murders.
TYNAN, who organised the Phoenix Park murders.
J MULLETT, convict.
T BRENNAN, who was secretary of the Land League, and paid some of the perpetrators of the Phoenix Park and other murders and outrages.
EDWARD M'CAFFERY, convict.
P J SHERIDAN, who was an organiser of the Land League, who organised outrages and acts of violence, and was implicated in the Phoenix Park murders.
M J BOYTON, organiser of the Land League and instigator of crime.

J W NALLY, convicted of crime.

J WALSH, of Middlesboro, organiser of the Invincible conspiracy in Ireland.

T F BOURKE, who was convicted of high treason on 24th April, '68.

J STEPHENS, the chief of the Fenian organisation.

J J BRESLIN, hospital superintendent of Richmond Jail, a member of the Irish Republican Brotherhood, who aided Stephens' escape.

HAMILTON WILLIAMS, the partner of Gallagher, the convicted dynamitard, and himself a dynamitard.

ALEXANDER SULLIVAN, a member of Clan Na Gael.

TRANSATLANTIC (Mooney).

AUGUSTINE FORD.

ELLEN FORD.

MARIA DOHERTY.

FATHER EUGENE SHEEHY.

DR WM CARROLL.

P A COLLINS.

C O 'M CONDON, sentenced to death for the murder of Sergeant Brett.

JOHN DEVOY, convicted of Fenianism, and a trustee of the Skirmishing Fund raised by the *Irish World*.

O'BRIEN, M'CARTHY and CHAMBERS, convicted Fenians.

JOHN FINNERTY, diynamitard.

JOHN DALY, do.

GENERAL MILLEN, do.

W F MACKAY-LOMASNEY, a convicted Fenian.

S J MEANEY, convicted Fenian,

J REDPATH, advocate of crime.

JEREMIAH O'DONOVAN ROSSA.

JOHN O'LEARY, convicted of Fenianism.

P J GORDON, F TULLY, FATHER EGAN, FATHER COEN, JOHN ROCHE OF WOODFORD; P N FITZGERALD, LAURENCE EGAN, J RIORDAN, J CONNELL, TIMOTHY HORAN, J RIORDAN, J DOWLING, PATRICK NALLY, M M O'SULLIVAN, J KELLY, T FITZPATRICK, MAURICE MURPHY, MARTIN EGAN, J M WALL, A M FORRESTER, J P QUINN, W F MOLONY, PEARSON REDDINGTON, members of the Land League and implicated in crime.

ANNA PARNELL, H REYNOLDS, H LYNCH, MRS MOLONY, CIARA STRITCH, MRS MOORE, members of the Ladies' Land League who paid for the commission of crime.

NAMING THE CULPRITS

Names of members of Parliament against whom it is proposed to give evidence of charges and allegations.

MESSRS SEXTON, COX, GILHOOLY, HOOPER, M HEALY, O'REA, M'CARTAN, ESMONDE, T HARRINGTON, FOLEY, SHEEHY, E. HARRINGTON, SHEEHAN, CHANCE, FOX, HAYDEN, FINUCANE, JUSTIN M'CARTHY, BIGGAR, WILLIAM O'BRIEN, J KENNY, PARNELL, O'DOHERTY, A O'CONNOR, CLANCY, T D SULLIVAN, WILLIAM REDMOND, HARRIS, STACK, KILBRIDE, LEAHY, QUINN, CONWAY, ABRAHAM O'KEEFFE, T HEALY, J NOLAN, CRILLY, JORDAN, F X O'BRIEN, LALER, COMMINS, P J O'BRIEN, J O'CONNOR, PYNE, TUITE, CONDON, J BARRY, T P O'CONNOR, TANNER, GILL, DEASY, DILLON, P O'BRIEN, O'KELLY, LEAMY, MAYNE, M KENNY, P J POWER, D SULLIVAN, J E REDMOND, BYRNE, FLYNN, LANE, and HENRY CAMPBELL.

The meetings at which particular members of Parliament made speeches are specified as under:

There followed a list of some hundred or more speeches, the names of those who made them, and the dates and places at which they were made.

Acknowledgements

MY THANKS GO TO two men for being the inspiration for this book. The first was Adrian Phypers. I never met Adrian, but as the originator of the Jack the Ripper Press Project it was his legacy which sparked my interest in the Newspaper reporting of the Ripper crimes. Sadly Adrian passed away in April of 2003. The other man is Andy Aliffe, whose interview on the Casebook website, described in his foreword to this book, gave me the impetus to get myself down to the National Library Newspaper Archive in Dublin.

This work initially resulted in an article in the January 2004 edition of *Ripperologist* magazine. My thanks to Paul Begg, the editor of that magazine, for his support, encouragement and help. Also to the rest of the staff, especially Adam Wood who kindly supplied many of the photographs and illustrations for this book. Thanks also to Stewart P. Evans who has been similarly generous in terms of both his time and in supplying illustrations from his own collection, including some never before published. Also to Dan Norder, editor of *Ripper Notes*, for supplying the cover image.

My thanks also go to the marvellous staff of the National Library of Ireland who must be sick of my face by this point. A special thank you to the genealogy service of that institution for their invaluable help to me in my attempt to track down Mary Kelly's birth records. Also to the staff of Trinity College Dublin, The National Archives of Ireland, the British Library Newspaper Library at Colindale, North London, and the National Archive in Kew.

I'm going to give a big thank you (she'll pout if I don't) to Lorraine Fox of the Histo-Pathology department of St James's Hospital, Dublin, for at least trying to help me make head or tail of all the medical stuff, and also for being a good mate and a long-suffering drinking buddy. Hey Foxy, time to get the little black dress out of the mothballs.

For help, advice, general encouragement and answering my sometimes bloody silly questions the following are a list of people in alphabetical order so they can't complain about favouritism. Glenn Andersson, Neil Bell, Alex Chisholm, John Hennessy, Liza Hopkinson, Loretta Lay, Robert Charles Linford, Estella McLoughlin, Caroline Morris, Stephen P. Ryder, Robert Smith, Chris Scott, Wolf Vanderlinden, A. P. Wolf, Eduardo Zinna.

Finally my thanks to my editor, Ruth Garvey, and to Susan Waine of the Ashfield Press for their hard work in making this book happen.

Bibliography and Sources

BOOKS USED:

Robert Anderson, *The Lighter Side of My Official Life*, London: Hodder & Stoughton, 1910

Paul Begg, *Jack the Ripper: The Definitive History*, London: Pearson Education, 2003

Paul Begg, Martin Fido & Keith Skinner, *The Jack the Ripper A-Z*, London: Headline, 1996

Philip Bull, *Land, Politics & Nationalism*, Dublin: Gill & Macmillan, 1996

Christie Campbell, *Fenian Fire*, London: HarperCollins, 2002

John J. Eddleston, *Jack the Ripper: An Encyclopaedia*, London: Metro Publishing, 2002

Stewart P. Evans & Keith Skinner, *The Ultimate Jack the Ripper Sourcebook*, London: Constable & Robinson, 2000

Stewart P. Evans & Keith Skinner, *Jack the Ripper: Letters from Hell*, Stroud: Sutton Publishing, 2001

D.J. Hickey & J.E. Doherty, *A New Dictionary of Irish History from 1800*, Dublin: Gill & Macmillan, 2003

Alvin Jackson, *Home Rule – An Irish History 1800-2000*, London: Wiedenfeld & Nicholson, 2003

Maxim Jakubowski & Nathan Braund, *The Mammoth Book of Jack the Ripper*, London: Constable & Robinson, 1999

Declan Kiberd, *Inventing Ireland*, London: Vintage, 1996

Major Henri le Caron, *Twenty-Five Years in the Secret Service*, London: William Heinemann, 1893

Marie-Louise Legg, *Newspapers and Nationalism: The Irish Provincial Press 1850-1892*, Dublin: Four Courts Press, 1999

Jack London, *People of the Abyss*, London: Macmillan, 1903

Ambrose Macauley, *The Holy See, British Policy and the Plan of Campaign in Ireland 1885-93*, Dublin: Four Courts Press, 2002

Sean McMahon, *Charles Stewart Parnell,* Cork: Mercier Press, 2000

Alan O'Day, *Irish Home Rule 1867-1921,* Manchester: University Press, 1998

R. Rees, *Nationalism and Unionism in 19th Century Ireland,* Newtownards: Colourpoint, 2001

Donald Rumbelow, *The Complete Jack the Ripper,* London: Penguin, 1988

Sir Henry Smith, *From Constable to Commissioner,* London: Chatto & Windus, 1910

Philip Sugden, *The Complete History of Jack the Ripper,* London: Constable & Robinson, 2002

Colin Wilson & Robin Odell, *Jack the Ripper: Summing Up and Verdict,* London: Bantam, 1987

NEWSPAPERS CONSULTED:

Armagh Standard (Armagh)
Ballina Journal and Connaught Advertiser (Ballina)
Ballinrobe Chronicle and Mayo Advertiser (Ballinrobe)
Ballymena Advertiser (Ballymena)
Ballymena Observer (Ballymena)
Belfast and Newry Standard (Belfast)
Belfast News-Letter (Belfast)
Bray Herald (Bray)
Carlow Sentinel (Carlow)
Clare Journal and Ennis Advertiser (Ennis)
Cork Examiner (Cork)
Daily Telegraph (London)
Derry Journal (Londonderry)
Derry Standard (Londonderry)
Drogheda Argus and Leinster Journal (Drogheda)
Drogheda Conservative (Drogheda)
Dublin Evening Mail (Dublin)
Eagle and County Cork Advertiser (Skibbereen)
Enniscorthy News (Enniscorthy)
Evening Telegraph (Belfast)
Evening Telegraph (Dublin)
Freeman's Journal and Daily Commercial Advertiser (Dublin)
Irish Catholic (Dublin)
Irish Times (Dublin)
Kerry Evening Post (Tralee)
Kerry Sentinel (Tralee)

Kerry Weekly Reporter and Commercial Advertiser (Tralee)
Kilkenny Journal and Leinster Commercial and Literary Adviser (Kilkenny)
Kilkenny Moderator and Leinster Advertiser (Kilkenny)
King's County Chronicle (Parsonstown)
Leitrim Advertiser (Mohill)
Limerick Chronicle (Limerick)
Limerick Reporter and Tipperary Vindicator (Limerick)
Longford Journal (Longford)
Meath Herald and Cavan Advertiser (Kells)
Midland Tribune and King's County Vindicator (Birr)
Morning News (Belfast)
Munster News and Limerick and Clare Advocate (Limerick)
Nation, The (Dublin)
Nationalist and Leinster Times (Athy, Newbridge and Naas)
People, The (Wexford)
Sligo Champion (Sligo)
Star, The (London)
Times, The (London)
United Ireland (Dublin)
Waterford Citizen (Waterford)
Waterford News and *General Advertiser* (Waterford)
Westmeath Examiner (Mullingar)

Index

Jack the Ripper